SHOOTERS

SHOOTERS

GUNS AND GANGS IN MANCHESTER
IN THE TWENTY-FIRST CENTURY

BEN BLACK

MILO BOOKS LTD

ABOUT THE AUTHOR

Ben Black is an investigative writer specialising in gun and gang crime. *Shooters* is his first book.

Published in June 2012 by Milo Books

ISBN 978-1-908479-00-6

Typeset by www.web-stars.co.uk

Printed in Great Britain by
CPI Group(UK) Ltd, Croydon, CR0 4YY

MILO BOOKS LTD
The Old Weighbridge
Station Road
Wrea Green
Lancs PR4 2PH
United Kingdom
www.milobooks.com

CONTENTS

Introduction 9

1 Bull 25

2 Street Wars 57

3 Special Delivery 72

4 Bloodbath at the Brass Handles 88

5 The Killing of Jessie James 95

6 Longsight Street Soldiers 107

7 Cabbo's Revenge 123

8 Life and Death 145

9 Gunchester Grime 165

10 Old Trafford Crips 180

11 Police and Thieves 207

12 The Man from Atlantis 223

13 The Angelzarke Murder 232

14 The Hitman 248

15 The Twins 281

Epilogue 297

Introduction

AT 1.50 P.M. ON Thursday, 20 April 2000, an anonymous phone caller told police that the Young Gooch Crew were planning to kidnap someone and hold them hostage in the Moss Side area of Manchester. The caller named Lee Amos as being involved, and gave an address on Ruskin Avenue, one of the rows of terraced streets situated roughly halfway between Manchester University and the site of Manchester City's old Maine Road stadium.

Five hours later, after mounting covert surveillance, armed police burst into the house. There was no hostage, but they did find seven men, six women and a formidable arsenal. In a back bedroom was a Skorpion machine gun capable of firing at a rate of 1,000 rounds a minute, its safety catch off. A fully loaded magazine was beside it. A Smith and Wesson .38 revolver, loaded with the safety catch off, plus five items of body armour, one of which was Greater Manchester Police issue, were also found in that room, alongside two scanners tuned to a police frequency and a pair of night vision binoculars. A Colt .45 with one bullet in the chamber, the safety catch off, was discovered in the living room.

The men and women present claimed the police had stormed a birthday party. Officers were confident they had in fact interrupted a council of war, part of a campaign of vengeance for the murder of a young man called Martin Bennett. Bennett had been tiring of gang life when he was blasted in the chest by a gunman from the rival Doddington gang. The Gooch had hit back quickly, shooting dead a young man called Dorrie McKie a few days later in Hulme and then blasting Anthony Cook, one of the most senior members of the Doddington, seven times in the head and body after a dramatic car chase. But it seemed their lust for vengeance had still not been sated.

The Gooch, the biggest and most powerful of south Manchester's four main street gangs, had been fighting two 'wars' simultaneously: against the Doddington, based, like them, in Moss Side, and against the younger Longsight Crew. Their own trigger-happy junior members, the so-called Young Gooch, had come of age in a period where the focus of the drug-dealing gangs was shifting from getting rich quickly to tribalism, vendetta and the outlaw lifestyle.

Two of them in particular, Lee 'Cabbo' Amos and Colin 'Piggy' Joyce, had seen their association with more seasoned players take them from young tearaways to dangerous enforcers. When they were arrested at the Ruskin Avenue raid, both were wearing jeans specially adapted to carry and conceal firearms. At that time, the pair had reputations as two of the Gooch's most active and ruthless soldiers, each with a series of shootings under his belt. Taxing other villains was a specialty. Just ten days before the swoop on the safehouse, an intelligence report recorded that Piggy had shot someone with a MAC-10 in the Big Western Pub after a squabble. Intelligent, manipulative characters who lived by their own code, their violent crimes consistently presented detectives with challenges that tested their wits and refined their techniques.

Until 2001, there was nothing on the criminal records of Joyce and Amos that matched their reputations. Yet their names had come up time and again in murder inquiries.

When Doddington gang leader Kevin Lewis was blasted in the head by an assassin on a mountain bike, the pair came under suspicion. When eighteen-year-old Julian Wagaba was brutally dispatched near his Levenshulme home, apparently after an argument over a car stereo, they were interviewed. Another case they were suspected of being mixed up in entered detective folklore, and is still used to test deduction skills. A man's body was found in a street in Longsight with a bullet in the back of his head. Detectives learnt that two men had been shot at by a gang of four, who had watched them pull up in a car. The two had escaped into a house unhurt. The dead man was in the position where the four gunmen had been standing, indicating he was one of them. But the bullet was in the back of his head, suggesting he had not been killed by returned fire. Analysis of gunshot residues on a nearby wall provided the breakthrough. The dead man had in fact been one of the gunmen, killed by 'friendly fire'; he had most likely risen from a crouch and been shot in the back of the head by one of his friends standing slightly behind him. The dead man was Zeus King, son of the lead singer of the Brit-soul group Sweet Sensation, who once topped the charts with the song 'Sad Sweet Dreamer'. No one has ever been convicted over his death, nor of the killings of Lewis and Wagaba.

Another man, thirty-five-year-old Roger Ormsby, was found in his burning BMW, a bullet in the back of his head, on a grassy path in Whalley Range. He had been shot at close range, evidently by someone he trusted, and had slumped forward onto the accelerator, revving the engine until it exploded in flame. It was suspected that the older Ormsby, who was known to police, had been trying to rein in the wild Young Gooch faction and they told him what they thought of his advice in the bluntest of terms. Joyce and Amos were seen in the vicinity. No-one has been convicted of this murder either.

In the end, Joyce and Amos were brought down by a prosecution that dispensed with ordinary witnesses and rested on evidence and experts. In the past, Greater Manchester Police had sought to deny the existence of the gangs. Now, they knitted together all the intelligence they had on their associations and activities to prove that a violent clique of drug dealers known as the Gooch existed, and that those arrested in the Ruskin Avenue raid were among them. The weight of evidence forced the gang members to concede the case against them at the eleventh hour. In 2001, Colin Joyce, then aged twenty-one, admitted joint possession of the revolver with Lee Amos, then twenty-five. The pair were jailed for nine years each.

In one swoop, GMP had removed what they regarded as the existing leadership of the Gooch. It was a major coup. The Doddington Gang was already in disarray, riven by internal feuding and shattered by the Gooch's war of attrition. The leader of the Longsight Crew was in jail for threatening to kill a witness in a gang trial. And the fourth of south Manchester's most active gangs, the impetuous Pitt Bull Crew, was about to be brought down with the help of 'supergrass' witnesses (see Chapter One). The police could have been forgiven for thinking that they had successfully closed a chapter in the city's gang wars. They were sadly wrong.

THE HISTORY OF the modern Manchester gang scene goes back to the midpoint of the 'money' decade: the 1980s. A rash of machete attacks led detectives to uncover a conflict between a well-armed, well-organised gang from Cheetham Hill, a largely ethnic neighbourhood to the north of the city centre, and criminals from the Moss Side area, to the south. Apparently the Moss Side armed robbers had struck a deal with their peers in Cheetham Hill, known as the Hillbillies, to each confine their crimes to their specified territories. The peace broke when one side committed a robbery on the 'territory' of another, and the bodies began racking up. Disputes over women exacerbated the conflict, as did the arrival of cheap crack cocaine a few years later.

Moss Side's Alexandra Park estate was built in the 1970s, replacing the Edwardian and Victorian terraces on the western half of Moss Side. It was designed according to the 'Radburn' style of public housing, an American offshoot of the English Garden City movement. Pioneered in the eponymous town of Radburn, New Jersey, the idea of the open-plan layout was to separate people from cars in a self-contained community of housing and green space. Local authorities across the English-speaking West gave the experiment a go. All too often it had the unintended consequence of ghettoising deprived people and fostering criminal subcultures – notably in Villawood in Sydney, Australia, and closer to home, The Meadows in Nottingham. The separation of people from their cars made them easy to take. The ginnels and walkways which connected houses became escape routes for muggers and burglars, and the profusion of dead ends isolated neighbours from outsiders and the authorities. Back gardens tended to face the street, with houses facing each other over open space. But, rather than create a sense of wellbeing, these splotches of grassland with no particular purpose seemed to erode the sense of community and ownership.

By the late eighties Moss Side had emerged as a highly lucrative street dealing patch, with dealers claiming the Alexandra Park estate in particular as their fiefdom. Some of the Hillbillies took to 'taxing' these local dealers of their profits at the point of a gun or a machete. A group of young toughs known as the Pepperhill Mob, named after a pub on the Alexandra Park estate, fought back. As the two sides went to war, others on the same estate continued to do business with the Hillbillies. In a street on the west side of the estate, Gooch Close, the gang whose name would become so emblematic of gang violence in Manchester sprang up. The Gooch lads, one of whom was related to a Cheetham Hill leader, continued to associate with the Hillbillies and so directly defied Pepperhill.

Now the Pepperhill and the Gooch fought their own 'war' for supremacy, a conflict fought out largely on the claustrophobic streets of the estate. At the height of the trouble, the Pepperhill pub was pulled down. The gang which had taken its name re-grouped at nearby Dodington Close and got a new, slightly mis-spelt name. A triangular conflict between the Hillbillies, the Doddington and the Gooch endured for years and set a template for gang warfare in the city.

The Doddington and Gooch would stick around, with bloody tenacity, long after the peak of their drug-dealing operations. In the late eighties and early nineties, the two rival factions turned Moss Side's Alexandra Park estate into a low-level war zone and the north of England's busiest hard drugs market. The estate eventually would be re-modelled to help eliminate the open-air peddling problem, but Greater Manchester Police found themselves still struggling with an embedded gang culture. In the nineties, the gangs exploited their violent reputations to beat the justice system. Trials collapsed amid suspicion of nobbled juries, some witnesses would rather go to jail for contempt of court than risk their lives giving evidence against the neighbourhood badmen.

Operation Chrome, the first research project of its kind into Manchester gangs, found boys as young as twelve were becoming involved. A desire to make money was only part of the story. Gangbanging had become a way of life. By the time a youth realised he was in too deep, it was often too late. The community had killers in its midst, young criminals fuelled as much by testosterone and a desire for 'respect' as they were by money, with little concept of consequence and with access to rapid-fire machine guns. Smugglers found a ready source of these weapons in the countries of the old Eastern Bloc. Meanwhile, deactivated weapons, which had been legally traded between collectors in Britain, were being brought back into use by amoral engineers. Young men, most of them of black Caribbean heritage, were being injured and killed with a fatiguing regularity on inner-south Manchester's estates. While young black men from these areas made up only a fraction of the city's offenders, the willingness to use firearms in disputes was more prevalent in their communities than in any other. Only the difficulties of belonging to a historically enslaved, subjugated and transplanted race of people could explain this cheapening of life.

In the years approaching the millennium the violence intensified. According to figures obtained by *The Manchester Evening News*, there were twenty-eight shootings in 1996, with twelve wounded and four killed. The year after saw sixty-eight confirmed shootings in the city, with thirty-nine injuries and six deaths, while 1998 brought seventy-four shootings, thirty-nine injuries and two deaths. In 1999, the number of shootings rocketed to 270, with forty-three woundings and seven murders. That year, police recovered sixty handguns, forty-five shotguns, eighteen rifles, three machine pistols and 1,200 rounds of ammunition.

A serving detective, unidentified because of the nature of his work, recalls the chaos of the late 1990s. 'In that really bad phase, almost every day we were going to the same streets for a shooting. You would go to the morgue and see this young lad lying there. He'd be otherwise fit and healthy, a perfect physique apart from the hole in his head. Rivalry among local groups accounted for a surge in shootings, there was an influx of firearms and ammunition on the streets and people were willing to put up with it. The violence could start over something trivial, like a dispute over a girl. The gang members were only young lads really and they were moving about on mountain bikes. Some of the older lads became vulnerable because of the emerging group of youngsters. They were very, very dangerous because they had big guns and were wearing them as fashion accessories. When they weren't carrying them they were putting pressure on young girls to hide them.

'They weren't really using the guns to further criminal aims, although that might have been how it started – it was about respect, they were trying to make a name for themselves, not fighting over a geographic turf, it was personal, there were certain streets where individuals would live and that would be their sort of area. It's about respect and disrespect. It comes in phases, different names come to the fore. It was about lifestyle, they weren't particularly rich guys at all …the older ones, as they got more sense, would get more into criminal enterprise.

'It was a different atmosphere in the community, one of fear and acceptance. It took us ages to get on top of them. There's almost a social acceptance in small pockets of areas where these boys go round in gangs. If you had a sex offender living next to you, you wouldn't accept it. But people who had a gunman next door, who could kill their son or daughter, were too scared to say anything against them.'

This book looks at the major episodes in Manchester's underworld in the first decade of the twenty-first century. An earlier book, *Gang War: The Inside Story of the Manchester Gangs*, by Peter Walsh, chronicles the period before this, and in many way *Shooters* is complementary to that work. By 2000, the year *Shooters* begins, there were at least four well-armed gangs active on the streets of inner south Manchester, each determined to prove it was the baddest. This area of a few square miles, dubbed the 'murder triangle', had Moss Side, plagued by the likes of the Young Gooch Crew and the Doddington, to the west. To the east was the Longsight area, which the Pitt Bull Crew and the Longsight Crew claimed as a battleground. In total, about 200 people, at varying levels of involvement, were judged to be mixed up in the gang scene in this area at the turn of the century. The rank-and-file of these gangs were scared and angry young boys, led by men barely out of their teens; thugs whose own schooldays had been punctuated by gunfire, whose best education had been in crime.

This period is described in the first chapter, 'Bull', from the point of view of Joseph 'Slips' Mensah, a gang member who made the rare decision to turn supergrass on his peers. Mensah joined the Pitt Bull Crew, whose members he had known as a young street tough, because he had nothing better to do when he came out of prison. He quickly found himself in the middle of a war. His testimony offers a rare insight into the stark realities of the gang lifestyle, all too often cloaked in secrecy or obscured by self-aggrandising fable.

Pitt Bull Crew leader Tommy Pitt, like his wheelchair-bound rival Julian Bell of the Longsight Crew, was at the top of a tightly structured street-dealing pyramid. Newer gangs would move away from this business model as the decade wore on and the relationship between their criminal activities and the violence they perpetuated would continue to diverge. Turn of the century gang members were just as likely to have a one-man cannabis sales operation as they were to engage in more lucrative 'class A' dealing. Car-jacking, home invasions and street robbery were other sources of income. With a good number of ordinary gang members at school age or near enough, many lived with their parents and had very little money at all. Even for reasonably successful drug dealers, like Narada Williams of the Longsight Street Soldiers (see Chapter Six), a rebel faction that split from the Longsight Crew and allied itself with the Gooch, the thug life was essentially a distraction from their racketeering, and played no part in furthering it.

Trivial disputes between gang members were much more likely to result in murder and serious injury when guns were abundant. As police took the MAC-10s and Uzis out of circulation, underworld arms dealers, generally white, fed demand by smuggling in replicas from Europe and converting them for lethal use. In the largest of these conspiracies, funded and masterminded by Michael 'Mickey the Fish' Sammon and Robert 'Bobby the Gun' Tyrer, at least 273 gas-firing 'sports guns' were brought to the UK. The firearms murder rate started to decline in 2002, but plots like Sammon and Tyrer's sowed the seeds for a surge in gun violence at the tail end of the decade. Their conspiracy, which ran from 2004 to 2005, is looked at in detail in Chapter Three.

Ian McLeod returned to notoriety after a few years away from local headlines. McLeod was one of the original Moss Side gangsters, having been at the heart of the Pepperhill and Doddington gangs in the eighties and nineties. He survived a series of attempts on his life and was jailed for running a major street drug dealing operation, before joining a number of the original gang heads in decamping to a quieter outer suburb. McLeod was running a security company when he was called upon by Bobby Spiers, a close associate of Salford face Paul Massey, to take out a local hardman in 2006. McLeod recruited two younger men for the job, which went spectacularly wrong. This episode is detailed in Chapter Four, 'Bloodbath at the Brass Handles'.

In 2006, the tragic death of an innocent would epitomise the dangers and pressures faced by youngsters in areas blighted by the gun. Jessie James was fifteen years old when he was gunned down in a park in a still-unsolved murder. His killing galvanised the city against gun crime in a way not seen since the death of Benjy Stanley, murdered buying a treat at a Moss Side bakery thirteen years earlier. This period is covered in Chapter Five, 'The Killing of Jessie James'.

In 2007, the *Manchester Evening News* published a list of names and photographs of people killed by the gun in Greater Manchester since 1999. Most of them were black males in their twenties or younger. The headline was 'How Many More?' The article would be printed on t-shirts in the community, and adorn the walls of senior police officers' rooms as a reminder of the human toll behind the statistics. In the same period, Manchester-based criminologists conducted scores of interviews in fieldwork which would inform several reports on gang culture. In the report *Youth Gangs In An English City*, the academics summarised the effect gangs had on the communities in which they lived and operated.

> The numbers of gang members were small, yet they had a large negative impact in and on their communities, both direct (e.g. victimisation, territorial restrictions on mobility) and indirect (e.g. stigmatisation of area and particularly young people). Community members consistently expressed the view that the violence should stop and that local young people should have mainstream aspirations rather than accept a life of crime. But equally, community members did not demonise gang members in the same way that others do; rather, they saw them as victims of the system. It was not surprising then to find a community willing to engage with them to get them away from gang activity, even if these efforts were limited by lack of sustainable funding, appropriate training, organised coordination, support from statutory agencies and opportunities for excluded young people.

Black community leaders were described as finding themselves 'between a rock and a hard place'. By acknowledging the gang violence in their communities, they were opening up the problem for sensible debate and increasing their prospects of getting funding to counteract it. On the other hand, they risked reinforcing negative stereotypes about black people and 'opened the door to simplistic and essentialist explanations'. There were no easy solutions.

The surge in gun violence in this period had as much to do with the emergence of Lee Amos and Colin Joyce from prison as it did with the availability of converted replica guns. Leaders of the Young Gooch, the second generation of the notorious gang, and veterans of ultra-violent, late nineties gangland, the two pals geed up the leaderless bands of Gooch-affiliated ragamuffins who had sprung up while they had been inside. Then they picked up the guns themselves in a campaign of vengeance against the Longsight Crew, who had killed Amos's brother in 2002. Their deadly spree climaxed in the killing of Tyrone Gilbert – among the city's most shocking, not because of the victim's age or innocence, but because of the occasion on which they chose to strike, at the funeral of a man Joyce had murdered.

Joyce and Amos stoked up gangland tensions, killing and maiming while on licence from prison. The system responded to this embarrassment by banging them up in a landmark prosecution. The police operation, codenamed Viola, and the trial which followed, involved a perfect storm of legal and technological advances, detailed in chapters Seven and Eight, 'Cabbo's Revenge' and 'Life and Death'. This case showed how the explosion in the use of mobile phones enabled police to retrace suspects' movements using cell-site evidence. Advanced forensic science and the network of surveillance cameras helped cops join the dots. Changes in the law allowed witnesses – in the past too terrified to give evidence against gangs – to give evidence anonymously. The rules about dealing with supergrasses were codified under the Serious Organised Crime and Police Act. Gangland insiders could win immunity from prosecution, or heavily discounted sentences, if they turned on their friends. Details of defendants' previous convictions could be aired even if they were prejudicial, if it was successfully argued they were relevant to the case, under the 'bad character' provisions of the Criminal Justice Act 2003, an overhaul of the system intended by the Labour government to tip the balance in favour of victims. The Criminal Justice Act bolstered the Firearms Act of 1968, and toughened sentencing for firearms possession. Anyone who lived in a house in which they knew guns were being kept by others, such as a partner, son or daughter, was considered to have possessed the weapon themselves and could expect a mandatory jail sentence of at least five years. Greater Manchester Police would trumpet their success, and controversially appeal for information on 'wanted' gun crime suspects, with huge billboards, often gloating in tone. These were condemned by civil liberties campaigners but few others had much sympathy.

Moss Side retained its image as the gangs' battleground because of high-profile murders like the killing of Jessie James, because it was where the conflict had started, because it was still home to a number of key figures, and because it was where gang members from across Manchester came to make trouble. However, in the first decade of the new century, younger cliques sprung up in previously relatively untroubled inner suburbs neighbouring Moss Side. These cliques, like the Old Trafford Crips and the Fallowfield Mad Dogs, were largely composed of lads who were too young to remember the original Gunchester era. Both new gangs were linked to the Gooch. The Old Trafford Crips were largely the violent sons of one extended local family and their associates, while the FMD's story was one of thwarted energies; members included talented MCs and disaffected suburban teens. These young gangs revived a practice first adopted in the nineties of allying themselves with Los Angeles gangs. Doddington's spawn, the Moss Side Bloods, took the colour red and claimed allegiance with their LA namesakes. The Old Trafford Crips sported blue bandanas accordingly.

When grime music travelled north from its east London birthplace, these young Manchester cliques found the perfect soundtrack for their lives. Groups of DJs and MCs tied to gangs by geography and shared experience formed, and for a brief period it seemed as if they could provide a creative outlet for the frustrations and hostilities which all too often ended in unnecessary bloodshed. Before long, though, old tensions resurfaced. In 2008, two young men lost their lives: Halton McCollin, a hardworking amateur footballer, and Louis Brathwaite, a handsome kid whose popularity on his estate placed him on the fringes of the gang scene. A group of teenagers would set out to avenge Brathwaite's murder, resulting in the death of a third youth, Giuseppe Gregory, a sixteen-year-old who had nothing to do with it. The killing of Gregory, and the culture at its backdrop, is looked at in Chapter Nine, 'Gunchester Grime'.

This was the period when gang rivalry and the fight against it moved into the internet. In the wake of those deaths, a slew of 'diss' tracks flew back and forth on YouTube. Detectives would scan these tracks for clues on unsolved murders, and use the same website for emotive appeals for information. Facebook was another frontier. Images of youths throwing up gang signs on the social networking site would be used in court to prove association and affiliation. Meanwhile, tribute sites and 'Gone Too Soon' memorial pages testified to the personal tragedies behind the shootings, away from the newspapers and the courtrooms.

While street gangs attracted attention with their internecine feuding and capacity for bloodshed, serious organised criminals were operating across the conurbation. A thieves' code in Salford meant that the reasons behind punishment shootings in the tough city, with its gritty housing estates and back-to-back terraces, were often hushed up. Outside elements, most infamously in the case of the bloodbath at the Brass Handles in 2006, could be brought in to settle internal disputes with extreme violence. Armed robbery, with the proceeds spent on the high-life or used to fund multi-kilo drug purchases, remained a Salford specialty. In the period this book covers, the authorities would attempt to hit back at bank robbers enjoying a lavish lifestyle using the Proceeds of Crime Act, which built on existing money laundering provisions to go after villains' assets. Meanwhile, provisions in the Criminal Justice Act 2003 allowed courts to label prolific robbers as 'dangerous', and lock them away indeterminately for the public protection. While the minimum tariffs on these sentences looked low, defence lawyers, criminals, and civil liberties campaigners hated this innovation. The minimum tariff was in fact only the time a villain must spend behind bars before he could apply for parole, and not the period that must be served before release. A villain could, in theory, spend the rest of his life behind bars if the Parole Board were not convinced he was no longer dangerous. Salford's bank robbers and their relationship with the authorities are looked at in the chapter 'Police and Thieves'.

The underworld in Bolton, the former mill town some ten miles north-west of the city of Manchester, also produced some dramatic crime stories. Wayne McDonald, henchman for a Lancashire-based Mr Big who made many millions from drugs, would spend years on the run after shooting two innocent people at a nightclub. McDonald was only caught after a robbery went wrong and he shot a policewoman, episodes detailed in the chapter 'The Man from Atlantis'.

The drugs scene in Bolton atomised after the murder of Billy Webb, who had ruthlessly dominated the trade there in the nineties. Rival gangs of Asian crooks seized pieces of the pie and a new conflict began. Organised Asian crime gangs were first identified in the north about 2000, and by the end of the decade they had begun shooting at one another. Oldham, the former cotton town to the north-east of Manchester, also had a lively underworld. It sprouted a number of regional headmen, and networks of Pakistani and Bangladeshi origin. Players from the backstreets of districts like Werneth and Glodwick were regular visitors to Pakistan, where they could set up heroin deals and disappear to if the heat got too much. With links to organised crime across the country, the leading Asian criminals were higher in the supply chain than inner-city south Manchester's lifestyle gangs, and Oldham became a destination for wholesale drug purchases. Taxings – targeting cannabis farms in particular – were common among the town's dealers, who cruised around in rented Lamborghinis while sharing two-up, two-downs with extended family.

A rash of shootings in 2009 would expose the Oldham underworld as a new frontier in Greater Manchester's gangland. The killing of innocent shopworker Nasar Hussain was the climax of underworld politicking and the bitter fruit of cooperation between gangsters from different areas: the murder took place in Salford but was coordinated in Oldham as a result of feuding in Bolton, and was carried out by criminals from Huddersfield, Longsight and Cheetham Hill. The wranglings and fall-outs of the Asian mill-town gangsters are looked at in the final three chapters.

The activities of the Asian gangs of Oldham and Bolton at the tail end of the decade prompted Peter Fahy, Chief Constable of Greater Manchester Police, to identify them as a firearms threat comparable to the inner-south Manchester gangs who brought unprecedented levels of violence and drug dealing to the streets in the late eighties and nineties. Thankfully, two-and-a-half years have passed since the last murder on the Oldham scene, and the guns have also fallen silent in Bolton. This has coincided with a long period of quiet in inner-city south Manchester, the area historically most troubled by gun crime. At time of writing, five-and-a-half years have elapsed without a gang-related murder in Moss Side, and nearly five years has passed since a murder in Longsight. The last gang-related killing in south Manchester, the murder of Giuseppe Gregory in Stretford, was three years ago. Gang activity is at its lowest levels for a generation, with only a few dozen, with limited access to firearms, buying into the lifestyle. The city hopes, with baited breath, that there will be no return to the bad old days.

1

Bull

THEY WEREN'T TALKING about the weather when they
said the streets were hot that summer, and Joshua Mensah walked out of jail into the thick of it. Longsight, the south
Manchester neighbourhood he headed for, was riddled with
feuding young drug dealers. Every few days, in just a couple of
square miles, someone shot at someone.

A tough twenty-something with Ghanaian heritage, Mensah was called 'Slips' because the first time he got locked up,
he was wearing his slippers; the cops had lifted him so quick
he hadn't time to reach for his Nikes. He did six years for a
double kidnapping and promised himself he wouldn't end up
back inside. Easier said than done, with a past like his. In his
early teens he had run with baby gangbangers who wore
bulletproof vests, slung class A drugs and carried radio scanners to keep one step ahead of the 'Five-oh'. On his release, the
old faces were still there, wreathed in smiles.

'Yes, Slips, you soldiered out your time. Respec' yo, you a
thugster,' they would say on the street, bumping fists before
passing him a freshly rolled spliff to burn. Tommy Pitt smiled
at him too, and Tommy wasn't much for smiling.

A mixed-race lad with a street reputation far bigger than
his stature, Tommy 'Bull' Pitt epitomised the new breed of

25

badman, schooled in crime at an age when some of his gangland peers had been attending Bible classes. Alongside his older brothers, Kenny and Ray, Tommy had worked the open-air drugs bazaar on the Alexandra Park estate, said to net the Doddington Gang up to £1 million a year, back in the early nineties. On the face of it, Tommy's youth offending record appeared to be textbook foot soldier stuff, with fire-arms, robbery and dishonesty to add to the drugs, but his attitude to crime was anything but. Most gangbangers are content making enough for an eighth of skunk and a few brandy and cokes at the weekend. Tommy was ruthless in an ambition to become the city's most feared, most powerful gangster. When his equally ferocious brother Ray, a Dodding-ton leader, was gunned down at age twenty by members of his own crew, Tommy was steeled with a lust for vengeance. And by the time Slips was back out, he had formed his own mob of violent drug dealers, armed with guns taxed from his former Doddington allies and named the Pitt Bull Crew, or PBC, in memory of Ray's street name, 'Pitbull'.

The Northmoor area of Longsight was mainly rows of terraces then, blighted by voids, but Tommy was proud to call it his territory. He recruited school truants and expellees to serve up crack and heroin to the local fiends, and made Fagin seem a model employer. A sad face on a kid was evidence only of them being a 'lazy cunt' as far as he was concerned. While just out of short trousers himself, he had answered to Ian McLeod, a Moss Side Original Gangster who had helped found first the Pepperhill Mob and then the notorious Dod-dington gang. Then, when barely into his teens, he had escaped from a bail hostel to join his brothers on the frontline of the crack and smack trade. Even if he hadn't been such an eager delinquent in his own youth, it would have been natural for Tommy to make use of kids in a criminal enterprise. They were easy to control, and he liked to be in control.

'Those kids were out slinging morning, noon and night,' a former Pitt Bull Crew insider said. 'They might have been promised money but I never saw them get any. They might have got the odd bit here and there, for a tracksuit or something, but not proper money. They made thousands selling drugs on the street and they would hand it all to Tommy, who said it was for "gang funds". Tommy decided not just when they worked but when they ate and slept as well. It was no life for them; they didn't have the freedom to go doing anything what a normal sixteen-year-old would do.'

Tommy may have had ambition but his operation was rooted firmly in the street, some distance away from the wholesale and importation sectors of the drug trade. The top tier of his gang consisted of older villains who controlled the dealers and were authorised to carry out extortions, or taxings. These men had been running with Bull since his days in the Doddington. Tommy now invited Slips to join them. 'There's a place for you Slips. The love's there, we need you,' the gang leader said. Slips wasn't immediately sold. While no stranger to gang culture, he liked to think of himself as his own man. Still, he was flattered to be invited. He prided himself on being a street soldier, the type you would want watching your back in a battle, and he knew that the Pitt Bulls were at war. They had traded shots with the faction of the Doddington blamed for Ray's death, had battled with the Gooch before brokering a peace, and were always busting at the Longsight Crew.

The beef with the Longsight Crew started out when the gang's dealers encroached into Northmoor, wise to how lucrative a patch it was for the PBC. The LSC's leader and founder, Julian Bell, had been dealt a trifecta of adversity by fate: he was poor, black and permanently disabled. He was also a streetwise young villain, who seconds before losing the use of his legs had been razzing around on a stolen motorbike. Fate dealt him a £500,000 compensation payment for his injuries, which he used to take control over the local thugs and street dealers from his secluded base on Langport Avenue, at the heart of a small housing estate. He bought a BMW specially adapted for his disability, and machines for processing cocaine in bulk.

Like the Pitt Bulls, the LSC were an offshoot of the Doddington, but unlike Tommy's mob they had stayed loyal to their Moss Side forefathers. The LSC had reasons of their own to beef with the Gooch, the traditional enemies of Doddington, since Julian's late brother Orville had been shot dead by a Goochie in 1996. Orville was the gang's talisman, the inspiration for its creation, enshrined in the memory of the local *yout'dem* as a Tony Montana figure. He was just seventeen when he was shot in the neck while sitting at the wheel of his Honda CRX; his assassin then snatched his blood-spattered gold chain.

Slips might never have got mixed up in the whole thing if he hadn't gone to the blues. A blues is what they call an underground party in inner city Manchester. They throw back to Moss Side's sixties scene, when shebeens served up lashings of rum and good music to West Indian locals, African students and white thrill-seekers. Over the years, the soundtracks have changed but the dingy unlicensed vibe of a front room given over stays the same. Gangbangers like blues parties; they give them the chance to flex in front of people who know who they are, and they don't have trouble getting in. Club doors are the last bastions of overt race prejudice in northern England; street thugs in dusty tracksuits stand the least chance, at least not without a sympathetic set of bouncers, of getting in the best clubs.

This blues was at Beresford Street, at the heart of the old terraced side of Moss Side to the east of Princess Road. Slips went there with Big D, a senior PBC banger who he had known from prison. Tommy had ordered that the whole crew turn out, and one by one they lined up to bump fists with

Slips, the returning hero: Big W, Little W, Little T, Little Snoop, Casper, Pinky, Trabbs, Chucky, Mango, Little Porky, Pork Chop, Scan, Chan, Bullet, Mickey, Mark and Mo. Slips had made vague plans to work for his sister's boyfriend now that he was free, but those plans evaporated amid the weed smoke, and the brandy, and the good vibes from the Pitt Bulls.

After bubbling at the blues, Slips found himself heading for the low-rise Alexandra Park housing estate, falling in line with Tommy's ragtag army as it crossed Princess Parkway, some soldiers on foot, others pedalling. Fronted by the distinct, yellow-brick terraces of Quinney Crescent, the Alex Park estate is far from the bleakest in Manchester, with many ordinary families proud to call it home. Still, it is a poor estate, poverty and crime are bedfellows, and its streets have seen many a bloody intrigue.

MOSS SIDE IS the geographical heart of the city's black community. Its people bear the scars of slavery and the colonial experience and have seen immigrant dreams dashed by racism and lack of opportunity. Like all deprived areas, low aspiration, casual violence and family breakdown are realities of life. The black people that settled on the eastern, 'old' side of Moss Side in the fifties and sixties were typical of the post-war generation: families who worked hard, bus drivers and factory workers, often guided by conservative Christian values. There were also rough and ready rudeboys, single males who engaged in slackness, like drinking, smoking weed, carrying blades and consorting with whores, but there was nothing like the wanton attitude to life and death that would be seen in the gang wars of the eighties and nineties.

The seeds for that were sown in the seventies, after slum clearance had shaken community bonds, when the badly planned housing estates that had replaced the back-to-backs were already beginning to decay, when Britain was heading for mass unemployment, when police beat black people up. Moss Side's young brothers found themselves disconnected both from British society and the West Indian islands they were brought up to call home. This potent mix of social and racial woes made Moss Side, and in particular the back passages and ginnels of the Alex Park estate, a crucible for gang crime.

That first generation of gangsters were by-products of the rapacious materialism of the Thatcher years, a period when it was difficult for young black men in the inner cities to achieve all, or indeed anything, they wanted. They were also products of the culture of resistance that the political and socio-economic climate of the time fostered. Away from the she-beens and the pimps of Moss Side, the majority of ordinary families in the neighbourhood were guided by a traditional West Indian morality which was compatible with the values of British society. But that society did not regard them as equals, fomenting a discontent among the young that exploded in the Moss Side riots of 1981. In such a climate, crime was easily justified as resistance. Violence furthered the goals of those involved in crime, and life became cheap. For those who inherited that thwarted culture of resistance, the violence became an end in itself. The Original Gangsters, those that survived, have mainly moved out of Moss Side. The more successful among them run legitimate businesses; some still engage in organised crime today. They left behind a bad reputation for the everyday people to live with and made their streets a magnet for thugs from other neighbourhoods.

Tommy Pitt and his mob hailed from all over Manchester, but they loved to come back to Moss Side to party, check their people, and make trouble. Tonight, they were heading for the Big Western, which sits at the 'back' of the Alexandra Park estate. Its name flickers images of the lawless world of cowboys and outlaws that influenced, in their rudeboy days, some of the older Jamaicans that patronise this saloon. The walls have seen more badmen than Strangeways prison, and if they could talk they would regale you with tales of the whole Manchester gang saga. The Big Western, more prosaically, is a big imposing boozer on the western side of Moss Side. It was here, just after the blues, that Slips got his first taste of what it meant to ride with the Pitt Bulls.

The lads were standing around near the car park, talking, some circling on bikes, waiting for something to happen, when a car pulled in. Tommy thought it looked shady, so he sent Little T over to have a look. Little T did not yet need to shave, but was the Pitt Bull's pitbull: a pup weaned by a cruel master. Three months earlier, he had been remanded on a charge of murdering Judah Dewar, a Longsight father of nine. The charge crumbled through lack of evidence and Little T was freed.

He rolled down the biker's balaclava he had been wearing like a hat to cover his face. Little T was high on ecstasy, as he often was. He produced an old gunslinger's .357 revolver from the small of his back, cocked back the hammer and bounced over to the vehicle. The innocent occupants threw up their hands. Little T saw there was no threat there and loped back to the ranks of his gang, gun in hand. Such hair-trigger moments were commonplace in such company.

Slips left the car park with a young lad called Pinky. Pinky was full of stories of how mad it was out here these days. The battles of the last few months had left him jumpy. It could kick off at any time. They only ever seemed to go to places where they might shoot somebody, or could end up getting shot, else they were selling drugs, or robbing somebody. Anywhere they went, they might run into LSC or Doddington. Pinky had come close to being killed himself, but he was trapped. His brother, Paul, was Tommy's lieutenant, but Pinky himself was rarely trusted with a gun.

In March of that year, Scan, a younger member of the PBC, had been caught in crossfire when Gooch gunmen opened fire on senior Doddington players at a blues party, and had been shot in his side. A couple of days later, Little Snoop had been blasted in the stomach. A fortnight after that, an LSC car chased the PBC's Volvo through Longsight, the passengers leaning out of the windows licking off shots at one another with automatic weapons. A patrol car got between the bullets, chasing down the Volvo until it sped off. Later that month in Old Trafford, an old friend of Ray Pitt's was found with shotgun holes in his leg.

Slips wasn't put off by what Pinky had told him. His plan to join the working population was fading every day. He couldn't face the boredom. It was easier to wake up, roll a zoot, switch on a scanner and go check the Pitt Bulls. One day, he went with Little T to his nan's, in a small row of houses running behind the Parkway. Little T had a MAC-10 stashed in the garden, wrapped in a gym bag, hidden under a pallet in the damp back yard. He carried the bag into the front room of the house, his arm pulled low by the weight of it, dropped the dull, grey weapon on the living room table and set about cleaning it expertly. He showed Slips the clip full of bullets, explaining that the weapon had a tendency to jam. Still, everybody in the Pitt Bulls was attached to that gun. They even had a nickname for it: 'the Nino'. It was the biggest weapon in their arsenal, and unless he said so, only Tommy was allowed to use it.

Little T might have been trusted to look after the Nino but Slips was already wise that the kid was a joey. All the kids in the outfit were. A joey, or grafter, or worker, is the lowest tier on the drug dealing ladder. They take the most risk and make the least money. Tommy had actually offered Slips Little T to work for him. That was the way it worked: if Tommy liked you he would set you up with your own flat, a connection for powder and some young workers who would do what you told them. Slips fancied a bit of that. None of the older gang members sold drugs on the street themselves; they bought in bulk, a kilo or two at a time, and gave them to the joeys to sell. Then they took the money off them. The top guys were under no illusions about what they were in the life for. Power and money, what went for it, on the unforgiving streets of Manchester's toughest neighbourhoods. The younger members might picture a day of hanging out, playing pool and eating crisps, smoking weed, chasing *gyal*, shooting the breeze. And then the call would come to get to work. Get here now. Even when they massed at a blues, it was never to relax but invariably to flex their muscle or war with their enemies. It was a rare night when it didn't kick off.

Slips soon became the driver for the top tier of the PBC. He would later become pissed off with his role, because it meant he was always at the heart of things without ever being asked his opinion, but in those early days he was happy because it meant Tommy trusted him with his cars. One night they drove out to Mr Smiths, a cavernous Warrington nightclub where monthly soul nights drew crowds from across the North. There was a particular DJ on, but really the Pitt Bulls were there because Longsight would be too. As soon as they pulled into the car park, they spotted enemy cars. Mo ran over and started popping the tyres.

Inside the club, the mood was tense enough even without the Longsight boys knowing what had happened to their ride home. The LSC were lined up near the entrance. Screwfacing, kissing of teeth and insults went back and forth. Slips, Pinky and one of the girls they were friendly with, Charmaine, got drinks from the bar and picked a quieter spot on the balcony to sip them. They tried to relax, to stop their minds and their eyes wandering down on the dancefloor where a cluster of LSC lurked. Slips saw his cousin among them, and another kid he had known for years, Baxter. His eyes moved from his rivals to a group of girls. When he next looked over at LSC, Baxter was gone. He was running straight at them on the balcony and then he was slamming down a bottle of Budweiser on Mo's head. Slips knocked Baxter off his feet with one punch. The club erupted into a chaos of smashing bottles and screaming dancers, cops and bouncers swarming. Everybody was hauled outside and the club was shut down.

On the M62 back to Manchester, Mo, who had Baxter's number, called him, and said he would ride on him. The Pitt Bulls also laughed and joked about Slips' punch. He had proved himself. 'I got out of prison and I felt as if they wanted me up there with them, you know,' Slips later said. 'They see me potentially to be on a level with them and they wanted me up there with them. It wasn't like I had moved up through the structure, it was more that I had known them for a long time, they knew what I was like, you know, like physical, and they wanted me with them.'

Staying in favour with Tommy was a full-time job. One time one of the boys pissed him off, so Tommy snatched the chain from his neck and tossed it to Slips. It was a thick chop and looked good. Slips hadn't had any money yet but he had a chain and access to a fleet of cars, so he felt like he was doing well. All of the top PBC guys wore chops.

His job at the wheel took Slips to all the different properties used by the gang. The homes of girlfriends and relatives were used to hide drugs, guns, and to provide houseroom, a hot bath, and laundry services in the aftermath of a shooting. Tommy also controlled a string of safehouses. Sometimes they were derelict properties that had been commandeered by the gang, other times they would be legitimately rented, or have an occupant too weak to resist the gang members who converged there. The joeys would ply their trade in back entries a mere shout away from the safehouses, so they could return quickly to restock when they ran out. Guns would be laid on the table as dust whirled from the cutting and the bagging process. The street-level dealers stuck together in small units of bikes and were always armed in case the LSC appeared. The kids had cold hard faces and were experienced gunmen. Inside though, they were more terrified than anybody.

Slips learnt this the hard way when Little T ran him over in a car. 'He was a bit mad,' said Slips, 'used to see things that was not there, because of the amount of drugs that was pumped into him. It was ecstasy that was making him mad, that was my opinion.' It happened down a dark street in Longsight. Little T was driving a car full of the youngers and was supposed to be meeting Slips. But when a black-clad figure stepped out in the road and pointed at him, Little T got spooked. He gunned the motor straight at Slips, scooping him onto the bonnet then dumping him with a crunch on the ground. Slips' foot was twisted at an awkward angle and his hand throbbed. His friends, realising their mistake, bundled him onto the back seat and headed for Manchester Royal Infirmary.

'I, I, thought you was one o' them lot,' said the flustered Little T.

At hospital, Slips begged to lie down but the staff told him he would have to book in. He was jumpy and antsy; the Longsight boys knew who he had been riding with. He had grown up with a lot of them, but none of that mattered since he had sparked out Baxter in Mr Smiths. If they saw him in the hospital, incapacitated, he would be a dead man. Slips mustered up all the strength he had and made a limping break for the ward. He didn't get far. The security men and a nurse and a doctor told him he was just going have to wait.

'I didn't feel at the time that they wanted to treat me,' Slips said. 'I felt like I was being looked upon as a stranger. I came in dressed in black, I had gloves on.'

The hospital staff knew what a gang member looked like. Gangbangers were regulars at MRI, which was located in the middle of their south Manchester neighbourhoods. Young men were always coming in with wounds, usually accompanied by posses of friends. Sometimes armed police would lock off the hospital. Slips wished there were some officers there now. The whole time he was in there he hoped and prayed there were no LSC visiting.

When Slips had got himself together again, Pinky called to say he was needed. By now he had moved to his girlfriend George's house in Rusholme, away from the eyes of his family. He cycled to the West Indian Sports and Social Club, where Pinky was waiting with a black eye. Slips didn't get the whole story at first: he was told Pinky had been in bed with this girl in Fallowfield, when a guy burst in and started battering him. Pinky knew where to find the man and together they cycled over.

It was a terraced house not far from the Beresford Road blues. Tommy and Little T were already there, interrogating two women at the door. It turned out that the guy who punched Pinky was the babyfather of a girl Tommy was running with. Her mother had reported her missing and told the police she had been keeping 'bad company'. The babyfather got involved, deciding to find her himself, because there was no way Tommy Pitt was getting involved with the mother of his kids. He tracked her down to a room at the Palace Hotel, where the gang leader had taken her for the night. Pinky and Slinger stayed in a nearby room. In the morning the lovebirds were woken by a loud rapping at the door and shouts for her to 'come home'. They waited until the man went away, and then they slipped out of the room and down a fire exit. The babyfather, at the other end of the corridor, turned and saw them. He caught up with them on the back stairs and shouted at Tommy; the young gangster smiled and raised his tee-shirt, flashing the butt of a pistol stuffed down his trousers. The babyfather watched as the girl drove off in a taxi with Tommy, Pinky and Slinger. Dogged in his desperation, he traced Pinky to a girlfriend's home in Fallowfield and gave him a slapping. Later the girl was tracked down to a homeless hostel, where she confessed her feelings for Tommy to the cops. The babyfather went back to Moss Side to wait for the inevitable PBC delegation.

He was round the back when the women gave him up. Little T was waving a shotgun about. Tommy snatched it from him and stormed round the back. But then, as unpredictable as he was, he decided he couldn't be bothered and came back round to the front of the house, tossing the shotgun back to Little T.

'Don't kill him, just take his knees off,' he said, before ducking into his car and speeding off.

The gang confronted the babyfather at the back door. A handy lad, he wasn't about to run and hide, but neither was he taking the risk of coming outside, not with that shotgun. Little T got pissed off and pointed the barrels directly in the man's face.

'Put it away, T,' begged Pinky, who wasn't the murderous type. 'Let me talk to him.'

The man was terrified now, his lips jabbering behind the glass, praying for his life.

'Look', said Little T, 'I could take your head off now. You might as well come out, yo.'

The man came out, and for a tense few seconds it seemed a terrible mistake; Little T was so keen to blow his head off. But Pinky managed to talk the kid out of such 'crazy madness' just long enough to lead the guy down the ginnel for a chat about a straightener, an old-school fist fight, to sort it out like men. Little T wasn't having it though.

'Fuck a straightener,' he started shouting. 'Forget a fucking straightener. Bull said what to do.'

Then he blasted the man in the leg. The guy crumpled to the cobbles before regaining his feet and hobbling off. His pain-wracked face struck a chord with Slips. He remembered that he knew the guy from way back, when they were kids.

He rode with Little T back to his nan's house, late at night. A terrible bang shot through Slip's nerves and split the wood of the door.

'Shit, soz,' said Little T. He had fired the shotgun by accident as he leapt from the bike with it.

The pair chilled out for a bit, smoking a couple of spliffs. There was talk of a house party in Levenshulme, so they went back to the car park of the Sports and Social, where Pinky was waiting at the wheel of a Renault 19. He shifted over to let Slips drive and the lads cruised the streets of south Manchester, stopping in at different girls' houses and picking up Mickey and Little W along the way.

When they got to the house party, it was already past midnight. Getting in was a long business, because it was in a flat above a shop and nobody could find the keys. Eventually the bars of the security gate were bent back and the Pitt Bulls bowled in, staring into people's faces. Lots of people lined the walls, high on spirits, cocaine and cannabis. In the middle of the front room, a girl was bawling that her purse had been stolen. Slips took control.

'No fucker's leaving till this gyal's purse has been found. You's all have gotta be searched.'

The gangbangers swaggered through the flat, frisking down the revellers crammed in each corner. Some were cheeky and wouldn't have it. Mickey didn't like this. He was Tommy's brother and shared some of his ways. He slipped away and left the others to it. The next time Slips saw him was when everybody had spilled out of the party and into the grey light of the early morning. First he saw an arm pumping up and down and heard the sound of metal on bone. Mickey was pistol-whipping somebody. He split the victim's head down to the skull with the butt of the Nino. When he was done he got on a mountain bike and rode off, firing a shot in the air. The witnesses scattered as the victim lay bleeding. He was one of those who had objected to being searched.

'He got battered senseless,' said Slips. 'He was on the floor not moving, thought he was dead.'

TOMMY WAS IN a bad mood. Some Jamaican had been sniffing around his late brother's babymother. Five years gone and there wasn't a day he didn't think of Ray. He was going to talk to the guy, the kind of talk you needed a gun for.

Unaware he was being watched, the Jamaican parked up opposite the Beresford Road blues in a Volkswagen Golf.

'Yo, where's that gun T? What you mean you ain't got it?'

Little T had given the loaded gun to Pinky, who didn't feel safe walking down the road late at night in Moss Side. Tommy was fuming.

'You don't give guns to Pinky.'

More importantly, he needed it now. Pinky was soon back with the gun. Once the pistol was in his grip, Tommy strode over to the car and pointed it at the Jamaican's forehead. Slips saw the man throw up his hands as he tried to reason with Tommy. Just when they were all thinking that Bull might whack the guy, he walked back to his minions with a smile on his face.

'Ten grand,' Tommy told them. 'I told him ten grand, in a month.'

Tommy's mood had switched. Happy now, he offered Slips the chance to make some 'serious money' of his own. Slips leapt at it. He'd been pepped for a while; it was high time he helped his girl with the bills. Tommy explained that he had a Moroccan connection who was coming up from London with a couple of grand for some guns. 'He trusts me,' said Tommy, 'it'll be easy.' The next day Slips met the guy in the city centre and drove him to Moss Side. He took the £2,000 from him as agreed and went to make the collect – except he slipped down a ginnel, walked to the next street and into the house where Tommy was waiting. Slips handed over the cash, eagerly awaiting the split. Tommy pocketed it all and said no more about it.

The next Saturday night, the Jamaican told Tommy he hadn't got the ten grand. Tommy was surprised, since he knew the guy had a footballer cousin who could have raised the money. The Pitt Bulls looked on as Tommy walked back to their corner of the blues empty handed. He seemed calm and said nothing more about the Jamaican. At the end of the night, he told Slips to take a ride with him. They pedalled north behind the Jamaican, watching him weave his way home, oblivious to the whirring of the bike chains behind him. When he got near Hulme's Millennium Bridge, their target leaned against a wall, spread his feet and unzipped himself for a drunken piss. Tommy dropped his bike and started running towards him. The Jamaican turned to see the thug bearing down on him, pistol in hand, and set off running, leaping over a fence and down an alleyway. Tommy stopped at the fence and fired his 9mm, licking off seven shots in rapid succession. The two Pitt Bulls then rode on through Hulme until the chain on Tommy's bike snapped. Slips offered him his own and they threw the broken bicycle in a garden before Tommy cycled off. Slips now found himself lost in Hulme, where most of the old tower blocks have been levelled to make way for new housing. Eventually though, he located the Henry Royce pub, not too far from where the carmaker had his works, and was picked up by Pinky.

Tommy was in a good mood the next day.

'Five out of seven,' he said to Slips.

'I got the impression he wanted me to know he was a good shot,' recalled Slips. At the time he had tried to sound uninterested, to not seem preoccupied by the text he had just received. It was his girlfriend George, and it was her cousin who had been shot.

AUGUST WAS HOT. Police clocked that the Beresford Road blues was full of various gangbangers, but the Armed Crime

Unit had no luck when they executed a strike on the shebeen. They also raided a PBC safehouse in Longsight that month. Owned by a helpless junkie, the house was used as a base for the young ones while they were dealing in the Northmoor Road area, and guns were usually knocking around. The day the police swooped, Little T had the Nino. As officers began pounding down the alleys, panic grew amongst the gang members who had been chilling in the house. One senior head told Little T to run straight out the front and into a nearby pub, the Garrick, and if he saw any police to '*bus* at them', meaning shoot at them. Fortunately he didn't need to.

Life in the PBC was taking its toll on Slips. His brother was beaten up by Longsight Crew members looking for him, his sister had a gun flashed at her by another LSC guy and his father's house was surrounded by armed youths, ballied up. When Slips arrived at the house, his father's car had been riddled with bullets. His family wanted less and less to do with him, and to cap it all he wasn't even making money. Tommy had offered him another chance to make 'serious money', this time by robbing a drug dealer who kept his weed in a shoebox under his bed. Slips refused a firearm, instead wresting the drugs from the dealer with his bare hands after going round on the pretext of buying a twenty bag. At Little T's nan's house they split the kilo of cannabis into ounces, and Slips was told that Little T would get him an income by selling it. Little T did sell it but passed the money directly to Tommy. When Slips asked why, he was told it was going to 'gang funds'. In the meantime he got by selling crack cocaine on the side, getting high on his own supply just the once.

Tommy wasn't slacking with the demands. The pair of them were at a daytime house party in West Gorton along with Little T. They were armed with the Nino and the .357, which Slips had taken to carrying. Sometime in the after-noon, Dean Eccleston stopped by. A bad boy who slept with a gun under his pillow, Eccleston had loose ties to the LSC and was despised by the Gooch and the PBC alike. He was a big, strong lad who no-one wanted to tackle in a fistfight. Tommy decided there and then that he wanted him dead. 'When he goes out in the street and goes past, whack him,' he said. He had already marked out a garden from where they could potshot.

As a nervous Slips and a hyperactive Little T readied themselves for the hit, Tommy kept Eccleston talking in his Mazda, even bumping fists with him in respect. When Eccleston turned the key and accelerated away, Tommy turned to the fence which Slips hid behind. Through a crack in the pallet, Slips saw Tommy jerk down his thumb, like a Roman emperor deciding the fate of a gladiator. Little T stood on a tree stump, waiting for Slips to fire first since he was the senior. But Slips' finger froze at the trigger and the car vanished from view.

Within a year, Dean Eccleston would be dead.

Bullets ricocheted around the avenues as the war assumed a new intensity. In early September, in the dog days of the summer, Slips was chilling out at a flat in West Gorton, idly listening to police frequencies on the scanner, when there was a buzz at the intercom. It was Tommy and Big D, sweating after racing there on their bikes. The pair had gone deep into enemy territory with the Nino. Tommy boasted that they had caught an LSC man – unarmed, exposed and alone – at Langport Avenue, yards from his HQ. Slips was pleased to hear the victim was the same LSC boy who had pulled a gun on his sister. Tommy said they would have killed him but they had to stop firing the MAC-10 when he picked up a toddler playing in the street and tried to use her as a shield.

The next day, the PBC massed at the home of Trabbs' sister, in the gang's Northmoor heartland. Trabbs, one of the younger members, had been daft enough to tell the others that his sister was going away, and it was decided there and then that there was going to be a party. The Pitt Bulls were soon dropping ash all over the living room carpet as they smoked weed and played computer games in their bullet-proof vests. Everyone was having a good time except Trabbs.

Then Tommy got a call from a spotter in Levenshulme that the LSC were riding down Northmoor Road, dressed in black and ballied up. Despite the shooting at Langport Avenue, the approach of the enemy surprised the Pitt Bulls, but they were not caught slipping: Slips had the .357, Tommy the Nino, and Big D was packing a nine-milli. All three, dressed in black to blend in with the night, rode up Northmoor Road. As they neared Crowcroft Park, they saw three men heading for them. Tommy and Big D leapt off their bikes and started shooting. Cartridges clattered from the clips as the opposing gunmen, facing each other in the middle of the road, unloaded. Slips dumped his bike and ran off in fear, ducking behind a car before bolting for an entry. Cowering in the darkness, he heard the staccato burst of the machine gun, punctuated by cracks from the handguns. He leapt into a garden, hands bunched around his ears. He stayed where he was for some time after the bullets stopped, until the insistent vibrating of his phone broke his peace. It was Tommy and he was angry.

'Go back and get that fucking bike where you left it. That's fucking evidence, that is.'

Slips ignored the order. Instead he went to the home of another gang member, Little D, where he caught his breath. Then he took a taxi and tried to head back down Northmoor Road, but was blocked by police officers sealing off the scene.

Mango, one of the younger PBC boys, hailed Slips from the road.

'It's over now, don't worry, just come back to it,' said Mango.

When he was back at the party, Tommy rang again, demanding Trabbs bring him the .357. Slips didn't ask the purpose, and Tommy said no more about the bike.

Slips was going through tough times with his girl George as well. She wanted them to make a home but they never got any time alone together. There was always a gang member at the door, on the phone, or worse, staying over. The Rusholme house had become just another of the PBC properties. George would make sure she was upstairs or in the kitchen when they came around, but would chew Slips' ear when they left.

A few days after the gunfight, Slips was coming to the end of a rare day to himself, spent cleaning to the humming of the police scanner, when Tommy called. There was anxiety in his voice. He was outside and he wanted to be let in. Slips checked George was upstairs before opening the door. The Tommy that he knew was 'always in his own little state', his mood switching for no apparent reason, twitching and mumbling to himself as he plotted, but the state he was in tonight was alarming. Below his ballie, rolled up like a hat, his face was slick with sweat. His hands trembled inside his black Golf Master gloves. Across his shoulder was slung a holdall from which the handle, the grip and the trigger of the MAC-10 jutted out. Tommy slapped the bag on the living room table, sat down on the sofa and demanded the scanner. The gang leader switched frequencies from Moss Side to Longsight.

'I just whacked a Longsight boy,' he said. 'That Marcus.'

Slips had known Marcus Greenidge all his life. They had gone to primary school together.

Tommy got a bath and a change of clothes at Slips' place. Later that day, he met up with Slips again, plus Little T, and the trio took a ride to a partyhouse.

'Bull's murderous, yo,' said Little T. 'Murderous. Rare, Bull's murderous y'know, proper murderous,' he kept rabbiting. 'Murderous innit, murderous.'

Tommy had killed Greenidge after going into the heart of Longsight Crew territory, alone but for the Nino. He had first tried to shoot two LSC members sitting in a car, but the gun locked up on him. By the time it was ready to fire, the targets had sped off, but Tommy was still eager for blood. Soon enough, around the corner at Flixton Walk he found two other Longsight boys on bikes. The two who'd had the lucky escape tried to warn Marcus but they never got through; he was shot twice in the head before he had time to draw his automatic. His mate lived to fight another day, leaping off his bike and running for his life, bullets clattering at his heels.

'Murderous, proper murderous, Bull, murderer, yo,' Little T rambled on, until Tommy slapped him and told him to shut the fuck up. From then on, Bull put it about that the Gooch boys had whacked Marcus and had done the PBC a special favour.

It was a plausible story, since the LSC and the Gooch despised each other. The LSC was an offshoot of the Doddington gang founded in memory of Orville Bell, murdered by the Gooch. Tommy was also ex-Doddington, but he hated the LSC as much as, if not more than, the Gooch did. He also hated a good number of the Doddington, since his brother Ray had been killed in the internal war of the nineties. Before his death, Ray was seen by surprised cops, bold as brass, on Gooch Close. At the time, he told them he was free to go there because he was a 'respected neutral'. Proof of this was seen years later when the home of Goochie Pierre Williams was raided. Williams would later become notorious as the killer of a nurse and her two young children in a horrific sex crime, but back then he was known to the police for his gang links. The officers were surprised then to find a commemorative picture of Ray Pitt on his wall.

Tommy worked hard to maintain whatever friendship and mutual respect with the Gooch his brother had established, conscious that a relatively small outfit like his, however aggressive, needed allies. On one occasion, when a street brawl involving dozens of young gang members broke out in Hulme, Tommy contacted Young Gooch Crew general Colin Joyce to act as mediator. Years later, Joyce, who was every bit as dangerous as Tommy Pitt, would be among a number of men convicted of the murder of Tyrone Gilbert, the younger brother of Marcus Greenidge.

A few days after the Greenidge killing, the PBC and the Gooch cemented their friendship with some sickening ultra-violence. They were standing around in the car park of the West Indian Sports and Social in Moss Side when the Gooch boys said they were going to the Levenshulme Palace night-club to find some Longsight boys. Some time later, the Gooch boys returned to Moss Side. Tommy's boys went over to a car. Inside was a Longsight boy.

'We've got no trouble with you, only PBC,' he bleated to the Gooch lads as they punched and kicked and rocked the car, unaware that the PBC were with them.

Bull rolled up his ballie.

'Get out the car!'

The young man was beaten to the floor, locked in a sleeper hold and punched all over his body. Then he was stamped on until Tommy ordered a pause, so that Pinky could go for another car. He came back with a Ford Mondeo and the battered victim was bundled into the boot. Tommy jumped in his Mitsubishi Shogun with Slips taking the wheel, while Little T and Mickey got in the Mondeo, with two of the joeys in the back, and they set off for Crowcroft Park with a platoon of foot soldiers heading there on bikes. Slips and Tommy got to the park first and waited for the others. At 1.30 a.m., Tommy phoned the other car to see where they were. There was a problem: the hostage had escaped. As the Mondeo was going through Rusholme at fifty miles an hour, the desperate man kicked open the boot and threw himself onto the road surface. His captors noticed that the thumping had stopped and screeched to a halt in the middle of the road. Mickey told Tommy to chill out, the 'prick' was being chased back down Wilmslow Road and, torn up as he was, he couldn't run very fast. A couple of minutes later, Mickey rang back and said he was back in the boot. By the time he was frogmarched into Crowcroft Park, punched and kneed every step of the way, the entire PBC had massed in the darkness.

The LSC boy pleaded with Slips not to let them kill him. Slips knew this guy as well, another face from the old days in Longsight. The PBC formed a circle around him, snickering as he sobbed and whined that he hadn't meant to get involved, that he was in too deep, that he was sorry.

'This is what gangbanging is all about, this is what it boils down to,' said Big D. 'If you wanna be a part of it, this is what you get.'

Tommy took the .357 from Little T and strode into the centre of the circle. He took the six bullets from the chamber of the old Western-style revolver before replacing one. Then he squatted close to the LSC boy's head and spun the chamber. He cocked back the weapon and pressed it to his ear.

'Is it your time?'

He pulled the trigger. In that instant, everyone froze. Click. The gun did not go off. Tommy spun the chamber again and asked again, 'Is this your time?' Everybody leapt back before Tommy pulled the trigger, as the victim whimpered softly. Click. Tommy spun the chamber one final time.

'Is it your time?'

It was not. The gun again did not discharge. They hauled the man to his feet and dragged him to the other side of the park, where they pushed him into a ditch by a fence.

'And he got battered,' said Slips. 'He got battered with bricks and stones, people jumping on him and bones breaking. Thomas Pitt was telling everyone to get in, to get in there, you know. Sticks, even that .357, the butt of that on his head, a big brick. I think Little T said, "Shall I whack him?" He was stood over him with the .357 and he said like, "Should I kill him?" and Thomas said, "No. Let him go back and tell them and let it be a warning to them all." He was still in the ditch. He hadn't moved. He couldn't move. He was in bits. So a few people have gone their own separate ways, some in cars, some on bikes. And I remember Trabbs coming over. He said that police was on Northmoor Road. We went after that. We all ran out the park after that.'

A few days later, the PBC were back at the West Indian Sports and Social car park, hanging around with the Gooch. It was said that the LSC were at the West Indian Centre, at Carmoor Road, Longsight, so the Gooch boys drove there with Tommy, Slips and Simmo following behind in a black Nissan. The Gooch got there first and went in while the PBC waited in the car park. They smashed up the place but came out without finding any Longsight. The Gooch moved on to the city centre Aquarium nightclub to continue the hunt. Tommy took the wheel of the Nissan, following close behind.

'I wasn't looking for anything,' said Slips. 'I expect that Thomas wanted to go along because he wanted to be, you know, seen to be allying with the Gooch.'

As the PBC men pulled up they saw the Gooch jumping out of cars, pulling down their balaclavas and barging into the club. It was just after midnight on a busy Saturday night in the city centre and merry groups were weaving their way through the streets. Slips heard the sound of smashing bottles and the rat-tat-tat of machine gun fire. Tommy started up the car and accelerated down the street. He kept one hand on the wheel, firing bullets out of the open window with the other. Then he turned the car around and fired more shots in the opposite direction, before braking sharply at the lights.

There, in front of them, in a white Nissan Bluebird, was the prey they sought. Tommy gave the order to 'mope' the car, which meant to riddle it with bullets. Then he gunned his vehicle until it was alongside the car and nudging its side. Slips squeezed most of his body out of the window and poised to pull the trigger of the Nino. But as the car scraped against the metal of the Bluebird, he got a good look into the faces of the horrified LSC men inside. One of them was his cousin, and as Slips held back, the car pulled away.

'What the fuck is going on?'

'It's me hand,' said Slips to Tommy. 'Remember when T ran me over? The Nino, it's way too heavy for me.'

Tommy kept a sullen silence as he sped back down Princess Parkway to Moss Side. They got out of the car at Little T's nan's house, where the kid and Mo were waiting. Slips repeated his excuses under Tommy's suspicious glare. 'He was just sat there staring me out, nodding his head,' Slips said.

Slips handed him the Nino and set off for his girl's house, wondering if he had got off lightly or if Tommy had something in store for him. If Slips had been one of the youngers, there was no question how Tommy would react. Little T usually copped the worst of it. Pitt would 'flip on' Little T over the slightest things. 'He would punch him, kick him, slap him and starve him, the way he was treated was bad, really bad,' Slips said. 'Every time he was in T's presence he would always have something to say to him, something to do to him, some gripe on him. He wasn't that clever, you know. He was slow and that, and losing drugs. He's always messing up.'

Little T had been given a flat at Bickerdike Court, Levenshulme, as a base for his drug racket. When Tommy had his back turned, Little T would bring back girls and throw parties. Tommy knew this and didn't like it. Then, on September 15, Tommy's worst fear was realised. Several PBC turned up at the flat to find the place had been raided by police and the door boarded up. They kicked in the door and found a copy of the search warrant and a record of the property seized by the police: an automatic Bronco handgun, two bullets, and some drugs. Tommy was furious. He blamed Little T for making the flat 'on top', as he put it. Tommy's prints were on the bullets, evidence which he had ordered Little T and Mango to drop down a drain a good while ago. Little T's face was badly lumped up by the time Tommy had finished with him.

Three days later, Little T went with Slips to an electrical store with money Tommy had given them to buy a scanner. They went back to Slips' place at Rusholme and smoked a little weed as they tested it out. It had a chip in it which stopped them accessing the police channels, so they made plans to go back the next day and have it taken out. As darkness fell, Bull called Little T and told him 'get your arse back'. Slips would never see the boy again.

The following morning, Slips cadged a lift into town, went to the electrical store and got the chip taken out. That evening, he heard over the scanner that shots had been fired near Levenshulme swimming baths and that police had found a male, dead, wearing a balaclava. Slips immediately thought of Little T, as the baths were on his drug patch. He rang T's phone. Tommy answered. Slips asked Tommy if he had his scanner on.

'Someone has been found at Levenshulme Baths, I think it's T, he might be gone,' Slips said.

'Serve him right if it's him. Won't be though, he'll get back to me,' said Tommy.

Slips rang every member of the crew to see if they had seen T. No-one had.

The dead boy was Little T. He had been shot. He was sixteen years old.

The next day, Mo, Mickey, Simmo and Tommy turned up at the front door. Mo was in a bad way, sobbing. It set the others off too, except Tommy. He told them to stop crying.

'Police suspect the cold-blooded assassination was a response to the murder less than two weeks ago of 21-year-old Marcus Greenidge,' read the report in the *Manchester Evening News*. 'Greenidge was known to run with a mob known as the Longsight crew and Thomas had associations with their rivals, the Pitt Bulls. The deadly inter-gang rivalry is a throwback to the days when small, but well-armed groups of yobs – the Gooch and the Doddington gangs – fought each other in Moss Side.'

It was a version of events that suited Tommy. 'At least now we can have peace,' he kept saying, suggesting Longsight had evened the score for Greenidge's murder. Little T had been found with the search papers from Bickerdike Court scrunched up in his hand. He had been shot twice from behind in the head and neck with a semi-automatic weapon. 'Thomas was basically saying that it served him right, that he had it coming to him,' said Slips. 'He was just being cold about it. T had been a liability to him, that is how I think Thomas seen him.'

Tommy changed his tune a few days later. Slips was chilling at Charmaine's house when there was a knock at the door from a member of the Longsight Crew. Charmaine wouldn't let him in while Slips was there. She agreed to charge up his phone for him though, and while they chatted at the doorstep the conversation turned quickly to the latest murder.

'Yeah, he was a white cunt, should be thrown in a bush. Got what was coming, [it was] one of my lot that did him.'

Slips went to a bedroom, put on his body armour. He loaded the .357 and rang Tommy to ask what to do.

'You've got the 357 innit, so kill him,' was the reply.

The conversation on the doorstep moved on from Little T. Tommy rang back again and said he was coming round. The Longsight boy had left, unharmed, by the time he arrived. Tommy waited until they had both left the house to say what he had to say.

'Listen, yeah, if I tell you do something, do it.'

Later that week the top-tier of the PBC drove down to Birmingham in convoy. Slips, at the wheel of one of the gang's old bangers, enjoyed the ride, since it took his mind off Little T. When they got to Birmingham, Slips pulled up outside a council house with loud music bumping from it. There was a party being thrown by one of Simmo's people, and here Tommy was to meet Fitzy, who had his own crew running things down here, the idea being that they would build a

Birmingham–Manchester alliance. They swapped stories about their local wars. Fitzy was out of 9mm bullets, had Tommy any? Tommy promised to help, before the Pitt Bulls went back to Manchester.

The next day, Mo, Simmo and Mickey called for Slips at his girl's house. Tommy pulled up outside shortly afterwards with his phone pressed to his ear. Slips signalled for him to come in but he ignored him, instead shooting up the road in his car.

Slips went back inside and told the rest of them about Tommy's disappearing act. No-one was surprised. In the living room they rolled up a few spliffs, and settled down to listen to the scanner. It had been crackling away in the background for some time when the news came through that an 'IC3' male had been shot. The victim was in a black Nissan. Hang on, Tommy was in a black Nissan ...

Mo leapt out of his seat and began pacing and clutching his head.

'No, no, this can't happen, shit no.'

The words 'walking wounded' popped up between the police-speak and the beeps of the scanner, and the Pitt Bulls breathed a little easier.

The next day, the *Manchester Evening News* reported:

> A man is recovering in hospital today after the latest in a wave of suspected gang-related shootings in Manchester.
>
> Thomas Pitt, 25, was shot in the thigh by a cyclist as he sat in a car at traffic lights at the junction of Upper Brook Street and Hathersage Road, Victoria Park.
>
> His injury is not life threatening. It is less than a week since his pal Thomas Ramsey, 16, was shot dead in a park in Levenshulme.
>
> Ten days before that Marcus Greenidge, 21, died when he was gunned down as he rode his bike in Longsight.

When the Pitt Bulls went to visit Tommy in hospital, police were everywhere. Tommy was in a secure unit, where he surprised the officers observing him with larger-than-life presence and chilling changes of mood. The Longsight boys had used a MAC-10 and still not killed Tommy. The PBC phoned them and taunted, 'Is that the best you can do? You can't end us y'know, you can't end our click.'

WHEN FITZY ANNOUNCED he was coming to Manchester the next day, the gang directed him to Slips' place. Fitzy wanted the bullets he had been promised, so Mo summoned Big D, who brought the Nino over with him. The deal was that Fitzy would take five bullets from the clip, but D wasn't sure because he thought he might need them. He suggested he would get some for Fitzy another time, but Slips could see Mo was keen for the deal to go ahead. Mo had taken charge while Tommy was in hospital. He told the others that Tommy had told him about this day for a long time; that if he was to get locked up or die, he was to fill his boots. Mo had been talking to all the dealers and telling everyone who had which gun. D gave in and handed the bullets to Fitzy. He asked them to come down to Birmingham the next day and the Pitt Bulls agreed for diplomacy's sake. Before they set off, Mo gave Slips fourteen wraps of crack cocaine, which Slips put in a sugar bowl.

Slips then drove over to Northmoor, where they dropped off some crack and heroin with two dealers. When they got to Birmingham, they parked up and Fitzy got in. He produced the 9mm that he had needed the bullets for before inviting the gang members into a nearby studio flat. The occupant was a fat bloke who Fitzy boasted was 'one of my DJs'. Then Fitzy left the room and returned with a .38 revolver, explaining that the bullets he had got from them the other day didn't fit his weapon. He wanted to swap a .38 and a 9mm Makarov for the Nino.

Mo asked his men what they thought. Mickey said the Nino had a 'personal meaning' and objected.

'It's logic to take two for one, innit,' argued Slips. 'It's logic.'

Everybody seemed swayed and Mo agreed they would do the deal. Slips thought Mo had a nicer style than Tommy. Fitzy said he would send a couple of girls down to Manchester for the handover but in the end he came down by himself with the fat DJ.

The following day, the Pitt Bulls had to go to London. Drug supplies were running low in Manchester without Tommy, whose contacts they couldn't use without him around. Mo said he could get some class A from down there, so Simmo and Mickey put in a few grand each and Slips drove them to Hackney, where they picked up a quarter-ki of cocaine. They got back late at night.

The following morning, Slips' home was raided at dawn by armed police. They found the 9mm Makarov under the sofa and the crack cocaine in the sugar bowl. Bail was refused. It was over.

ON REMAND FOR drugs and firearms offences, Slips got a visit from Big D and Little W. 'I was told Thomas had sent a message from another wing, Cat A wing, that I was to go to the police station, that the police was doing us, they was on to PBC, they were getting everyone out, interviewing us bit by bit, and that because the police was on to it I should just say anything that I knew, just blame it on Zeeka.'

Zeeka had turned his back on the PBC a while back and had been labelled a 'dead man' ever since. It was agreed that Big D and Little W would write letters backing up the unlikely claim that Zeeka was the leader of the outfit and was responsible for the murder of Marcus Greenidge, the shooting of the Jamaican, and every other shooting Tommy had been involved in that crazy summer. But the evidence against the Pitt Bulls was strong. Enough guns, ammo, body armour, ballies and golf gloves had been seized in raids to link them to a string of crimes.

Police had been trying to nail the PBC since at least September 1999, when thirty-five-year-old Judah Dewar was found dead at Bletchley Close. It had been a confusing scene: a body in a BMW, a bike, a bullet and a fingerprint, arrayed in such a way that it was tricky to work out where the gunman had been standing. Detectives worked out that the gun had been fired over the car and a bullet had bounced off the roof and hit Dewar, who had apparently attracted the attention of a PBC patrol simply for being a dread in a car. The bullet found had markings which suggested it had been racked off twice, and the gun it came from could be linked to a shooting which targeted the home of Gooch enforcer Lee Amos, so police knew it wasn't a Gooch weapon. With intelligence suggesting that the PBC were behind the killing, the police eventually questioned Little T, who was seen near the scene on CCTV, and Simmo, whose DNA was found on the bullet. But when Simmo learnt from disclosure that the bullet had those distinctive rifling marks, he claimed to have racked it off the first time but not the second. He still served a year for possessing ammunition, while the case against Little T was dropped for lack of evidence.

In interview, Slips obediently ran down everything he knew, inserting Zeeka's name where Tommy Pitt's should have been. Then he changed his mind. The epiphany came halfway through a gruelling November 10 interview. His family, besieged by the LSC, had all but cut him off because of his association with the Pitt Bulls. Old faces from his past had been injured and killed by the gang. And what had he got to show for it but a gold chain snatched from Pinky's neck? He had no money and no respect. He drove the PBC here and there, gave house room to anyone in the shit, always showed respect, yet Tommy spoke to him like a dog. He thought of Little T's face after the Bickerdike raid, mashed up where Tommy had punched him. And then there was his girlfriend's news: she was pregnant. Here he was, a prospective dad looking at a long stretch for drugs and firearms offences.

'I did it for a while, and then I realised that I couldn't do it no more. Some of the things that Thomas had done, I couldn't tell them Zeeka had done that, it was wrong to do that, so I told them the truth.'

Pitt himself, having been released from hospital after his wounding, had been arrested at a house in Hulme, wearing combat trousers with shotgun residue on them. He was soon charged with the murders of Marcus Greenidge and Thomas 'Little T' Ramsey. Detectives were convinced he had murdered the youngster – who had been so loyal to him – for messing up one too many times.

Slips' decision to tell the truth helped finish the Pitt Bull Crew. In 2002, swayed partly by the twenty-four-year-old's testimony, a jury at Preston Crown Court found Thomas Pitt guilty of the murder of Marcus Greenidge, three attempted murders, conspiracy to possess firearms with intent to endanger life and conspiracy to possess class A drugs with intent to supply. He was acquitted of the murder of Thomas 'Little T' Ramsey but was jailed for life and told he would not be eligible for parole until 2031. The rest of the Pitt Bulls all copped substantial sentences after Gregory 'Pinky' Day, Warren 'Big W' Coudjoe, Mark 'Simmo' Simons, Douglas 'Big D' Thorne and Sandra Thorne were convicted of conspiracy to possess firearms with intent to endanger life and plotting to deal drugs, while Stefan 'Mango' Proverbs and Moses 'Mo' Boakye admitted firearms and drugs offences.

Slips, who admitted drugs and firearms offences, was reported to have a 'price on his head' after turning supergrass and went into the witness protection programme. Thomas Pitt continued to exert influence from behind bars, coaxing a young legal secretary who fell in love with him into trying to smuggle heroin into Whitemoor prison for him. The war on the streets carried on in his absence.

2

Street Wars

REMNANTS OF THE Pitt Bull Crew remained at large, thrashing on like a chicken with its head cut off. Abdul 'Chan' Butt took the helm. Looked up to by the troops, he was said to have bested feared Gooch gunman Colin Joyce in a prison brawl, which did his street reputation no harm. He was also as ruthless as Bull had been.

On the afternoon of Saturday, March 24, 2001, Mohammed Ahmed, a cab driver who moonlighted as a Longsight Crew courier, took LSC man Lee Fielding to a meeting in Fallowfield. They had just arrived when Abdul Butt and his wild young sidekick Paul 'Casper' Day burst on the scene, armed with a MAC-10. They hijacked the car and forced Ahmed, a father of three, to drive around Manchester and Stockport for two hours, visiting various addresses in the hunt for LSC members higher up the chain. Having no success, they stopped the taxi back in Levenshulme and bundled the captive Fielding into a stolen car.

Ahmed, still in the driver's seat of his cab, was executed with four shots to the back of his head.

The Pitt Bulls then drove around with their terrified hostage while they debated what to do with him. They decided to take him to a disused railway line in Longsight, where no-one would be about. There, he was shot with a sawn-off shotgun, doused in petrol and set on fire. Though his clothes and hair were ablaze, he played dead until his attackers had gone, then managed to extricate himself from his smouldering garments. He survived despite horrific burns.

His survival marked the end of the Pitt Bulls: Fielding agreed to give evidence against his attackers and was put in the witness protection programme. Butt and Day, who was described as the gang's chief hit man and torturer, were later caught and jailed for life, joining Tommy Pitt and the rest of the now defunct crew in prison.

The jailing of the Gooch leadership and the destruction of the PBC, following as it did the voluntary relocation of some of the main Doddington faces to Sheffield, a less hazardous location, should have heralded a hiatus in the violence. For a short while, it seemed that was true. But the Gooch especially was by this time a vast gang, dozens strong, and seemed determined to stamp out their enemies in the Longsight Crew and what remained of the Doddington once and for all. While their PBC allies had taken the fight to Longsight, elements of the Gooch attempted to eradicate the Doddington's most active figures. A particular target was Gavin Donald, a young man whose father, Ian McLeod, had been instrumental in the rise of the Doddington in the 1990s. In continuing the family tradition, Donald had incurred the enmity of his father's old foes.

Tensions grew, as they often did, in the weeks running up to the annual Moss Side carnival in July 2001. A young Doddie was cornered and marched into an alley one night by a group of armed, balaclava'd Gooch, who demanded to know the whereabouts of 'Darrell and Winnie'. They were referring to Darrell Laycock and Winston Brownlow, two feared Doddington figures. The youth suffered a pistol-whipping but stuck to his story that he didn't 'chill' with them. 'What have you got to say before you die?' asked one of his assailants. Then he was given the chance to run and shots were fired at him as he zig-zagged down the street. Fortunately, they missed.

It was, however, a deadly summer. Teenager Alan Byron was cut down by a MAC-10 in Longsight in June. Daniel Dale was killed when a gunman opened fire on a group of young people in Miles Platting in July. Ex-armed robber Alphonso Madden, a former Gooch associate, died at the wheel when machine gun bullets raked his car as he drove through Longsight in August. And in October, twenty-four-year-old Dean Eccleston and father-of-six George Lynch were killed in separate shootings in Chorlton-on-Medlock and Longsight respectively. No-one has ever been convicted of the Madden, Eccleston and Lynch killings. Eccleston, who had previously incurred the wrath of the Pitt Bulls, was believed to have been killed by the Gooch. One man snatched his jewellery at the scene, another prayed for him as he breathed his last.

The Gooch attacks on the Doddington faction resumed in January 2002, when a young man who had previously been shot at had his car smashed up with hammers and set alight by a masked gang. The same young man was threatened again with a gun two weeks later. 'Don't you know it is zero tolerance?' one of his tormentors said. He lied about his identity and managed to escape again. The young man was part of Gavin Donald's Doddington faction. The Gooch repeatedly drove through the Cowesby Street area of Moss Side, where some of this faction still hung out, pointing guns out of car windows. After numerous threats and shootings in which no-one was hurt, it seemed as if the Gooch were toying with their rivals. Their enemies would raise the stakes higher with a killing that showed there were no rules of engagement in the Manchester gang conflict.

STEPHEN AMOS WAS a sometime DJ who had been a good enough footballer to play for Manchester City in his youth.

He was also the brother of Lee Amos, one of the dominant figures in the Young Gooch who was at the time behind bars, and that made him a target. On February 18, 2002, Stephen, aged twenty-one, was outside Bexx Bar in Ashton under Lyne, east Manchester, when he was targeted by the Longsight Crew. Richard Soloman, one of the LSC's top enforcers and the personal henchman of gang leader Julian Bell, opened fire. Amos was fatally wounded.

Gang members loyal to the Gooch rushed to the hospital where the stricken man was taken. Armed officers despatched to the hospital in case of more gunplay quickly arrested Ricardo Williams and Kelvin Taylor, based on intelligence that linked them to the rival Longsight Crew. In fact, they belonged to the Longsight Street Soldiers, or L$$, as they styled themselves, a new gang which had split from the Longsight Crew after apparently becoming 'disillusioned'. They quickly allied themselves with the Gooch, hence their presence at the hospital.

The L$$ were led by Bobby Phipps. He and his mates had knocked about with Gooch members as kids, before they allied themselves with different camps. Their about-face came at a time when tensions were particularly high. Dean Eccleston had been shot dead in Longsight and an active Young Gooch soldier was in the frame for the murder. The Longsight Crew had hit back, catching a Young Gooch runner on his own in the Brunswick area and shooting him in the leg. To add to the drama, Doddington boys were also making regular forays into Longsight, offering back-up to their allies in the LSC.

The fledgling L$$ set up headquarters at Ernley Close, Belle Vue, muscling their way into a house and forcing the tenant out into the night. When they weren't dealing drugs from a nearby phone box, in the shadow of the dog racing track, they were skirmishing with the Longsight Crew in the street. Phipps, a dangerous young man, somehow acquired a MAC-

10, with which he was reported to be 'threatening people in Longsight'. In response, the LSC smashed up his car.

The MAC-10, a compact machine pistol made by the Ingram company in the United States, was as much a status symbol as a viable weapon. According to a report commissioned by the Home Office, *Gun Crime: the market in and use of illegal firearms*, it tended to be wielded by those most wedded to the thug life: 'the symbolic value, overwhelming power and often indiscriminate aim of these guns seems to conform to a "gangster" stereotype not aspired to by the majority'. Indeed one Manchester gang member complained to the report's authors that the weapon was not excessive for most purposes, but was too expensive. 'I had a MAC-10 back in 2002 – well, I was offered it,' he said. 'But the only thing was the price of the fucking bullets; it is not viable, you know what I mean? I was offered £5 a bullet. And you know you have got thirty in a clip. One spray is £150. Because it is a road sweeper, you don't use it for shooting someone or doing a robbery, it's a waste of time … you can't aim it, it goes everywhere, so it is stupid.'

In the days after the murder of Stephen Amos, police found another MAC-10, loaded with twenty rounds, on the passenger seat of a clapped out Renault. Then a sixteen-year-old member of the Longsight Crew was hit in the chest when the L$$ opened fire on a terraced house full of partygoers in Gorton in the early hours. Days later, in another Gooch/L$$ sortie, a gunman on a motorbike sped down Winterford Avenue, in the heart of Longsight Crew territory, and licked off shots at two Doddington boys who were in the area. The Doddies were armed and fired back at the rider as he screeched out of the cul-de-sac.

The Gooch also stepped up their attacks on Gavin Donald and his Doddington foot soldiers in Moss Side. They lured one carload of Doddies into an ambush on Broadfield Road and emptied a handgun at them, only to see them ram a blocking car out of the way and speed off. A few days later, on March 9, seventeen-year-old Denzil Byfield, one of those targeted by the Gooch, was driving Donald through Moss Side when they passed a youth on a mountain bike. The youth was so small that his balaclava hung off his face, but he suddenly opened fire on them with a handgun. One of the bullets went through the driver's door and hit Byfield above the right knee. Donald took the wheel and drove him to hospital.

Four days later, a young man driving a Honda with the word 'Venom' painted on one of the doors threatened some Doddington men in a car on Princess Parkway. A car chase later ensued, with the Doddington hitting seventy miles an hour in a bid to throw off their pursuers. As they streaked towards the city centre, the front passenger of the Gooch car was seen leaning from his window and firing at them. His aim was good enough to blow out two of their tyres. The driver of the lead car managed to retain control before spinning to a sudden halt at a roundabout at the bottom of the Mancunian Way. Their rivals drove off. On inspection, the Doddington car was found to have nine bullet holes in both sides, more in the boot, a hole in the back of the driver's seat, and three blown out tyres. A young back seat passenger, hit in the left thigh and buttock, managed to limp home and was taken to the Royal Infirmary.

Less than a week after that, Gooch and Doddington gunmen in cars exchanged more fire in the street, one of them shooting for the sunroof. No-one was hurt, though a stray bullet smashed a house window and went through a TV set on the sill, shattering the screen.

On April 7, Denzil Byfield was in his front porch in Cowesby Street, while some of his friends were outside. Byfield looked down the street and saw a Rover parked at the junction that he recognised from earlier attacks. A youth in the front passenger seat, who he knew by the streetname

'Dirty', pointed his fingers at them in the shape of a gun. Byfield thought this might be a deliberate attempt to draw his attention and looked around warily. From an alley behind him, he saw a gunman run out and point his weapon in both hands at him and his friends. He wore a bandana across his face. The gunman tried to cock the gun but it seemed to be jammed, then he fired five shots in quick succession. Everyone sprang for cover. Police later recovered the bullets and found they had come from a Tokarev, a semi-automatic pistol designed for the Soviet military.

On April 9, the Gooch opened fire again in Cowesby Street. This time two young men and a woman were hit by bullets and were later detained in hospital. Four members of Gooch were involved, using bikes to keep track of the movements of their prey and relating intelligence to a gunman and a lookout, who pulled on balaclavas at the crucial time. Police recovered numerous fragments and cartridge cases from the scene.

The next fatality was not long in coming. On April 11, the Gooch staged an all-out assault on the Longsight Crew's base in Langport Avenue, in the heart of a small housing estate in a working class, multi-ethnic neighbourhood. Eighteen-year-old Aeon Shirley was driving a friend's car when he was spotted by the Gooch and chased. He sped back to Langport Avenue, parked up and made a dash for the house that was their HQ. He never made it. Shirley was shot four times in the back. One of the bullets pierced his heart and killed him. The LSC fired back and there followed what was later described as a 'sustained gun battle' in the residential street.

Though Shirley was found to have nine 'wraps' of heroin on him, Detective Superintendent Tony Brett told his inquest that he was not known to police specifically as a gang member. After a five-month inquiry involving sixty officers taking 136 statements, the investigation failed to find any hard evidence against the main suspects and was closed. 'We found

reticence and unwillingness to assist the police among witnesses,' said Mr Brett. A man was subsequently shot in the
arm as he drove past Shirley's wake at a south Manchester
pub.

THE INITIAL POLICE response to Shirley's death, to the
spate of other shootings and to an increase in cases of their
own officers being threatened with firearms, was Operation
Goodwood. Armed officers accompanied their unarmed colleagues on foot patrols, using stop-and-search powers under
the Criminal and Public Order Act, and a number of covert
operations were planned. GMP revealed they had recovered
an extraordinary 623 firearms, air weapons, replica guns, stun
guns and ammunition in Greater Manchester in the first four
months of 2002 alone.

At the same time, they made inroads into the gang leadership. Julian Bell, the wheelchair-bound leader of the Longsight Crew, had relocated to Lostock Hall, near Preston in
Lancashire, to conduct his drug business. On April 14, he was
arrested along with £38,000 in cash and his henchman Richard Soloman, who was wanted for the murder of Stephen
Amos. Both men were subsequently jailed. The Gooch members believed to be most active in attacking the Doddington
were also targeted. Several of them were arrested in early
morning raids that also turned up weapons, body armour
and documents detailing two websites, one for the Young
Gooch Close gang and one for the 'Gooch Close Original
Gangsters'. The gangs were moving into the internet age. True
to form, none of those arrested would speak to the police.

In May 2003, the Gooch's allies, the Longsight Street Sol-
diers, were also taken out in dawn raids. L$$ leader Bobby
Phipps was eventually jailed for eighteen years after admit-
ting firearms offences, although not before making headlines
nationwide when he was let out of Strangeways Prison by

mistake while awaiting trial. He spent a month on the run, getting involved in a shootout three days before his recapture.

A new weapon, the anti-social behaviour order, or Asbo, was also used against the gangs. Manchester had welcomed New Labour's justice policies with the same enthusiasm with which it had waved in the party's election victory. Asbos promised to transform grim estates into tree-lined utopias by 'curbing' neighbourhood nuisances with restrictions backed by jail sentences of up to five years. They were relatively easy for prosecuting authorities to obtain and newspapers loved them, the increasingly wacky restrictions and the quirky human dramas behind them making great copy. Fifteen-year-old Nathan 'Natnat' Wadley, identified as an L$$ rider, was banned from wearing a ski mask, showing his gang tattoo and wearing a single golf glove, in a story which had the whirr of *A Clockwork Orange*. A year later, police put the L$$ on ice for a while with an operation aimed at curbing drug dealing in the Gorton and Levenshulme area. Asbos were also used against some of the most prominent Gooch members in yet another police operation, this time called Breakthrough.

Many of the younger gang members did not even know why they were fighting. The origins of their feuds were now so distant, and so opaque, that they had become irrelevant. All they knew was that they were *supposed* to hate each other, and so they did. 'My opinion? I don't think any of us know why we don't like each other,' one convicted gang member told researchers compiling a Home Office report. 'It was over girls, it was over this and that. But it's just a bigger escalation.' The cycle was pointlessly repetitive. "If someone gets shot, obviously the someone who shot them will have to get shot,' said another gang member. 'Like tit for tat really.' That was all there was to it.

Competition in the drugs trade had once fuelled the violence between the gangs. But for the new gang members, who had been small boys when their elders were jostling for supremacy, the spoils of the drug trade would diminish as violence got in the way and police activity disrupted inner-city markets. While some gangs still had reasonably profitable drug operations, dealers without gang connections were flourishing. A growing number of gang members took to robbing and extorting successful dealers, travelling as far afield as Preston, some thirty miles north of Manchester, for victims. Closer to home, personal squabbles between individuals over girls, bikes, petty debts and 'disrespect' continued to assume an unwarranted significance because of the gang rivalry that formed the backdrop. Each shooting fed the long-held hatred, creating a new excuse for bloodshed.

Most of the foot soldiers in this street war came from poor or troubled backgrounds, or had grown up in areas where the lifestyle had been normalised. They had been lured into gangs by the promise of money, girls, excitement, brotherhood and respect. By the time they found how dangerous a game they were playing, it was too late. They were marked men as far as their enemies were concerned. Gang membership was para-doxically both their protection and the biggest threat to their safety.

One 'veteran' of the period described his experiences this way: 'Them guys always had weed and gyal, and when you're at that age, teenager, that's attractive. And if you rolled with them no-one fucked with you. I didn't see it like I was joining anything, I was just like chilling with them, they was alright guys and I known 'em from years ago anyway. I was safe with everybody, but I was from that side of the estate, so when I got a certain age people would say that to you anyway, like, "Rare, you're with them, innit."

'I was expelled from school and would chill with these guys, like anybody moves between mates at that age. We never had too much money at home and these older guys would say, "Go here, go there", and I started making a little change here and there. They made me feel important. Then I got a name 'cos of who I got seen with, and when you get notorious it's a bit like being famous. Then it got on top 'cos I got shot at and I had a kid and wanted a new start for me and my gyal, but I already had the name. Two-twos, I can't really stand here and say that I got into it because, oh, life's harder when you poor, you black, you dad gone or things ain't right at home or whatever. Feeling like there was nothing out there might've made it easier for me to make them wrong choices, but I did know the difference between right and wrong, me mam did teach me. I knew them guys did wrong, I knew where they got the reputation. And I made a choice like you do at that age, like you try things back then, fourteen, fifteen, even when you're not supposed to. But I don't care what you say, don't care if he's from a palace or the ghetto, every little boy thinks about being a gangster, same way he might think about being a spaceman or a fireman sometime. 'Cept where I lived you could make it real at an age when you didn't even know what you was getting involved with. It was just easier to get into serious trouble.

'In what you might call more white areas of Manchester there are lads who start robbing from ten, eleven, the older lads use them to squeeze through windows, and they get into ram-raiding and armed robberies and stuff like that. In my area the thing was gangbanging. There was kids I grew up with who had dads, uncles, cousins who had been in it from day, from that time when you couldn't get no job. From these older guys you get influenced and everything got upped a level. And these was alright kids, the generation under them, they weren't monsters. But they didn't know no better because them that should have been showing them the way had lost their way themselves. And these kids come smiling and you don't know how real it all is till it's too late and by then you're already part of the problem, doing things you never thought you would be.'

And so the conflicts continued, often with startling levels of brazenness. In April 2004, Young Gooch Crew stalwart Leon Johnson attended Manchester Royal Infirmary as an out-patient, receiving treatment in the fracture clinic for injuries he had suffered in a hit-and-run incident. By chance, a man with ties to the Longsight Crew was also being treated that day, having been shot in the same week that Johnson had been run over. A Gooch teenager was also in the hospital, having been admitted the previous day after a drive-by shooting in Hulme. It was a potent mix of personalities that made a tinderbox of the hospital.

Fellow gang members and family alike had flocked there to visit the afflicted. Word spread quickly that the 'bwoidem' were on the wards and more gang members were summoned, swarming at the entrance to A&E. Staff, patients and visitors began scattering in panic as the thugs began prowling and even pedalling on bikes down the corridors, 'ballied' or hooded up. At a stairwell outside one ward, a trio of LSC came face-to-face with their Gooch enemies. The rivals squared off with weapons – including a gun and a hammer – but no shots were fired. They fled when a police officer and security guards came on the scene. Leon Johnson and his visitors heard the clamour on the corridor and came out of the fracture clinic to find five Longsight boys gurning at them. A scuffle was followed by a chase, with youths using hospital trolleys as battering rams. Nurses determined to protect patients had to wedge shut doors to keep the marauders at bay. The chaos ended when the gangbangers fled the hospital.

As the activities of the gangs threatened public safety, Greater Manchester Police set up Operation Xcalibre, its biggest-ever campaign against gun and gang violence. The initiative would evolve into a successful anti-gun crime task force at the heart of most of the major shooting investigations detailed in this book. In its early days Xcalibre set the template for the multi-agency approach which would become the norm by the end of the decade, forging alliances with community groups and organisations like Manchester Multi-Agency Gang Strategy, at the time the only gang intervention project of its kind in the UK. The new approach was timely. By the mid-point of the decade conflict could break out anywhere, even in broad daylight in Manchester city centre's legal district. One summer afternoon the Gooch and Doddington met on their way back from court hearings, creating a scene which one witness described as 'like downtown Los Angeles'. The Gooch lay in wait by a Volkswagen car that belonged to the Doddington before ambushing them in Byrom Street. Office workers and passers-by gawped as the Polo was battered with carjacks in the build-up to a brawl. The Doddington contingent eventually sped off in the damaged car but were chased to nearby Quay Street, where the skirmishing continued. A Gooch gang member fired a gun at the Polo before the thugs scattered, watched by horrified bystanders, one of whom vomited in terror.

Known faces who stepped outside their established territory risked their lives. A couple of months after the clash at Quay Street, the day before his nineteenth birthday, Ramone Cumberbatch went with his girlfriend and three-month-old son to his aunt's house in Hulme to borrow a barbecue for his party. Ramone had previous links with the Doddington gang, and had been picked up by the police in Operation Breakthrough, but the birth of his son had seemed to have a salutary effect on him. His previous associations, however, would cost him his life.

He was spotted outside the house by Errol Junior Reynolds, a particularly violent gang member known as 'Little EJ' (the original 'EJ', Errol Jones, was serving life for a murder in Bristol). A robbery specialist, twenty-year-old Reynolds had been practically born into the Gooch. Like his Doddington rival Gavin Donald, Little EJ had a polite, intelligent side, but made a fearsome enemy. He had been riding with the heavy hitters like Colin Joyce and Lee Amos from a young age, and an older brother, Malachi, had spent the bulk of his early adulthood locked up for threatening a police officer with a machine gun.

Reynolds flew into a murderous rage when he saw Cumberbatch in Hulme, which the Gooch gang claimed for its own. Words were exchanged before he pulled a handgun from his waistband and began pistol-whipping Ramone. The teenager ran into the kitchen of the house and held the door shut, but Reynolds fired two bullets through the door, striking him in the heart and killing him.

Little EJ was by now out of control. Over a three-month period, he and his homies launched twenty-eight raids on shops, petrol stations and jewellers. They would strike under cover of darkness, armed with guns, iron bars, hammers, weighted ropes, knives and metal poles. Resistance or delay would be met with a gun to the head or a beating. But they also left behind a trail of clues, which eventually led police directly to their door in an operation codenamed Cupboard. Shoeprints, CCTV footage and a getaway car bought using a combination of their personal details tied the raiders to their crimes. Crucially, witnesses also came forward to implicate Reynolds in the murder of Ramone Cumberbatch. Errol Reynolds was jailed for thirty years for murder, and would also get forty-five months for robbery, to run concurrently. Others in his immediate crew were also jailed, while his brother Malachi would end up back inside for seven years for stealing a woman's car at gunpoint.

Police celebrated the jailing of the prolific Gooch robbery team with a giant poster in Moss Side. Intelligence from the public had played a significant role in their demise, according to the billboard, which was titled *Enough is Enough.* 'These men are all members of a gang,' it read. 'They have used firearms to commit crime in Moss Side and surrounding areas. Ordinary decent people stood up when it mattered because they had enough of the intimidation and fear in the community. With their assistance the police successfully prosecuted these dangerous men. They are all behind bars making the community a safer place. These convictions prove it – these men thought they were untouchable and above the law: they relied on people being too scared to stand up against them. THEY WERE WRONG.' The poster, GMP said at the time, was intended as a 'reality check'. John O'Hare, then the top officer in the inner-city Metropolitan division, told *The Times*, 'I hope that young people will see it and will not want to be on it. These offenders are in prison during the years they should be enjoying themselves.'

The capture of Little EJ and his busy team of bandits was undoubtedly a coup for the police. But if they were really to neutralise the gangs, they had to stop the supply of guns. Police seizures had seen the number of MAC-10s dry up, but another, different type of weapon had come to replace the spray-and-pray machine guns. Converted replica firearms were now being linked to ever more shootings in the city. The weapons were falling into many different hands, including those of young inner-city gang members. Their source was a small group of middle-aged white guys.

3

Special Delivery

IF LOOKS COULD kill, David McCulloch would have dropped dead in the dock. Every so often, Henry Grunwald QC would urge the gruff Scotsman to lean forward, so the court could see more of him. Michael Sammon's small eyes burned through the glass at McCulloch, the man giving evidence against him.

If you were to draw a picture of an old school villain, he could well look like Michael Sammon. A strapping, red-faced, moustachioed fellow with a dyspeptic permanent glower, he wore a green jacket, white shirt and loosened tie. His woman, Fiona McIntyre, a solidly built redhead who looked the image of the Blackpool pub landlady she actually was, sat beside him in the dock, slack-jawed in mute indignation.

Their nemesis, David McCulloch, was a man who could be bought. In the eighties he had been an overseer in the diamond and gold mines of apartheid South Africa, where he had learnt how to use a gun. By the nineties, the qualified engineer was living in Manchester and running DMC Engineering, a 'jobbing shop' at Pollard Street in Ancoats, then an area of decaying mills and forgotten housing in the eastern armpit of the city. McCulloch took pride in the metalwork he turned out for Asian businessmen. Most of the jobs never went through the books.

After work he supped in the Magpie, an ugly, smoky boozer frequented by working men and working girls, scallywags and gutter rats. Sometimes, after a couple, he would talk about his time in South Africa and the guns he had owned there. It was one of his favourite subjects. He had once told a friend called Pete about those days. Pete gave him the odd bit of work, like making security grilles for his 'recording studio', but no tracks were ever laid at the premises, only rows and rows of ganja plants under hydroponic lamps. McCulloch later said he wouldn't have done the job if he had known. But he had no such qualms about looking over an Uzi machine gun for the same customer a while later.

The problem with the Uzi was that it would fire only one bullet at a time, said Pete, looking him dead in the eye. McCulloch felt excited as he fingered the cold, slightly greasy metal. He hadn't been as close to a machine gun since his days in Africa. He looked over the weapon without asking any questions, as he made it a policy not to snoop in other people's business. Taking the weapon apart, he found it a very simple piece of engineering. There were no obvious faults. Pete left him a couple of bullets and he fired them into some sandbags in his yard, sending rats scattering in panic. Back in his forge, with pigeons cooing in the eaves and cuts and rolls of metal littering the floor, he handled the machine gun until he stumbled on the switch. He laughed as the penny dropped: put the switch one way and the gun was semi-automatic, put it the other way and it emptied the full clip. When Pete left the mill a week or so later, his wallet £200 lighter, he was satisfied McCulloch had 'fixed the problem'.

Pete returned some time later with a pen that doubled as a gun, the kind of weapon that could be bought for pennies in the Pashtun market stalls of Pakistan. Pete wanted to know if

McCulloch would manufacture a line of them, but the engineer wasn't keen. 'The end's gonna blow out as soon as you fire it,' he told his dodgy customer. 'It'll put a hole in your hand.' Pete left the gun behind on the bench and mentioned nothing of it when he returned with some slightly more 'legitimate' work. It lay there amongst the bits and bobs in the workshop for years. Now and then, McCulloch would pick the little pen gun up, write with it and remember.

By the summer of 2004, McCulloch's life was on the skids. His business had once had twelve employees but now there was only him. Every morning he dusted the metal filings from his clothes after a night spent drunk on the hard floor of his forge. His marriage had crumbled and he was boozing more than he was eating. The engineer had a sore head the day Robert Tyrer visited with his mate Mick. McCulloch had known Tyrer for about fifteen years from drinking in the Magpie. Balding, with glasses, they called him Bobby the Gun. True to his nickname, he pulled two gas-firing alarm guns from his jacket pocket. Ostensibly they were for sending distress flares from boats, and had been bought legally on the Continent. They were also useful for criminal purposes. They looked enough like real guns to convince in robberies, and with the right expertise, Bobby and Mick hoped, they could be adapted to shoot real bullets. Bobby handed McCulloch one and asked if he knew how to get anything out of it. McCulloch said it couldn't be done.

A car pulled up at the mill and gave McCulloch the breathing space he wanted. He told the two men to come back later, so they picked up the guns and left. When they returned, the customer had gone and they were just as keen.

'It can't be done, it's hardened steel. You can't drill through it,' protested McCulloch.

But Bobby was insistent. 'He kept mithering me to have a go at it,' McCulloch later testified.

Back in the echoey seclusion of the old mill, Bobby the Gun and Mick, who was brooding silently, stood over McCulloch while he demonstrated. The drill bits broke the first few times he tried to penetrate the end of the gun. Bobby wanted to know if he had a better drill. McCulloch got out the £100 cutter he kept for special jobs. It wobbled a bit in the barrel and ground out a little metal before the end of it snapped and dropped uselessly to the floor. When the two men had gone, McCulloch continued his efforts to drill out the gun barrel. Soon enough he had unblocked the barrel using a computerised lathe, and fitted a new cylinder.

'He kept coming back and I got dragged into it,' the engineer turned armourer said of Bobby. 'It was a bad time in my life. I had split up with the missus. I was quite depressed, business wasn't doing so well and I just said to him, "I'll give it a go." At the end of the day I thought I could do with the money anyway. My heart wasn't in it when he started talking about big quantities … It's not a proper type of job.'

BOBBY THE GUN and his mate Mick had already brought dozens of guns into the country by the time they approached McCulloch. In fact one of their couriers, Thomas Ravenscroft, had been stopped at Dover carrying twenty-five ME38 blank-firing handguns. Undeterred, they aimed to convert 200 weapons a week. Between spring 2004 and summer 2005, Tyrer and his associates made a string of trips to Germany, meeting a supplier based near Cologne. Tyrer himself made at least ten journeys, paying no more than fifty euros each for the pistols, which the gang smuggled back in rucksacks on the cross-channel ferry. McCulloch was promised £100 to convert each weapon: the Umarex Reck Cobra, the Kimar Competitive Alarm, the ME9 Mod Para, the ME P08, the ME38 Compact, Pocket and Magnum. The .38s were the worst; they had a tendency to blow apart when someone pulled the trigger. Sammon and Tyrer helped McCulloch to drill out the cylinders when the operation was in its infancy, and another backstreet armourer, Kenneth Lloyd, also helped. Sammon and Tyrer also supervised test-firings.

McCulloch wasn't proud of himself – he thought 'the handiwork was crap' – and a number of the weapons fell apart in the drilling process. He also reckoned he had been short-changed: for the nearly 300 guns he worked on he was given less than five grand, plus whisky, and he had been dragged into repairing power tools and generators from one of Sammon's shops. McCulloch's paymasters were more than happy, though. The guns fetched up to £700 a time. Mick started to talk of expanding the operation, of setting up a factory in Spain and importing thousands more. He and Tyrer even brought a silencer to the factory and asked if McCulloch could knock out a line of them.

At one stage, McCulloch made the mistake of pulling out the pen gun – they had walked past it dozens of times and not known what it was – and they asked if he could make a line of those. They obtained the parts and McCulloch obediently knocked out a line of them. Tyrer hurt himself firing one of them – which gave Sammon a good laugh – and the guns were never sold. The engineer also put thumb grips on some of the guns when the pair suggested it would make them look more like original firearms. He had been reluctant, describing it as 'a waste of an operation', but they had been as insistent as ever. Bobby and Mick even bought some metal dye to make the guns look more real, but the painting was unsuccessful.

After the arrest of Ravenscroft, the plotters had started bringing in the guns through the post. At first, they simply mailed them to their own addresses, before developing a more elaborate, but equally risky system. They put false names and addresses on the packages so that they would be returned undelivered to the postal depot and then be returned to 'sender' – the sender's address marked on the parcels being one they controlled. By spring of 2005, at Tyrer's orders, McCulloch had been sent to Spain as part of a plan to set up an operation on the Costa del Sol. He met up with Sammon in Malaga and inspected gun-making machinery, leaving Kenneth Lloyd in charge of converting 150 weapons on the home front. Halfway through his stay on the Costa, McCulloch was sent back to Manchester to inspect Lloyd's work. He found Lloyd had completed 100 guns and then went back to Spain. The Spanish enterprise never got off the ground though.

So blatant was the smuggling that it was only a matter of time before the operation unravelled. The gang was leaving a string of clues. When Thomas Ravenscroft was stopped with twenty-five guns, which exploded when test-fired, he had been carrying a diary with telephone numbers in it linked to his paymasters. Three months later, a customs officer intercepted a parcel at a depot at Dover containing three .38 blank-firing revolvers and addressed to the engineer Lloyd, who was then living with Tyrer and his brother Jamie. Less than three months later another parcel – this one sent to 'Tyrer' – was stolen from the mail hub in Coventry. It contained three .38s and three Luger blank-firers. In July 2005, an undelivered package was left at a shop in Levenshulme, close to one of the gang's addresses. The shopkeeper discovered fourteen Cuno Melcher pistols inside. Fingerprint evidence linked Tyrer to the package. Two more parcels, containing nineteen guns, were intercepted at a Parcelforce depot in Manchester, the sender being 'K Lloyd' of Telfer Avenue, Longsight; later Bobby the Gun was seen letting himself into the same address with a key. When police caught up with him in early September, a German postage receipt with Mick Sammon's fingerprints on it was found in his wallet. A raid at Tyrer's Gorton home recovered items connected to firearms' conversion, including parts of pen guns, while German travel tickets and post office receipts were found at his girlfriend's address. Invoices for specialist tooling bought from a firm in Birmingham and given to McCulloch for the job could also be linked to Tyrer.

The game was up.

'Clear out, Bobby's been arrested,' was all Mick said to McCulloch on the phone.

The engineer tried to destroy any evidence, but the task was daunting. 'As the weeks went by I started clearing stuff out, but it's very difficult in an engineering workshop,' he recalled. 'There's bits and bobs lying about all over the place.' These bits and bobs included parts of Derringers, bullets from the 'sackfuls' Bobby and Mick had brought to the jobbing shops, a magazine from a semi-automatic, a funnel and cup used for measuring gun powder, the original cylinders from the ME38s, the boxes from the cutters used to drill the barrels and a piece of wood which he had test-fired bullets into. Even the most innocuous of items, like a yellow duster on the floor, told a story. Bobby and Mick were in the habit of turning up with rolls of them. When a weapon was finished and ready for collection, they would wrap it in a duster, seal it with a couple of elastic bands and then slip it into their pocket or a carrier bag.

Anything that was flammable, McCulloch burned in the yard. He also packed incriminating metal parts into a steel tube which he welded at both sides and dumped in a skip. But in March 2006, when police raided the jobbing shop, he had not done as thorough a clean-up job as he had thought: among the evidence left behind for the detectives was a gun in the photocopier drawer, converted by his own hand. He would later insist that he kept the gun for protection in case his paymasters turned on him.

In ten interviews conducted over two days, McCulloch said nothing. 'Well, you keep your mouth shut, see what evidence comes back, it's the normal thing to do,' he said later. He was charged and remanded to Strangeways, where he had a change of heart. 'I had a reason to look after myself after receiving threats. The others turned against me and have got a lot of friends in there, so I decided to go my own way and look after myself.' McCulloch had found himself on a wing surrounded by associates of Tyrer, one of whom he actually shared a cell with. He believed Tyrer's cronies were going to put everything on him because they were 'all family' and he was an outsider. Three months to the day he had been charged, he turned supergrass, signing an agreement under the Serious Organised Crime and Police Act to implicate Bobby and Mick.

As for Mick, McCulloch didn't actually know his identity despite all the times he had met him. He only learned who he was while watching an episode of the TV show *Manhunt* in prison in Bristol. Mick – or Michael 'Mickey the Fish' Sammon, to give him his full name and underworld monicker – had vanished as the net closed in. Unbeknown to McCulloch, he had already been on the run for seven years when they first met in 2004, and had brazenly returned to his old stomping ground to oversee the gun-making conspiracy that he was funding.

Born in 1960 and raised in the Longsight district of Manchester, Sammon was a street scallywag who first came to the attention of the law when he was sixteen. He troubled the courts and prisons, mainly for offences of dishonesty, on and off until 1983, then for several years he appeared to go straight, making money from legitimate businesses. But in 1992, he came to the attention of police again with a massive long-firm fraud which left creditors millions in the red while earning him a reputed £1.6 million. Convicted in 1997, he vanished before sentence. An intelligent, charismatic, overbearing man, Sammon was of Irish travelling stock and had links to the notorious Quality Street gang, the dominant force in Manchester's underworld in the 1970s and early eighties. He was known to have connections to Malaga, Torremolinos,

Benalmadena and the Irish Republic, as well as Croydon, Leicester, Blackpool and Manchester. Now, after returning to mastermind one of the biggest firearms importation rackets the country had ever seen, he was on the run again.

Investigators could anecdotally trace a weapon back to Sammon by telltale injuries like bullet wounds to a victim's feet or to a gunman's hand, since they were so prone to misfiring. Yet the availability of his guns trumped their unreliability, and for a time they became the favoured weapon of trigger-happy criminals across the North. A report in the *Daily Mirror* had police sources attributing 4,000 crimes to his weapons, including 'kidnap, armed robbery, torture and extortion'. There were also killings, like the murder of Thuy Van Le in 2005. The thirty-year-old had left his wife and young sons behind two years earlier in North Vietnam to earn money in the West. He was gunned down and left to bleed to death by robbers he tried to stop from raiding the till of his brother's wine store in Stretford, south Manchester.

Sammon's batch even got the seal of approval from Domenyk Noonan, of the notorious Manchester crime family. The security boss, who adopted the surname Lattlay-Fottfoy for his court appearances, was caught with an adapted gas-firer and five .357 Magnum bullets after police stopped his Jaguar near Darlington. In the same month, Brian Walsh, a lorry driver from Droylsden, Manchester, shot his estranged wife in the head in a fit of depression before turning the gun on himself. Pauline Walsh was leaving for work when he opened fire. He then went to his relatives' home and told them he planned to kill himself, asking a nephew to 'finish him off' if the suicide bid failed. After saying goodbye to his father and brother, he went to the Moravian Churchyard in Openshaw and shot himself in the chest. Mrs Walsh survived, her husband did not.

Sammon's guns also turned up in a raid on a post office in Rochdale in October 2005, in which the owner was pistol-whipped and shot; the bullet grazed his head. Villains used one of the ME38s in a kidnapping in Liverpool in which the victim was tortured with an iron. Gunmen pulled them on a police officer in the Kirkdale area of Liverpool in September 2007, and on a landlord in Bolton in October 2005. They turned up in a wheelie bin at Heathcote Road in Gorton, in a boozer in Wythenshawe, in a man's underpants in Manchester city centre, a café in St Helens, woodland in Sheffield, a Newcastle allotment, a golf course in Liverpool.

The Sammon-Tyrer conspiracy was just one of a number of underworld arms-dealing plots active at the time. In August 2005, weeks before Tyrer's arrest, armed police swooped on a garage in Stretford and caught a British-Lithuanian gang stood about a Volvo as a mechanic tried to free its cargo: thirty guns with silencers and 1,220 rounds of ammo. Like the Sammon-Tyrer consignment that had been discovered by the postmaster, the guns had been made by Cuno Melcher. Ringleader Richard Saltmarsh, a drug dealer from Coventry, had paid £30,000 for the blank-firing pistols, which had been converted to fire bullets before being smuggled to these shores, headed for Manchester's underworld. Dawson Wray was the local contact who had arranged for the guns to be extracted from the Volvo. Behind an alley in his Eccles home, they tried to get rid of the guns, but didn't have the right tools for the job and were wary of being spotted. The following day, plotters Wray, James Parker and Marius Renke drove to the Stretford garage, where a mechanic had been lined up for the job. Police had them under surveillance and arrested them. Twenty-seven-year-old Saltmarsh was arrested six months later and was jailed for twenty years after being found guilty of conspiring to import the weapons.

Ex-serviceman Paul Alexander also saw the moneymaking potential of supplying the underworld with guns. The former Royal Artillery sergeant, born in Bury, north of Manchester, put together assassins' kits consisting of laser-sighted gasfirers he had converted himself, silencers, magazine clips and ammunition. By the time Greater Manchester Police, Merseyside Police and Serious Organised Crime Agency investigations brought him down, his weapons had been linked to twenty-eight shootings, including six in Manchester. Members of the Doddington gang and its offshoot, the Haydock Crew, were caught dealing the weapons to three men from London. Ten convictions resulted. When Merseyside Police launched an anti-gun crime operation in the wake of the death of Rhys Jones, the eleven-year-old gunned down in Liverpool, an innocent victim of the conflict between street gangs based in the Croxteth and Norris Green areas of the city, a DNA profile for Alexander was recovered from one of the pistols. It was passed on to SOCA who raided his gun factory and arrested him. At the age of fifty-three, Alexander was jailed indeterminately for the public protection and ordered to serve seven years and 320 days.

By then, Bobby Tyrer and his cohorts were also incarcerated. In the face of the evidence against them and McCulloch's damning testimony, they admitted a litany of charges, including conspiring to possess firearms with intent to endanger life, conspiring to import firearms, conspiring to manufacture firearms and conspiring to possess ammunition. Tyrer, then aged fifty-one, of Gorton, got nineteen years, Kenneth Lloyd, fifty-five, of Levenshulme, got thirteen years, and Jamie Tyrer, thirty-seven, got five years. Courier Thomas Ravenscroft, who was sixty-two, got a two-year suspended sentence because he was gravely ill, and died soon afterwards. At the time, about 140 of the 273 weapons they brought into the country had still not been traced. 'These men are not what you would typically expect of individuals involved in this kind of operation,' said a detective inspector with the Armed Crime Unit, on hearing of their sentences. 'They are mature individuals, some of them working, and were quite a surprise to us.'

David McCulloch admitted conspiracy to possess firearms with intent to endanger life, conspiracy to manufacture firearms and conspiracy to possess ammunition. He was given a six-year jail term, reduced because of the help he had given to the authorities.

McCulloch had assumed Mick was in Spain, but his former boss was on sands much closer to home. Fiona McIntyre was running the Sun Inn public house in Blackpool when she met Michael Sammon, who at the time was using the alias John Eugene McDonagh, taken from a dead friend and backed up by fake documents. McIntyre, one of a small army of Scots to settle in the seaside resort, fell in love with the errant arms dealer. Brazen as ever, he ran a shop selling tools at Waterloo Road in the town. It was one of a number he had opened in the North and Midlands since fleeing his sentence for long-firm fraud in the late nineties. At one point he even travelled to Spain with McIntyre, and by early 2007 she knew he was wanted. That February, she was spoken to by police but denied knowing him.

Brian Kinsley was a drifter with mental health problems and a booze addiction who had moved to Blackpool a few years earlier, the latest in a number of stints in the seaside town. A regular at Bev's Café, he got to know the owner, Beverley Hughes, and her husband, Colin. Fiona McIntyre's pub was a short distance from the café, so he also came to know their friend Mick. The show *Manhunt* – watched by David McCulloch in jail – was also seen by Brian Kinsley when it aired in May 2007. Watching the trailer in his flat, he recognised the 'wanted' man named as Michael Sammon as the Mick he knew. Soon after, Mick himself turned up, accompanied by Colin Hughes and another member of their circle, Anthony Key. Mick said that he and Tony Key needed somewhere to stay and put pressure on Kinsley into letting them stay. The men shared a bottle of whisky and Mick insisted on watching the news channels.

Kinsley would later testify, 'We watched Sky News, we watched Granada News, we watched every news programme possible to find out what was going on and we read the newspapers together.'

Mick was not on the news, as he had expected, so they switched to the BBC, where *Manhunt* was about to start, 'There I am, I told you I was on it,' said Sammon as his mugshot was shown. 'I don't look like that anymore though.' The programme described how his accomplices had been jailed for converting weapons, and he remarked on their sentences, which he had read about in the paper. He said he felt sorry for one of them, a lackey who 'did nothing really', possibly Kenneth Lloyd or Jamie Tyrer. Another of those jailed he described as old and sick; undoubtedly Thomas Ravenscroft, who would die soon after in prison. Asked by Kinsley whether he agreed with what had been said about him on the show, Sammon said 'most of it', though he complained that the programme implied they had smuggled the guns in containers, when they had sent them from Germany in parcels. He described the mistakes they made – sending the guns repeatedly to the same address, getting caught out eventually because someone had sent a parcel to his own home. Otherwise, they would never have been caught, he claimed. For his own part, he said he was 'just the money man', not an armourer like the show made out.

Sammon laid low at Kinsley's flat for just over a week after the appeal was broadcast. Then he was spirited away in Colin Hughes's BMW, stretched out on the back seat under a coat.

On January 7, 2008, Brian Kinsley turned up at Blackpool police station and said he wanted to 'help with Mike Sammon', who he described as 'wanted by Crimewatch'. He said Sammon had been running guns from Germany and growing cannabis on an industrial scale, and told a detective that he was staying with Tony Key in a flat on the seafront at

Lytham St Annes. The information was passed on to Greater Manchester Police, by which time Kinsley had moved on to Southampton.

Sammon seemed to know that the net was closing in, and switched identities with McIntyre's help. She got a crooked accountant to endorse a bogus Irish ID card application in the name of 'Dermot Monaghan'. She also got a job at a caravan park near Portsmouth, where he hid out for a couple of months. Meanwhile, Kinsey was tracked down and convinced to return to Manchester, where he admitted in interview that he had also harboured Sammon in his own place. Eight days later, Michael Sammon was tracked down to the Southsea Leisure Park. His faithful mistress tried to put the detectives off the scent, by showing them the fraudulent passport, but the game was up and Sammon was arrested. Kinsley would be put on the witness protection programme, which gave him a home and a stability he had not enjoyed in twenty years, he said.

Sammon's trial began a year and a half after that of his co-conspirators. The arms dealer and fraudster, who had so nimbly avoided justice for so long, was gouty, troubled by a dicky heart, and forced to begin serving the four-year fraud sentence he had skipped from back in 1997. Trial was delayed by Sammon's poor health, and had to be moved to the modern Preston Crown Court where his frailties could be better accommodated. McCulloch had finished serving his time but was still bound by the supergrass agreement and compelled to testify.

McCulloch told the jury what the man he knew only as Mick had, along with Tyrer, paid him to do, reeling off the facts with an engineer's precision. A firearm found from the Greenwood Tree pub in Wythenshawe in January 2005? 'Yes, this was one of the early batch of firearms ... different from the ME38.' A Reck Cobra found inside a Volkswagen Passat in Merseyside? 'I remember doing this as well. I don't think there's so many of these – I think there's only half a dozen or ten of this model. It's been fully converted, capable of firing live ammunition.'

Kinsley would give evidence about Sammon's stay at his house and his admissions while they watched TV. However, he got the name of the show wrong, describing it as *Crimewatch*, and the date of broadcast a year out. Despite the confusion, the prosecution were allowed to play the *Manhunt* programme in court, with the defence argument that to do so was prejudicial and unnecessary rejected by the judge after he had viewed the recording privately.

Sammon stood trial alongside McIntyre, Colin Francis Hughes and Anthony Key, who were all charged with assisting an offender. Hughes had driven Sammon from a property at Shaw Road in Blackpool to a new lair after the Manhunt TV appeal identified the crime boss as one of Britain's most wanted. Key had provided food and drink for Sammon after he moved south to Hampshire. All four were found guilty at trial.

Sentencing Sammon to thirty years, Judge Martin Steiger, QC, dubbed him a 'Merchant of Death' – as he had his cohorts just over three years earlier. The judge described how over 100 guns brought in by the gang remained in circulation – 'still waiting to do their lethal work to innocent victims'. Sammon's role had been to head the 'sinister commercial organisation', and he was, in the judge's view, 'a man of considerable commercial acumen'. 'He is a man of considerable intelligence, he is described by others who have testified as overbearing and a bully. No doubt whatsoever he's a man of great charm and persuasion when he chooses to use it. A man who is both ruthless and manipulative,' Judge Steiger added.

Fiona McIntyre, Sammon's 'devoted mistress', in the words of the judge, had already had a taste of jail by this stage. In May 2009, she was jailed for twelve months for a £200,000 benefits fraud, having set up a cleaning company with her father and brother that employed people under false names. They then used the fake workers to claim benefits, boosting their coffers and allowing them to undercut honest rivals. For helping Sammon, McIntyre got another thirty months behind bars. The fact that a former partner of hers had been shot in 1995 was deemed by the judge to be an aggravating feature.

After he had been locked up, Sammon would appeal his conviction on a number of grounds, among them the argument that showing the programme *Manhunt* to the jury had prejudiced them against him. The programme featured a senior detective saying how firearms had fallen into the hands of criminals across the UK and been involved in a 'variety of horrendous incidents'. It graphically described the toll of gun crime, depicting a watermelon exploding as it was shot at, a dramatic reconstruction in which a Sammon-like character, played by an actor, pressured an engineer to do his dirty work, and another in which a hoodie on a bike was seen buying a gun. Sammon was described by a detective as being at the 'very top' of the conspiracy, surrounded by a 'climate of fear'. The Court of Appeal rejected Sammon's arguments, concluding that everything had been done properly and he had had a fair trial. Robert Tyrer had appealed his nineteen-year sentence, but that was refused in 2007. Sammon tried to appeal his thirty-year sentence as well, arguing the difference between his and Tyrer's sentence was unjustified, even allowing for the discount the latter got in return for pleading guilty. This was also refused. Far from merely being the 'money man', the Court of Appeal found that he 'was also the source of supply of the guns … also involved in their distribution after conversion'.

Even without scores of Sammon's untraced weapons swirling about in the criminal underworld there was enough beef on the streets to feed another frenzy of gun violence. A double murder at a Salford public house was the first in a new wave of killings.

4

Bloodbath at the Brass Handles

THE UNITED MATCH was on the TV when gunmen burst into the Brass Handles pub and opened fire. Armed with two powerful handguns, they left behind a scene of carnage: two men badly injured, upended stools and tables, smashed glass, blood and lager mixing on the floor. They also ended up dead, sprawled out on the grass outside.

The local children, circling on bikes in black tracksuits and Reds' shirts, were full of it in the minutes afterwards, as reporters invaded the little square in the Pendleton district of Salford. They claimed that one of the injured men had given out banknotes as he waited for the ambulance, bleeding from the holes in his face. 'Remember me, I'll always look after you, remember me, that was what he were saying,' claimed one of the kids. By then a white tent had been placed over the bodies of the two would-be hitmen, and only their Nike trainers stuck out.

Carlton Alveranga and Richard Donny Austin were killed doing someone else's dirty work. Some months before, Bobby Spiers, a well-known older face in Salford gangland, had been on a night out in Manchester with one of the city's up-and-coming hardmen. It was all good until the younger man was

88

refused entry at the door of a club. He told the bouncers that he was with Spiers, but when Spiers was asked if it was true, for a joke he denied knowing his companion.

From this trivial incident sprang a deadly feud. Rancour increased to the point that, when shots were fired in Spiers's direction, he suspected the younger man was behind it, though this has never been proven. The younger man also took to drinking in the Brass Handles, Spiers's local pub. Spiers took this is as a direct threat and decided to have his rival removed. However, given the sensitivities in Salford – both men had mutual friends and acquaintances – he went outside his own circle. He turned to Ian McLeod.

McLeod was an intelligent but ruthless man who had shunned a respectable background to become a major league drug dealer. He had been part of the black Moss Side 'mafia' who had started the city's gang culture for real in the eighties, first at the heart of the Pepperhill Mob, then a founder member of its offshoot, the Doddington gang. He warred with the rowdy Hillbillies from Cheetham Hill, then with the fledgling Gooch, and carried the scars of several attempts on his life. He had once been shot through the skull, which some said changed his personality, for the worse. He had also served a lengthy prison term for running the Doddington's 'drug market' on the Alexandra park estate.

Both Spiers and McLeod had moved into security work as they got older, and detectives believe they met at a training session organised by the Security Industry Authority, the quango set up to professionalise the door trade. Security was an attractive business for someone with their background, credentials and contacts. McLeod's firm, IMAC, employed Doddington boys for jobs. Spiers's firm won high-profile contracts including guarding the site of a police station, despite Spiers's background and his close friendship with Paul Massey, once dubbed Salford's 'Mr Big'. Indeed, his firm was called PMS, which officially stood for Professionally Manned Security but which many took to be an acronym for Paul Massey Security.

McLeod took a £10,000 contractor's fee to handle Spiers's 'problem' and recruited two inexperienced Moss Side lads, Carlton Alveranga and Richard Austin, to do the job. Constance Howarth, who handled administration at PMS, was another key conspirator. No ordinary secretary, she had a conviction for transporting MAC-10 machine guns and had links to many underworld characters. She was also Paul Massey's cousin. As a regular at the Brass Handles, the blonde was the perfect person to direct the out-of-town hitmen to the target.

In the run-up to the assassination bid, McLeod was seen driving Austin, aged nineteen, and Alveranga, twenty, in his black Mondeo. Both of them had been in trouble before, but this job was way out of their league. Still, they hailed from streets where gun crime was a reality of life. Austin was a friend of McLeod's son, Gavin Donald, an active Doddington head who had been introduced into the gang by his father when barely into his teens, and had also knocked about with Ramone Cumberbatch, who had been shot dead nine months earlier. His mother moved to Wythenshawe, hoping to keep him away from the gang milieu, but the attempt had failed. Carlton Alveranga was a talented artist whose family also hoped for a better life for him.

On the morning of Sunday, March 12, 2006, McLeod called Austin to collect him. They filled the tank of the Mondeo at an Asda near McLeod's home in the Radcliffe area of Bury, then drove south to Moss Side to get Alveranga. It was after 2 p.m. when they arrived at Salford, by which time the two young men may have got cold feet: McLeod was seen shoving them out of the car. They trudged across the croft in front of the ugly, low-rise pub, tower blocks looming above them, and entered the Brass Handles.

Constance Howarth had spent much of her time inside the pub talking on her phone, keeping McLeod informed of their target's movements as the pub filled with regulars eager to watch Manchester United play Newcastle United live on television. Shortly after the half-time whistle, Alveranga and Austin entered the vault. Constance Howarth was conveniently in the toilet, touching up her lipstick. Bobby Spiers was in an executive box at Old Trafford, watching the game. McLeod was waiting in the Mondeo outside.

Shortly afterwards, following a burst of gunfire, the two would-be hitmen ran, badly wounded, from the pub before both collapsing on the grass. There they died, where minutes before youngsters had been playing in the spring sunshine, the Netto opposite milling with shoppers.

The investigation was led by an experienced, cerebral senior detective, Andy Tattersall. It unravelled one of the more extraordinary episodes in recent gangland history. The two young men, both armed with handguns, had entered the pub 'ballied up' and started shooting. Their target, a Salford villain who cannot be named for legal reasons at time of writing, was at a small corner table. The novice hitmen held their guns in an odd way, holding them horizontally side-on, as if in a Hollywood movie. Men, women and children screamed and dived for cover. Six shots were fired at the man; his face and upper body were peppered with bullets from Austin's gun. The table was upended as Aaron Travers, the target's friend, leapt up and took two in the chest for his drinking buddy. Alveranga's Glock misfired, and somebody grabbed hold of him. Alveranga ended up on his back on the floor, the gun fired again as the men battled over it. The Glock was wrenched from him at some point in the melee, which may also have involved a Gooch gang member, who by sheer chance had been drinking with the two victims that day.

Someone, who has never been identified, then shot both Austin and Alveranga. They managed to run from the pub but fell on the grass before they could reach McLeod's getaway car. McLeod was heard to shout, 'Are they dead?' before going to check the bodies, removing their guns, and speeding off.

The wounded men were rushed to Hope Hospital where, thanks to the expertise of the staff, they survived their injuries.

ARRIVING REPORTERS were perplexed by the fact that the dead men's legs were crossed. Already, everybody was saying the name of the intended target. The scene was abuzz with chatter over some sort of feud between black lads from south Manchester and locals, possibly sparked by the stabbing of one of the dead men's pals. More than one bystander remarked that the black lads had been cheeky 'coming up here with guns' when Man United were playing, that they had bitten off more than they could chew and got what they deserved. Locally, the rumour spread that their accomplice had taken their guns from them and deliberately crossed their legs in some bizarre gesture, when in fact it was the beating they got as they lay dead or dying that contorted their limbs that way.

In the aftermath of the shooting, the drinkers fled the pub and its shutters were drawn down. Whatever CCTV footage there may have been of the bloodbath could not be found. The investigation began, as the lead detective put it, with just 'two mobile phones, two dead bodies and a car registration'. Two unregistered phones were at the heart of the case. One ended in the digits 420, the other 752. Detectives found evidence linking '420' to McLeod, who would later admit using it up until lunchtime on the day of the murder. Connie Howarth would be forced to admit that '752' was her phone. In the month leading up to the attack, the pair had spoken more than forty times. In a series of calls between 2.06 and 2.19 p.m., Howarth kept the assassination squad informed of the target's movements and the layout of the pub.

The police established that the men were either shot inside the pub or on their way out, not on the grass. They also knew that they were looking for a black Ford Mondeo. By the end of the month, McLeod had been dragged from his bed on suspicion of attempted murder, and police had learnt that a conflict of underworld egos lay behind the carnage. McLeod was soon charged with conspiracy to murder. A week after his arrest, police secured the pub's closure, and Howarth was brought in.

After a four-week trial at Preston Crown Court, Ian McLeod and Constance Howarth were convicted of conspiracy to murder. McLeod was ordered to serve twenty-one years before parole could be considered, Howarth twenty years. The trial confined itself to the conspiracy and did not look at who had killed the two would-be assassins, though special measures were promised to anybody who could provide information on their execution. An open verdict was recorded in their inquest by coroner Janet Leeming, who said she was unable to rule they had been killed unlawfully because of the possibility that they were shot dead in self-defence.

True to the code, the target of the shooting never breathed a word about his ordeal to detectives and never made a complaint. Spiers had vanished in the aftermath of the shooting but was tracked down to a bar in Benidorm and arrested on a European warrant a couple of years later. He stood trial, was found guilty, and was jailed for life as supporters shouted, 'Keep your chin up, Bobby,' from the gallery. The Brass Handles was later ear-marked for demolition, to make way for a regeneration scheme.

In the months directly after the bloodbath at the Brass Handles, gun violence continued in Ian McLeod's old south Manchester stomping ground. The bungled hit he had orchestrated was just one incident that year where gunmen struck in broad daylight. And the killings of Alveranga and

Richard Austin were only the first in a series of senseless deaths linked to gang activity. In the most shocking of these incidents, a schoolboy would lose his life to the gun.

5

The Killing of
Jessie James

A T THE END of May 2006, two-and-a-half months after the bloodbath at the Brass Handles pub, the Gooch and Doddington gangs clashed at a 'family fun day' at the West Indian Centre in Moss Side. Older Gooch member Leon Johnson, who had been involved in the notorious multi-gang brawl at Manchester Royal Infirmary, had returned from a family holiday in Turkey just hours before. Johnson was an old pal of Colin 'Piggy' Joyce and Lee Amos, and back in the day he had been suspected, although not convicted, of accidentally killing his friend Zeus King at a shoot-out in Longsight. He had eventually been relocated from Moss Side to a housing estate in Preston, and had been placed under surveillance by Lancashire Constabulary's Serious and Organised Crime Unit. A covert bug had also been placed in his Seat car. Officers listened as he met up with associates before driving in convoy to Moss Side. It was a Bank Holiday Monday and the fun day was just winding down. Hundreds of parents and children had enjoyed music, a merry-go-round and a bouncy castle.

The Gooch mob sped through safety barriers onto the club's car park, where they saw two of the Doddington on foot. Bullets cracked back and forth. In the panic and the scramble to escape, a heavily pregnant woman collapsed and had to be rushed to hospital, while a man had an epileptic fit. The Gooch ploughed on, trying to hunt their rivals down. 'Man can't war with me,' the bug caught Johnson boasting. 'I've been hanging them shots, I ain't gonna fall.' He told two fourteen-year-old boys that when they were older he would 'show them how the hot boys do it'. He also talked about 'daybanging' – daylight shooting. In the wake of the incident, Lancashire Police pooled their information with their GMP colleagues, leading to Johnson's capture the year after. Described in court as a 'leading light' in the Young Gooch Crew, he was jailed for an indeterminate sentence after being convicted of possessing a firearm with intent to endanger life.

That same month as the 'fun day' fracas, shots were fired at a car, showering the occupants with glass, in Stamford Street, an area where a new, Gooch-affiliated gang called the Old Trafford Crips hung out. It was one of a number of incidents which were casually depicted as a 'drugs turf war', though they were in fact typically street 'respect' squabbles which escalated into him-or-me situations. In one such case, a fifteen-year-old boy was lucky to survive when a gunman leapt out of a car in Ardwick, grabbed him and pumped five bullets into his body. A thirteen-year-old boy, Giuseppe Gregory, was also injured. Gregory mixed in bad company, something that would later cost him his life.

The murder of Ernest 'Ruddy' Gifford was relatively unusual that year because it was directly linked to acquisitive crime. Gifford was a forty-five-year-old small-time dealer targeted by local hot boys on a taxing mission. A masked gang, believed to be linked to the Doddington, barged into a house in Raby Street, Moss Side, and rounded up the family, bundling Gifford's partner and her two daughters into an upstairs bedroom. They shoved Gifford into another room, where they shot him on the bed. His family, cowering next door in the darkness, heard the whole thing. One of the young men pursued by the Gooch at the family fun day was later convicted of his murder but was acquitted after a retrial ordered by the Court of Appeal.

Those in the know say the Gooch's deadly ascendancy can be traced back to the late nineties, when they perfected drive-by shootings on bicycles. The Doddington and the Longsight Crew would match them bullet for bullet, but the cold fact was that the Gooch gang was bigger and killed more people. This had little to do with the original guys from the nineties; it was those young enough to be their sons who took on the name and inherited the rivalries without knowing what they were all about. The Old Trafford Crips revived the waning practice of wearing gang colours. They wore blue, like the Los Angeles gang that inspired them, while their Doddington enemies wore red in imitation of the rival Bloods gang. At the core of the OT Crips were brothers and cousins from a local family who were matey with YGC types like Leon Johnson. The gang was also home to a manic young clique of car-jackers who would cackle with glee as they gratutiously pistol-whipped their victims, including a fourteen-year-old boy who was taped by his mates loading a sawn-off shotgun in seconds. Hanging around at Arch Bar in Hulme, the terraced streets of Old Trafford, the 'Seven Sisters' tower blocks, and the west end of the Alexandra Park estate, the Old Trafford Crips would be linked to everything from nuisance noise complaints, to robbing Jamaican pensioners of their 'pardner' saving scheme money, to cold-blooded murder.

Three shootings within twenty-four hours, the result of a dispute between these self-styled Crips and their 'Bloods' rivals, rocked inner south Manchester in mid-August. In the first, at Pepperhill Road, the heart of Doddington territory, a passenger leaned out of a speeding car and opened fire at four lads on bicycles. As they pedalled off, one of them returned fire, drawing a machine pistol and shooting behind him without turning or looking at his target. Cars and houses were peppered with bullets. The twenty cartridges and abandoned bikes recovered by police told the story of the terrifying if brief intensity of the gunfight.

The next month came a killing that horrified even the trauma-weary residents of the Alexandra Park estate.

BARBARA REID barely had time to sit down. Her neat home at Greame Street, on the east side of the Alex Park estate, was packed with visitors, well-wishers eating and drinking from the spread she had laid on. They had come because the night before last, her son had been shot dead in the park. A growing lad, his toothy, mega-watt grin shone out of the pictures on the dresser. Jessie James was fifteen years old when he was cut down by a ruthless, experienced gunman.

That Friday night, Jessie's mother had not wanted him to stay out late but he had begged her for permission, since all his friends were allowed. He was growing up fast, becoming a fitness fanatic, picky about what he ate and working out as he neared the cusp of adulthood. He told his mother about the party when he returned from the gym for a meal, heading back out again into the night with his close-knit group of friends. Five of them headed over to the party, at Caythorpe Street, before relocating to the West Indian Sports and Social Club a short distance away, where an event was going on. They talked for a while on the car park before going into the club to buy fizzy drinks. They then decided to return to Caythorpe Street.

Jessie lingered with another group of lads while his friends pedalled off to the first party. It was now one o'clock in the morning, a good couple of hours past the time he should have been back, but Jessie knew his mum wouldn't stay cross with him for long, and like any teenage boy he pushed the boundaries of his freedom. At a minute past one, Jessie passed by the basketball courts of Rec Park, the green space between the Sports and Social and the Edwardian terraces of eastern Moss Side. A gunman and his accomplice lurked in the bushes. Shots rang out in the darkness. Jessie's friends were ahead of him and scattered at the bangs, cycling fast. Jessie lagged behind. It was hard to tell where the shots were coming from and by mistake he steered into them. He tumbled from his bike on a grass verge, hit by four bullets from a powerful 9mm, Browning-type Parabellum handgun. He died just a few feet from the Powerhouse, the local centre set up to improve the opportunities of the area's young, the place where he went to train and to tackle his homework.

As the news spread, the inevitable questions – this being a Moss Side murder – were raised about the victim's innocence. After all, some asked, what had a fifteen-year-old boy been doing out so late? In the community, people knew that at night the park was a 'Doddington park'. But they also knew Jessie James, and what they knew of him was at odds with the manner of his death. A nice boy from a hard-working Jamaican family, he liked swimming, he liked Manchester City, and he liked to help people, especially with technical stuff. Give him anything broken and he could take it apart and fix it, from a bicycle to a computer. He would wash windows and cut grass in the warm weather when the estate was alive with the smell of barbecue smoke and the sound of black music. He lived with his widowed mum, his elder sister, Rose, and his brother, Elmo. His only connection to gangs was geography. Invisible to outsiders, a dividing line placed his home on what was considered to be Doddington territory. For a young man raised here, the malign influence of the gangs was nearly impossible to escape.

At a press conference on September 10, police said that Jessie had been fatally unlucky. Tony Cook, the senior gang-buster heading the investigation, said there was 'not one shred of intelligence' to suggest Jessie was a member or affiliate of any gang. 'I think, to be honest, it perhaps was mistaken identity,' he said.

The investigation had got off to a bad start. Minutes after the shooting, a detective was tipped off by an informant but did not do anything about it. The witness, who would later give evidence under a pseudonym at the inquest, claimed to have witnessed the shooting from a car parked close by. The events he described in the half-hour before Jessie was murdered were, to a trained eye, typical of the prelude to a gang-related shooting.

A blue car with alloy wheels and a spoiler drove along Raby Street and then braked sharply. Two young men who had been standing with a large group by the Sports and Social ran over to the car and briefly got in, then out again. The car sped off and the young men returned to the group. The witness said that he 'thought straightaway that something was not right, and these men did not belong in the area'. A lad then rode away from the group on a bike, heading for the entrance to the park. He was followed by one of the men who had been in the back of the car. The hood of his grey top was up and he wore tracksuit bottoms and black trainers, his hands in his pockets. Shortly afterwards, two more young men left the same group and walked towards the park. One of these men had earlier got in the front passenger side of the car.

As soon as the two men entered the park, the witness heard five gunshots. The witness claimed to have then seen the gunman standing by the play area and taking aim with his arm outstretched. The firing stopped when a figure went down. 'I had seen sparks coming from the gun, and the gunman appeared to be running backwards,' said the witness. Immediately afterwards, someone cycled at speed from the park, standing up in the saddle.

The witness appeared to describe gang footsoldiers receiving a gun or instructions from a senior gang member before going into the park to fire at rivals. The odd detail was slightly out-of-kilter – two men captured on nearby CCTV at a critical time, believed to be the killers, were both on bikes. But moments later, at 1.19 a.m., the witness rang the detective to report what he believed was a shooting. It was the first such report that night but it was not followed up. The detective was contacted on his mobile phone by the witness, who at the time was central to a number of other investigations. The witness, the detective would later tell Jessie's inquest, sounded scared or excited and spoke in a 'rhythmic monotone'. The officer's account of what he had been told differed from what the witness told the inquest, although it still sounded a lot like a shooting. 'In essence', the detective said of his informant, 'they said there had been a dispute, initially inside the chicken shop on Great Western Street. Numerous males from the area had been there, and a small blue vehicle had attended at the scene. A male went into the park followed by another male. At some point there was a flash or flashes within the park. At some point a male had fallen over. At no point did they say anyone was injured, shot or killed.'

The detective said that he had received the call while groggy and drowsy from a cocktail of wine and antihistamines. 'From the information conveyed to me, I believed what was said to me didn't warrant further police response.' The Independent Police Complaints Commission described his conduct as a failure of duty.

The bullets had destroyed Jessie's vital organs on a deadly path through his body. No doctor could have saved him. But a second opportunity to secure the scene, corral witnesses and halt the killer's flight in what is known to detectives as the 'golden hour' was also squandered, this time more through ill luck than ineptitude. Police were called to the West Indian Sports and Social to a report of a disturbance around twenty minutes after Jessie was shot. They left without knowing that the teenager was dead or dying yards away. The sirens that had heralded their arrival meant that local people who had heard the shots thought police were already following them up, and so didn't report them. No 999 call was received until ninety minutes after the murder.

Barbara Reid would also have to wait for the police. She heard pounding on her door in the early hours and thought Jessie had forgotten his key. She was cross that it was so late. But when she opened the door, it was one of Jessie's tearful friends on the step. She went to the scene and waited in shock for news of what had happened. She was told that someone would come to see her but they did not turn up until 1 p.m.

As the story dominated the headlines, one police officer told a newspaper that the city's gun and gang problem was 'getting out of control', with gangbangers prowling about untroubled by the fear of being stopped and searched, while officers busied themselves meeting targets by chasing soft public order offences. In response, the force insisted that gun crime was a priority.

THE YOUNG MEN of the Doddington gang interpreted Jessie James's death as an attempted attack on them. They sought revenge on the Old Trafford Crip they held responsible, catching up with Reydell Waite about a fortnight later and shooting him in the knee; he escaped by crawling through an alleyway. It would be the first of three attempts at his life. A few days later, fifteen of the Doddington rode on bikes into the Gooch side of the Alexandra Park estate. One of them opened fire, hitting a sixteen-year-old girl in the shoulder. 'If you aren't Gooch, why are you running?' shouted the gunman as he fired. The injured girl had nothing to do with the Gooch and was not even from the area.

In such an atmosphere, witnesses were reluctant to come forward. The police tried an appeal to conscience, unveiling a giant poster of Jessie James in Hulme and asking for three

girls, who they believed had seen the murder, to come forward. The story had attracted the attention of the national
press, echoing the case of Benji Stanley, the fifteen-year-old
shot dead in 1993 whilst buying a snack at a bakery, most
probably because he was mistaken for a Doddington member
who wore a similar style of jacket. Heated discussions on the
problem took place everywhere, from barber shops to street
corners, churches to community halls. Youngsters wept in the
schools and the colleges, and Christians organised a candlelit
vigil, praying in Jessie's memory at a shrine in the park where
he died. Even the veteran US hip hop group Public Enemy,
famed for their politically conscious lyrics, visited the spot
where Jessie died, hype man Flavor Flav's blunt message for
the kids being, 'Get the hell out the gangs.'

The women of Jessie's family, his mother, sister Rose, and
aunt Milly, spoke widely and eloquently about their own
grief, while a host of community leaders spoke of the pain,
shock and exasperation at the plague that threatened young
black men. It was only a tiny minority who were involved, but
their eagerness to use violence against their own kind, risking
the lives of anyone within the vicinity, was disturbing not just
for those from the same streets or the same colour. It wasn't
only the loss of innocent youth that troubled residents; the
murder revived Moss Side's reputation as a national hotspot
for deadly crime when much time and money had been spent
on regenerating the area and improving the prospects for
local youngsters. At community meetings, people were keen
to stress that this wasn't 'just a black problem'. And, it was
true, there seemed a disproportionate amount of attention
when there was a shooting in a black area, and very little when
shots were fired in a 'white' area.

The sad reality, though, was that young black men were
much more likely to end up dead. A report backed by the
National Union of Teachers, co-authored by veteran community activist Professor Gus John, of Strathclyde University,

said life expectancy was as low as twenty-five for Afro-Caribbean males in some parts of Manchester. John called for an investigation into the effects of street culture, calling on fathers to take greater responsibility for their sons' educations, looking at the low academic attainment of black boys – only 36.6 per cent were leaving school with five GCSEs at grades A to C when the national average was fifty-seven per cent at the time.

'For young people to live their lives and not have any expectation of growing into adulthood and making any useful contribution to society is a terrible thing,' he told the *Manchester Evening News*. 'It has got to be down to families, and particularly fathers, to take a greater responsibility for their children's education and turn this around. There is a culture of low expectations on the part of the young students themselves and on the part of those who teach them. I believe schools should start from the premise that they are institutionally racist.'

The highpoint of the community response came when dozens of people came together to erect a 1,500-capacity marquee for Jessie's funeral in the park. The event drew thousands to see his coffin borne by a white carriage, drawn by plumed horses in a cortege led by a bagpiper. Those that could not get in the marquee lined the streets outside, listening to poignant eulogies and highly charged preaching and prayer. Jessie's mother believed her son had been shot for refusing to join a gang, and paid tribute to her 'lion' in a eulogy. After a two-hour service, 200 balloons were released into the sky, and the procession set off for the cemetery, led by Jessie's friends on bikes. A dozen white doves were released at the graveside as mourners wept.

Yet the information trickling into the police incident room did not match the tide of outrage and grief on the streets. Those closest to the killers were not minded to do anything about it. Barbara Reid made another of the many appeals she would make as Bev Knott, another Moss Side mum, got the justice she craved for her son, Ramone Cumberbatch. Two months after the death of Jesse James, the two women embraced at a press conference held after Ramone's killer, Errol 'Little EJ' Reynolds, was jailed for life. But Barbara Reid was exasperated, wondering if the community she called her friends were really her friends. She was 'sickened, distraught and ashamed' at the silence that shielded her son's killer, or killers. 'People of Moss Side, it's time to search your conscience and talk … someone must have seen or heard something,' she said. Witness anonymity provisions had been used for the first time in Manchester to nail Reynolds, a seasoned Gooch gangster. Witness anonymity promised to remove one of the gangs' most potent weapons, the power to intimidate witnesses. It even prompted one senior detective, John Piekos, to say the gangs' days were numbered. GMP also said the 'net was closing' in on Jesse's killers.

For the team working on the investigation still had reason to believe they would find the murder weapon, that a bike or a mobile seized might turn up a clue, that a girlfriend or a relative whose loved one was acting strangely might pick up the phone, share their suspicions and yield that vital clue. GMP released CCTV footage from the scene of the killing in an attempt to jog memories. The delay in releasing these images, so grainy they had to be sent to specialists in America to enhance them, attracted some criticism but they breathed life into the investigation. They depicted two hooded figures cycling into Broadfield Park moments before the shooting, two people police were confident were the killers. The images were premiered on television on *Crimewatch*. Police had already campaigned for information via YouTube and had scoured internet tribute sites for tidbits of information. The images were accompanied by an interview with Barbara Reid and a harrowing 999 call in which one of Jessie's pals told an operator, 'He's been shot! He's a dead man.' About a dozen calls came in to police directly after, three of which were hailed as 'significant'.

While the police followed up the new leads, the shootings continued. Another teenager was shot in a park after being ambushed by youngsters with ties to the Haydock Close gang, an offshoot of the Doddington. They took their name from a street in the suburb of Stretford which had itself been the scene of a murder in 2004. The shooting of the teenager had trivial origins: his crime had been to text a girl. Her jealous boyfriend hatched a plot to exact revenge. He was sent a text purporting to be from the girl and cycled to meet her in Longford Park, on the leafy border of Manchester and Trafford, only to be shot in the back, leg and stomach. He was lucky to survive. His assailant was later caught and jailed, but the gun was not recovered and would be linked by ballistics to two subsequent shootings.

Barbara Reid spent Christmas Day 2006 by her son's graveside. In the New Year, the family criticised the police, saying the months of delay in releasing the footage was the latest in a litany of blunders that was damaging the force's credibility in Moss Side. Local people were confused about why two people whose names had been going round had not been arrested. 'Police have dismissed the information as hearsay and rumour,' complained Jessie's aunt, Milly Henry, 'but hearsay and rumour catches killers.' Top brass at Chester House, the headquarters of GMP, said they were satisfied the images had been released at the 'most beneficial' time.

Then Reydell Waite was shot for the second time, and a new cycle of killing began.

6

Longsight Street Soldiers

ONE DAY AN ex-jailbird sat in Karen Scotland's living room in the Fallowfield area of south Manchester, chatting with her partner. The two men had been in prison together. Karen noticed the man had a tattoo on his arm which said, 'Young Gooch Crew.' She had heard of them; everybody had in south Manchester. A jolly, easygoing woman, Scotland (a pseudonym; her real name has been changed to protect her identity) did not worry about such things too much. Nor did she mind when the tattooed man returned to her home and brought with him the odd mate. Mostly the lads just hung round outside the gate, sitting in cars.

Her partner eventually got locked up again and the tattooed man faded from the scene, but Narada Williams, one of the lads he had brought with him, continued to mooch about. He was just out of prison too. She liked Narada, who went by the sobriquet 'Yardie' because he had come from 'Yard' – Clarendon, Jamaica – when he was a small boy. His family were what Jamaicans would call 'coolie', people descended from Indians brought to Jamaica as indentured workers in the 19th and early 20th century, the people who brought ganja and curry to the island. Narada still retained a whisper of the accent behind heavy Mancunian tones. Solidly built, with a goatee beard and a bearing of jocular pugnacity, he bore a passing resemblance to the legendary boxer Roberto 'Hands of Stone' Duran. He had been part of a small, Gooch-affiliated group called the Longsight Street Soldiers, who had been involved in shootings and drug dealing. Yardie was all right to be around, especially on his own. His younger brother, Ricardo, who sometimes came with him, was more serious. Karen had little truck with the sullen type and so didn't warm to Ricardo so much. She could never quite pronounce his name properly either: she called him *Ricaldo*, which after a while wound him up.

Scotland came from a big Irish family, and by her thirties had five children. Since many of her cousins lived locally and were willing to help out with her brood, there was a steady stream of girls coming in and out of the house. The Williams brothers were always trying to 'cop off' with her babysitters. Sometimes they would bring a lad called Chucky, a Pakistani kid from Longsight. Scotland liked banter but Chucky wasn't much for banter, not with her anyway. She thought of him as a 'wisp', floating in and out, saying and doing nothing, often just sitting and smoking with his mate, Gonoo Hussain.

Karen had lived life on the edge. Some of her children had been in care and she had a social worker. Still, she did what she thought was best. She wasn't entirely happy about all these young men traipsing into her sitting room to lounge about, poker-faced, as if it were the vault of a boozer with a bad reputation. She liked a 'family environment to be a family environment', she would later say. 'But half the time the door was off the latch and they would just walk in anyway.'

Soon the dubious visitors no longer came in trickles but in groups. It was getting too hectic. 'There was too many people coming and going,' she said. 'I just didn't have my own space, my kids didn't have their own space. I was getting stressed about the house. The house was deteriorating. People were just in and out, pleasing themselves.' The visitors wouldn't stop coming, not just Yardie and his lot but her own nieces and nephews too. Cars pulled up at all hours, and with the ripe smell of skunk weed, the smashed glass on the driveway and the noise, her neighbours were soon complaining. Poor school attendance and the lifestyle at Yew Tree Road even led to one of her children being put on the Child Protection Register. So Scotland went to the council and gave up the tenancy, spending time in hostels to get herself back together. She was getting too old for partying and wanted a settled life.

She was moved a couple of times by the council, ending up in a three-storey council terrace on Princess Parkway in Moss Side. Princess Parkway, the A5103, cuts through south Manchester heading towards Cheshire, the M6 motorway and, ultimately, London. On its way from the city centre it bisects Moss Side. Behind shops on the main drag lies the east side, or 'old' Moss Side, with its two-up, two-down housing. On the other side is the Alexandra Park estate. Keep heading south and you pass Alexandra Park itself, once the strutting ground of the wealthy Mancunians who built the mansions – still grand if slightly down-at-heel – of Whalley Range. Inner south Manchester's estates – Alex Park, the Fallowfield, Withington's Old Moat and Chorlton's Merseybank – all border the parkway as it leads south. There is a large youth population here and gangs are active. It would never be a place where someone like Karen Scotland could live quietly.

It turned out that Yardie knocked about just around the corner. He was soon coming round to play computer games and watch DVDs with her son Robert. His brother Ricardo was soon 'bobbing in and out' too, as well as Chucky, Gonoo and the odd other visitor whose demeanour she didn't like. At first, the situation was manageable. Things weren't as out of control as they had been at Yew Tree Road, with the house falling to bits and the constant partying. Something was playing on her mind though, a creeping sense that she was being watched.

'Don't you reckon summat's up?' she asked her social worker. 'I mean, my landlords, they look like coppers to me. Summat about them, I dunno.'

The social worker's reply was ominous. 'She told me they were setting me up for a fall,' Scotland would later recall.

Being as close to street life as she was, the notion 'gang' didn't have the same resonance for her as it would for some-one from the suburbs, or a wide-eyed teenager raised on rap videos. She knew the personalities of Yardie and his mates better than she knew their reputations, though there was no doubt she was clued-up to the reality of their lives. It was in the little things, like the way they talked and their habits, like always using the back door, weaving the way to her house through a network of ginnels and alleys because it wouldn't be safe to use the street. The 'bwoidem' might see you. As she understood it, being in a gang was all about who your mates were, and how you were seen by their enemies – *your* enemies. 'I assumed that Ricardo and Narada were part of [the gang scene] through their association with some people in the Fallowfield area,' she later said. 'They never said they were Gooch gang members.' They didn't need to.

Scotland knew that if the police wanted to keep gang members under observation, her house was a good place to watch. It might have been paranoia but she couldn't help questioning why the people at the homeless families unit put her in Moss Side, where gangs were so active. Still, it wasn't as if she actually saw any 'gang activity'. Just occasionally though, as she put her head to the pillow in the small hours, she couldn't help worrying about those 'housing officers' who looked like coppers, and whether the 'bwoidem' might come and shoot up her house.

One day she walked into her kitchen and found the Williams boys cutting heroin, bagging the brown dust into £10 wraps. She did nothing. She discovered they were slinging it in the ginnel, taking their time to get up from the Playstation to meet the shivering addicts. Soon, white and yellowish rocks of crack cocaine were also a fixture on the living room table, being sorted into deals. Scotland later maintained that she was 'stressing', desperate for the Williams and their clique to get out of the house and take the gear with them. In reality, things were less clear-cut. Yardie was giving her crack cocaine to test for him, and while she and people around her maintained she was not a 'crackhead', she was an experienced enough smoker to give the product marks out of ten, while her older brother, Chris, was kept sweet with heroin.

One night, the Williams brothers left the house, only to come back ten minutes later in a state of high excitement. A car had drawn close to theirs and someone inside had shot at them. Only a screech of wheels and a white-knuckle manoeuvre had got them away from the drive-by gunmen, undoubtedly Doddington or Longsight boys. The shocked but pumped brothers told her how lucky they had been: they were not wearing bulletproof vests or carrying weapons.

Scotland left Princess Parkway without telling a soul outside her family. In July 2006, her social worker found her a new house in Moston, on the other side of the city. She welcomed this as a 'nice cosy environment for me and the kids' and after a few months, she was settled. Settled enough to see Yardie in the street and not worry too much about it. It turned out he was living nearby with a girlfriend. He did not seem annoyed about the cloak-and-dagger way she had left Moss Side. In fact, when she asked him a favour, he obliged. Moving house, for a mother-of-five on benefits, had been an expensive business, and then there were the visits to her partner in prison. 'I needed basic things – bread, milk, plus cigs – and I thought if anybody would lend me anything it was Narada, he was all right, we got on like that. So I asked Narada – he was always up in pocket.'

He lent her the money. Once he had been paid back, he phoned and asked politely if he might pop round now and again. Karen didn't want him calling in the daytime in case her social worker found out, but evenings were okay. She and her son liked his company and there was no harm in him sticking his head in while walking the dog. This went on for a few weeks without any problems. Narada alone, she thought, posed no problem. Nor did she make a fuss when he started to bring his 'driver', a lad called Scotch John. Then they brought round a couple of girls. As it turned out, the girls were all right too and Karen got friendly with them. Then Ricardo appeared again.

The inevitable happened. As time went on, the little group, who spent much of the time smoking weed, got more and more excitable. They talked about people they knew who were due out of prison and how 'everything is going to be partying and going to be great'. Scotland, concerned about her family, did not want to know.

OUT ON THE street, things were hotting up. Lee 'Cabbo' Amos had been out since May 2006, and Colin 'Piggy' Joyce's release was imminent. The converted firearms supplied by gun-runners like Michael Sammon and Bob Tyrer were fuelling conflict between the various factions claiming allegiance to Gooch and Doddington; their firecracker-like sound became commonplace. The Williams brothers and their mates readied themselves for battle. The L$$ would ride again.

'There was a time Chucky came to me all hyper, asking me to destroy some clothing for him, which I didn't do. I was not happy, there was a lot of bad words said. I never really liked

Chucky. I don't like his demeanour. The kids were on the Child Protection Register as well and I didn't want the social worker seeing all these people round the house.'

Then, on February 2, 2007, Reydell Waite, the Old Trafford Crip who was top of the Doddington's 'wanted' list, was shot again. This time his own posse and their allies in the Gooch sought swift payback. Narada Williams, armed with a handgun, led a small group into Wilcock Street, in the heart of the east side of the Alexandra Park estate. He was in the company of Kayael Wint, the younger brother of a Young Gooch veteran, and Tyler Mullings, then just fifteen years old. They confronted a phalanx of Doddies on bikes, most of them teenagers.

Shortly before 8 p.m., a male neighbour standing on his doorstep heard one of the boys on bikes shout something and saw him point with a silver handgun. 'I tried to open my door to get in,' the man later told a jury. 'I went in and told my wife to lie down, there's a problem outside. Then we heard the firing of shots so we lay down on the floor.' When he looked outside, he saw abandoned bicycles on the ground.

At one end of the street were the Gooch and the OT Crips, at the other was the Doddington. Both sides had opened fire in what a prosecutor later called 'a scene reminiscent of a Wild West movie'. Narada Williams, then in his mid-twenties, and his teenage friend Kayael Wint, were both hit with bullets from a Russian-made converted Baikal handgun.

By chance, two detectives drove along Alexandra Road in an unmarked car minutes later. They saw a group of five or six hooded young men moving with urgency towards Bold Street, in Gooch territory. One of them was dragging his left leg. The unmarked car followed the group along the street as a radio report came over that there had been a shooting at Wilcock Street. The detectives drove there and found nine bullet casings, a discharged cartridge and a fragment scattered around the three bikes, with one training shoe and a baseball cap. Four guns had been fired.

When officers arrived at a Gooch safehouse on Bold Street, Wint was found writhing in agony with bulletholes in both his legs. A bloodstained panel of Kevlar body armour lay next to him in the hallway. There were a few other lads in and outside the house. The cops told the young men around him to move out of the way while he was given oxygen. Then he fainted. Shortly afterwards, Yardie was driven up to an ambulance parked at a junction on the Whalley Range side of the Alex Park estate. The crew had been called out but were waiting, as was routine for firearms incidents, for a police escort before moving to Bold Street. Yardie had been shot in the big toe of his right foot. A bullet fell from his bloodsoaked sock and into the palm of a paramedic's hand as he was treated.

The victim, who had been armed with a revolver that night, spun a yarn for the police officers he saw. He claimed to have been crossing the Alexandra Park estate, minding his own business, when he was confronted by a gang of up to six masked males. Somebody shouted, 'Yo,' he heard a bang, and felt a sharp pain in his right foot. Two black men with dreadlocks had let him into their car before seeing the ambulance, he lied. Yardie also lied about his injury to Karen Scotland, telling her he had been on the street when someone rode up wearing a balaclava and shot him for no reason.

OT Crip Reydell Waite would end up in jail after police trailed him to Wythenshawe and watched him buy a 9mm converted replica for protection. He was arrested at a house, where he threw the gun into the garden. Remanded in custody, he was heard to say in the back of a prison van, 'They don't know it's me who chucked the baby out the window.' The prison officer who heard him thought he was admitting to a child murder, when in fact he was referring to the gun. Waite refused to tell the police who shot him.

THE STREETS CRACKLED with gunfire for the rest of that month. A man was shot in the leg at Upper Chorlton Road, a short distance from the OT Crips' base. An eighteen-year-old was shot in the back after gunmen opened fire on youths standing outside the Powerhouse, the Moss Side community centre for young people close to the spot where Jessie James died. In Longsight, two men were shot in a drive-by as their car stopped at traffic lights. Neither was seriously hurt. Indeed, the fact that so many people survived shootings was to some extent due to the unreliability of the converted replicas and older guns, loaded with home-made ammunition, that were doing the rounds at the time. Manchester detectives even travelled to Germany to try and urge Cuno Melcher, one of the major manufacturers of blank-firers, to change the way they made them. Dave Keller, then the Chief Superintendent of the Metropolitan Division, blasted the 'macho culture' which surrounded these guns and the 'playground aggression' that led to their use, in a front-page interview with the *Manchester Evening News.*

'Over the last two or three years things have changed in this area,' he said. 'This is not about organised gangs. It is now more about youths hanging around on street corners, but with access to guns. They are young, aged fifteen upwards. They pose with guns to enhance their reputation but they often have no money and are not really involved in turf wars or drugs. It seems to be more about them hanging around on street corners being visible with their guns. In reality it is a pathetic, hopeless lifestyle. There is no real hierarchy or structure, they are just a loose connection of people. It makes for a more chaotic setup. These are children who as they grow older – if they make it – will reflect on their lives and realise how pathetic it has been.'

The CCTV network in Moss Side, Old Trafford and Whalley Range was boosted by twenty-three cameras, and armed patrols and extra community support officers were drafted into these areas. And while Chief Supt Keller had talked tough over street thugs, the attitude of police was becoming more nuanced. They knew that many of these youngsters came from troubled, deprived family backgrounds, may have been isolated from the education system, had been arrested at a young age, and often stuck together on the streets for protection. As Jessie James's case would eventually show, youngsters living in areas infested by gangs could easily come under pressure to pick a side, whether they wanted to or not.

Guns and gangs had become a hot political issue. In late February, both the Labour Prime Minister, Tony Blair, and David Cameron, then Opposition leader, visited Manchester on the same day to talk about gun crime. Cameron stole the show, but for the wrong reasons. The day had started out as an opportunity for him to appeal to the northern working-class support that his party traditionally lacked. At a community centre on the vast Wythenshawe housing estate, he was welcomed by local activists who had fallen out of love with the Labour-dominated council. The work done by volunteers at the centre chimed neatly with Cameron's nascent vision of the Big Society, and he talked that day about how society had 'broken down' and needed to 'rebuild itself from the bottom up' with 'strong role models, families and communities'. He was reluctant, however, to be drawn on specific plans for tackling gang crime, promising more detail at the end of the visit, then huffing, 'Families and communities, will that do?'

Near the end of his visit, Cameron went on walkabout for the cameras. The tie-less, loafer-shod Prime Minister-in-waiting must have heard the shouts of, 'Ee aar, who's 'e?' from the lads in black tracksuits lurking about the avenues, but was unaware of the cheeky youth who made a 'gunfingers' gesture behind his head. The moment, captured by a photographer, would make an iconic picture that appeared in all the national press the next day. Cameron's calls for greater understanding of young offenders had already been labelled 'hug a hoodie' by sceptical pundits; now, he had first-hand experience of what might happen should he attempt it. Dressed in the standard-issue black tracksuit, the hooded youngster screw-faced and shaped his right-hand into a gun, trained on Cameron's back, his left hand down the front of his pants, fumbling with his privates at the same time. Seventeen-year-old Ryan Florence, who didn't even know who Cameron was, later boasted to newspapers that he was in a gang called Benchill Mad Dogs and had made the 'click, bang' gesture for 'a buzz'.

Tony Blair's visit went off with less incident. At the Zion Arts Centre, he met Manchester United and England footballer Rio Ferdinand, who had been raised on a tough estate in Peckham, south London, and was putting himself forward as a positive role model. Community members discussed the deadly combination of deprivation, poverty of aspiration, educational under-achievement, police mistrust and the ready availability of guns. Then Blair went to the Saltshaker, the community centre on the site of the notorious, now-demolished Pepperhill pub, where Moss Side's Original Gangsters used to knock about. There, he met four former gang members in a private meeting. Blair's rhetoric was tougher than Cameron's. He too stressed the importance of the Government supporting the community, but said those carrying firearms should face the 'full force of the law'.

In such a media and political spotlight, Manchester's anti-gun crime movement was galvanised. Among its most articulate and most-quoted members were Patsy McKie, a social worker who co-founded Mothers Against Violence (MAV) after her own son, Dorrie, was murdered, most probably by the Gooch, in 1999, and Erinma Bell, a former social worker who had dedicated herself to tackling gun crime in the city, along with her husband, Raymond, and their organisation Carisma. MAV and Carisma specialised in grassroots work and acted as go-betweens for the community, police and politicians. Carisma started an annual event called Peace Week in 2003, with the aim being to get the gangs to put down their guns for seven days. It evolved into a week of activities to celebrate talent in the community, educating youngsters about the perils of thuglife and improving the relationship between locals and the authorities.

In yet another 'crackdown', the police targeted the places where gang members stashed their guns, executing 300 search warrants. By now, it was a common tactic for gangs to hide their weapons in the gardens and sheds of innocent people who lived on the streets they regarded as their territory. Shaun Donnellan, a senior detective who had worked on Operation Xcalibre, which targeted gun crime in the inner-city Metropolitan division, which included the hotspots of Moss Side and Longsight, was brought in as the new broom on the Jessie James investigation, and promised more raids to root out the killers and their arsenals. Donnellan took solving the murder personally. He was confident that the gunman was experienced – the gun had such a powerful kick that no novice could have used it with such deadly accuracy. It was a fresh weapon, not used before or since, and a real firearm, not a converted replica, suggesting its owner was well-connected criminally. Donnellan was confident that this man could kill again 'in the blink of an eye'. But ultimately, the evidence that would have led him to the killer's door was still not there. The weapon had vanished, no clear motive had been established and the calls weren't coming in. The people least likely to pick up the phone were those most likely to have known who did it and why.

In the first week of March, as more shots were fired in Blackley, Levenshulme and Longsight, GMP announced it was trying to boost the number of trained firearms officers by more than a quarter, to 164. It also put up a £20,000 reward for information about Jessie James's killing, stressing that the identity of witnesses could be protected. However, Barbara

Reid's frustration was growing. The disappointing response to the pleas for help prompted her withdrawal from the community she had once been at the heart of. It was even suggested to her when she was out and about in Moss Side that she ought to 'forget about' getting justice and move on. She and her family faced cruel accusations that they were attention-seekers, that they thought they were better than everybody now they had been on the TV and in the papers. She expressed her despair in a newspaper appeal.

'The police can only do so much,' she said. 'They don't live in Moss Side and if the community is not willing to support them they will not get very far. We think of Jessie every day, but I haven't cried. I let out a shout just after he died but I can't cry properly because I'm too hurt. It's so difficult living in the same area where Jessie was killed. The murderer could be walking past me. I am pleading for my neighbours in Moss Side and Manchester to give up the killer, so we can finally mourn.'

The violence raged on. Residents of the Alexandra Park estate were lucky to escape unhurt when shots were fired after a blues party. The gun violence was also spreading across the conurbation, to areas relatively untouched by gang conflict. Two teenagers were shot in the leg in separate incidents in Moston and Droylsden. In Hattersley, a deprived overspill estate on the road to the Derbyshire Peak District, a house was shot at by a man on a motorbike.

In April 2007, twelve-year-old Kamilah Peniston was accidentally shot dead by her fifteen-year-old brother. Kasha Peniston had been left in charge of Kamilah, a polite, intelligent little girl, and her two younger sisters while their mother went to a funeral. Before she left, she told Kasha about a gun she was hiding in the garden and warned him not to touch it. At some point Kasha dug up the revolver from its hiding place and began fiddling with it as his younger sisters ate snacks in front of the TV. He thought that when he pulled the trigger nothing would happen.

Through the spring and summer of 2007, GMP were responding to up to seven firearms incidents a day. A boy was shot in the leg as he fled gunfire in Moss Side, a guest was shot in the stomach after a row at a Muslim wedding, two teenagers were shot in a Moss Side drive-by, shots were fired after a comedy show in Newton Heath and at a car in Gorton.

KAREN SCOTLAND'S HOME in Moston had by now become a fully fledged L$$ safehouse. The Williams brothers had the run of the place, and Aaron Alexander was someone they thought of as a 'good kid'. When he and his best mate, Stefan 'Tricks' Melia, said they had nowhere to stay, Narada Williams offered them a place to live and a job. He also promised Scotland that they would only be around for a few days, but it ended up being weeks. If her son didn't let them in, they would prise open the patio doors or wriggle through a window. Sometimes Scotland would come back and find them with girls and she would 'kick off'. They would then go out, only to come back a couple of hours later. One time she got so frustrated she picked up a chair and threw it, but all they did was laugh.

Crack cocaine and heroin would be sorted or chopped by Aaron and Stefan in her kitchen. If she stumbled in on them sorting the gear she would leave the room, though not before taking a rock for herself. Once it had been sorted into wraps, the dealers would take up to thirty each to sell on the streets. They had carved out new markets in the towns east of Manchester which skirted the Peak District. For boys raised on the toughest streets of Longsight and Gorton, used to thugging it in Moss Side, these backwaters were easy meat: the locals posed no threat, while the combination of small town isolation and post-industrial boredom fuelled heroin abuse, and on the weekends, plenty of clubbers keen for cocaine.

Karen knew something was going on in the attic. The gang members were always going upstairs, watching DVDs in her son's room. It was the chair that made her suspicious. She would go out, come back and find it beneath the attic door. She would move it, and two days later, there it was again. She asked Narada what was going on. He said he had not been up there. She was minded to take a look herself, but was no good at climbing. She argued with Narada about it. She was fed up of him, she wanted peace, and no-one called when he wasn't around. She told him to stay away.

Chucky dropped by, told her to 'stop stressing', and marched straight upstairs. Narada started coming round again. She would see him coming down the stairs with a small bag that looked heavy. It was her son Robert, then just eleven, who eventually found the semi-automatic machine gun in the attic. He had already watched Narada handling a sawn-off shotgun. An arsenal, including handguns and revolvers, was being kept in the house.

For a while now, the lads had been enthusing about 'mans getting out'. They included Kelvin Taylor, an original L$$ member and Narada's best mate. Known and respected on the street as 'Kray', Taylor was released from a drug-dealing sentence and placed in a bail hostel with an 11 p.m. curfew. He hated the hostel and threw himself back into the life, getting involved in Yardie's expanding operation and treating himself to a high-powered motorbike. Kray and Yardie also asked around the Longsight area if anybody had seen Tyrone Gilbert, an old enemy from the Longsight Crew.

On May 29, Kelvin Taylor was killed in a motorbike accident at the age of twenty-four. Narada Williams would say his 'heart died' with Kray. More significant, for the Gooch gang's enemies, was the release that spring of Colin 'Piggy' Joyce on licence from a nine-year term. In hindsight, it was a terrible mistake: reunited with his old sparring partner, Lee 'Cabbo' Amos, Joyce represented a terrible threat. Police already believed that Amos had been quietly stirring up tensions. Now, it seemed, Joyce – who had walked out of prison and given a cheeky wink to watching surveillance cameras – was handing out guns to young gang members and telling them to do their worst. Detectives were also told that a Doddington gang leader from the bad old days, who had vanished from the city to Sheffield years before, had made a surprise return to Manchester, cruising the streets in a yellow Lamborghini in a bid to cook a snook at the release of his old foes.

Joyce and Amos had been wild young men when they were locked up back in 2001; they returned to the streets as elder statesmen. Their Young Gooch Close gang were no longer the new kids on the block; a crop of new Gooch-affiliated gangs like the Fallowfield Mandem and Old Trafford Crips had sprung up in their absence. To these youngsters, Piggy and Cabbo were the stuff of legend, and with old hostilities still smouldering, the pair picked up where they had left off.

Piggy and Cabbo had known the Williams brothers when they first came to England from Jamaica; the four were among a number of primary-school-age toughs who hung around on Mount Road, which runs from Gorton down to Levenshulme. The friendship was strengthened when the Williamses, along with Kelvin Taylor, Karl Reid and Bobby Phipps, fell out with the Longsight Crew and affiliated with the Gooch. The bond had been cemented with the death of Stephen Amos, with the L$$ paying their respects to the dead man and stepping up the violence against the LSC in the days afterwards. When Kelvin Taylor died, Colin Joyce helped arrange the funeral and the L$$ all put money towards the costs. On the day itself, the L$$ made sure Kray got a send-off fitting for a 'true soldier'. Each of them wore hoodies emblazoned with the words 'Longsight Street Soldiers'.

With L$$ as their foot soldiers, Joyce and Amos now planned a fresh orgy of killing.

7

Cabbo's Revenge

ON JUNE 10, 2007, five lads from Manchester bought a silver Audi S3 from a car dealer in Bedfordshire. Among them were Lee Amos, of the Gooch, and Amir Hussain, one of three brothers from Cheetham Hill who were closely associated with the gang. It was six years to the day that Colin Joyce, Amos and their Gooch cohorts had been sentenced after being caught with an arsenal of weapons in Moss Side. Five days after they bought the car, Joyce and Amos met in the Radcliffe area, on the north side of Manchester, before travelling south for a friend's funeral. They spent the afternoon together before Joyce returned to south Manchester, cruising the streets in the newly bought Audi.

Ucal Chin, a twenty-four-year-old man from Longsight, was out that day too, in a Renault Megane. He gave his friend Marlon Cameron a lift to the job centre in Stockport, then shortly afterwards took another friend, Edward Simpson, to Levenshulme to see his girl. Ucal and Marlon then went back to Ucal's house on the Longsight estate, before the pair returned to pick up Edward. At some point in the course of this zigzagging across south Manchester, the three men were spotted by Colin Joyce and a carload of Gooch gunmen.

The Megane was travelling along Anson Road, Victoria Park, when the Gooch's silver Audi finally pulled alongside it. The rear passenger window of the Audi wound down and a gloved and masked man pointed a Russian Baikal self-loading pistol at the offside of the Renault. He fired seven shots. Three 9mm bullets hit Ucal Chin. One passed through his right upper arm, another entered his right upper back near his shoulder, while the third and fatal shot blistered his heart, liver and lungs as it coursed through his chest, causing massive internal bleeding. His friend Marlon, the front seat passenger, was hit in the hand. Chin lost control of the vehicle, which mounted the kerb before crashing into an electrical box at the side of the road. The Audi sped towards the city centre, taking a roundabout route to Cheetham Hill before disappearing from the CCTV network.

Ucal Chin had been identified by police as an LSC associate way back in 2001. However, at the time of the shooting his family denied suggestions that he was in a gang, maintaining that he was a well-loved 'peacemaker'. He was pronounced dead on arrival at Manchester Royal Infirmary, a few hundred yards from where he had been ambushed. It was the fifth shooting in Manchester that week and the first fatality.

Back in Cheetham Hill, a veritable Who's Who of Gooch and L$$ gang members converged for a summit in the aftermath of the killing. There was Lee Amos, Antonio Wint, the Williams brothers, Hassan 'Chucky' Shah, drivers Gonoo Hussain and Michael Wilkinson, and grafters Aaron Alexander, Ricci Moss and Stefan Melia. High on adrenaline, and utterly unremorseful, it seems the gang began making plans for another attack almost immediately. They were on a mission to eliminate the Longsight Crew in revenge for the murder of Cabbo's beloved brother, Stephen, and nothing was going to stop them.

As the Gooch revelled in their murderous adventure, police began piecing together the few clues they had. CCTV showed the moment the silver Audi pulled alongside the Renault Megane as Ucal's killer opened fire. A witness remembered part of the numberplate, and with this fragment cops were able to trace the vehicle back to Luton. The man who sold it recalled that the buyers had come from Manchester. The victim's associations, plus the manner and location of his death hinted at a gangland motive. At the time the Gooch gang, the Longsight Crew's natural enemies, were fond of Russian Baikal handguns, converted replicas sold for as little as £200. Ballistics experts at the Northern Firearms Unit test-fired bullets from a Baikal and compared the rifling marks on it with those on bullets from the scene. They matched.

Within days of Chin's murder, Narada 'Yardie' Williams was sending out for 'riding gear', his term for black, waterproof clothing which did not shed fibres and could be burned. He also wanted 'cold killer gloves'. Two pairs of waterproof pants and jackets were duly bought, paid for with the clique's drug money. From then on, if they went to a club or to a party they made sure they were strapped in case 'the boys were in'. They used girls to smuggle the guns past club doormen.

In consultation with Colin Joyce, Yardie Williams contacted a car dealer who was advertising a Honda Legend for sale. The next day Ricardo Williams, Chucky and Gonoo visited the dealer in the Lancashire town of Nelson, where they test drove and bought the car for £650. Ricky drove it into the garage of Karen Scotland's house at Kilmayne Avenue in Moston, asking her to mind the registration documents. She noticed that he wore gloves to handle the car and the documents, and Chucky told her it was 'hot'. A couple of days later, they took it to have its windows tinted. A nosey neighbour had been asking about the car, so it was not returned to Karen's address.

The following week, the Hussains set up a meeting between Colin Joyce and another car dealer who was advertising an Audi S4. By the next day, the car had been bought and was parked behind Joyce's Walkden address. The day after that, it was taken to a garage in Stockport for new brake discs. Two men, who wanted the work done urgently, signed their initials 'C' and 'P' in the garage diary. That evening, Lee 'Cabbo' Amos and Colin 'Piggy' Joyce met with Yardie and the Hussain brothers in Cheetham Hill.

THE FUNERAL OF Ucal Chin had taken place that day, July 27, in Longsight, having been delayed by the police investigation. At 11 a.m., Oleanda Mason, mother of Ucal's two children and his partner of eight years, went to his mother's home on the estate. There was a photo of Ucal she wanted to put in the coffin, but when she got there the casket was sealed. The service was held at the church of St Luke the Physician, before burial at Southern Cemetery and a wake at the West Indian Centre in Carmoor Road.

Later that evening Oleanda went to her mother's home to change into a white pair of jeans, a jumper with a picture of Ucal on the back, and a white jacket which said 'gone but not forgotten, rest in peace', with the outline of Ucal's face. She took cards with pictures of Ucal on to hand out at the wake. At the end of the night, everybody went back to Frobisher Close for more food and drink. Oleanda took a carload of children from Carmoor Road to Mrs Chin's home, and then returned to pick up more family and friends, including Racquel, Ucal's sister, and Beatrice, a family friend. Oleanda joked that she hoped police did not stop them because they had so many people in the car. When she pulled up by the house, she saw two cars parked parallel to each other on the opposite side of the close, further up. A number of people were chatting in and outside of cars at the time. Two of Ucal's friends, Tyrone Gilbert and Michael Gordon, were among them.

Oleanda was asked for food by the men. Ucal's mum Viv said they could have drinks but the rice was still boiling. Oleanda went upstairs to a bedroom, where she sat and talked with some friends for about forty minutes. Her son came in and asked if he could play outside with his cousin. She said no, it was too late. Concerned for her little cousin, she opened the window and shouted after him. She heard a loud bang. She thought someone had knocked over a wheelie bin, but when more bangs followed, she realised it was gunfire. The women in the room rushed to the window.

On the street below, they saw screaming people. Beatrice was among them. She had been talking outside the gate when she heard six or seven bangs in quick succession. She thought at first they were fireworks, but the panic told her otherwise. She got on her knees and ducked down outside the gate. As she crawled to the door she felt people jumping on her back, desperate to get into the house.

'I called police and told the operator that a gun had been fired but I didn't think anyone had been hurt,' recalled Oleanda. 'At this point, I saw a male figure being carried. My mobile phone began ringing, it was my mother, she'd heard the gunshots and was ringing to check I was okay. I ran downstairs but soon realised how everyone was trying to run inside. People had been just clambering over the baby gate. People were crammed in Viv's hallway. I heard Natalie say, "They have taken him in my car." '

Natalie had known Ucal Chin all her life. After the funeral she sat in her car at Frobisher Close with the door open, chatting with other mourners. It had been, she thought, a 'nice funeral'. Then someone said, 'Who's that in the green Honda?' As she glanced in her rear-view mirror, she saw the long, dark vehicle drive up. Then she heard the first shot. The Honda had stopped. She thought she saw another car coming up just behind it.

Carlie, aged fourteen, had been hovering about Tyrone and his friends. She was leaning on a car as they laughed together, oblivious to the danger drawing near. It was only when the green Honda pulled closer and its windows dropped down that anybody realised anything was wrong.

'It's the bwoidem! It's the bwoidem!' Carlie heard somebody shout in the instant before she heard what she called 'pop, pop gunshots'. Bullets ricocheted off the walls of nearby houses. Glass flew everywhere and everybody scattered.

Carlie noticed that Tyrone Gilbert looked strange. He was on his feet, but appeared to have been wounded.

'Tyrone, what's wrong with you?' she asked.

'Help me, help me,' he gasped. 'I've been shot.'

Blood started coming out of his mouth. The girl held his face, telling him to breathe and that he was going to be alright. 'Tyrone's been shot,' she shouted out. As people ran over to help, he collapsed.

Natalie and her friend crouched on the floor of their car, keeping their heads down until they heard tyres screeching. Natalie thought she heard eight shots, then two more. Her friend got out of the passenger side first, but when Natalie tried to follow the door handle snapped. She squeezed out of the window and stood dazed in the street.

Keith, a local resident whose niece and nephew had been at the funeral, was washing dinner plates in his house when he heard the shots, and went outside. Two cars were speeding away, with shots still ringing out. Another neighbour watched the two vehicles that had caused the panic. She thought one of them was silver, and as it sped down Markfield Avenue and onto Plymouth Road West, she made eye contact with the driver, a black man with short hair and a screwfaced expression. Then she went inside and put the kettle on.

Tyrone Gilbert was unconscious on the ground. Another neighbour saw him curled on the floor at the bottom of a ginnel and recognised Gilbert as someone he had been to junior school with. He and two others picked up the stricken man and carried him down the ginnel as blood ran from his nose and mouth. Natalie's car was nearest and the door was open, so the mourners picked him up and put him in the front passenger side. Natalie was too panicky to take the wheel. One of the men drove Tyrone to the hospital. Natalie ran behind the car, sobbing all the way.

Carlie was among the many at the hospital. 'I was waiting outside. His mum came out and started crying, I knew that he was dead. I had a feeling something was going to happen that day.'

Tyrone was pronounced dead at 12.30 a.m., a single bullet having destroyed his liver, heart and right lung. His friend Michael Gordon had been shot twice in the leg, but survived. Up to ninety people had been at the scene at the point the Gooch pulled up at the junction and opened fire. The shooting meant that Keicha Greenidge, an elegant, eloquent young woman, had lost two brothers to the gun. First it had been Marcus, gunned down by Tommy Pitt, and now Tyrone. In the ITV documentary *Bringing Down the Gooch*, she summed up the mentality of Tyrone's killers.

'It says a lot to me that they could go past a wake and shoot into an open street with women and children. They were just unbiased with who they might hit with those bullets – I think it comes down to them having no self respect, so they have no respect for the life of other people. They have no value on life so anyone is for the taking.'

The Honda Legend was spotted after leaving the scene of the shooting by a police officer who was driving through Fallowfield. The driver's face was covered and the front passenger was wearing a balaclava. At Ladybarn Road, an officer in a parked car saw the same vehicle with the tinted windows. The Honda did not have its lights on and he lost them a few yards away at Kingsway. A third police officer saw the Audi and two vehicles heading for Kingsway; he caught only the last part of the Audi's reg number, S831, because of the speed they were going. The cars crossed Kingsway and went into Firethorn Avenue in Burnage, south Manchester, where the Honda was dumped. Four men got out of it. Two sprinted towards the Audi, which hared away with its lights off. Two other men in dark clothing were seen trying to escape through the rear gardens of the little street before running back to a third car, another Audi with tinted windows. This car sped away, leaving the two men behind. The pair were seen sprinting just as a police vehicle passed by. One of the men crouched by the side of a parked car, the other leapt over a barbed wire fence. The two men then ran from Firethorn Avenue and into the driveway of some flats. There, they were spotted by yet another officer, who shortly afterwards found the abandoned Honda. The men escaped.

THE NEXT MORNING, as the mourners digested the terrible events of the night before, tributes appeared at the bottom of the ginnel at Frobisher Close where Tyrone Gilbert had slumped to his death after running a few yards, a bullet in his side. The patch, still spotted with blood, was marked with flowers, bottles of liquor, and tributes written in felt-tip pen, which soon began to smudge in the drizzle. As friends of the dead man converged at the scene, fragments from the story of his life emerged.

Gilbert had been born in Slough, Berkshire, the second youngest of five children. His family moved to Manchester when he was five years old. He had attended Coverdale Crescent Church and St Luke's C of E School, where he was remembered as a sociable child who liked football and art. He grew up on Langport Avenue, the street where the Longsight Crew hung out. He matured into a serious player in the outfit, and extreme violence punctuated his young life. His brother Marcus Greenidge was shot dead by the Pitt Bull Crew in

2001, while Gilbert himself had been at the High Society night club when his friend Fabian Flowers was mysteriously killed by a single shot to the head from a key-fob gun in 2004. And he had been involved in the notorious gang fight with the Gooch at Manchester Royal Infirmary, serving twenty months for affray. The Gooch believed that Gilbert had been there on the night Stephen Amos was murdered by the LSC. That was the event that sealed his fate.

Gilbert had apparently been trying to put the thug life behind him, moving to Blackpool before returning to Manchester and settling on a new street, away from the Longsight estate. He already had three boys with his childhood sweetheart, Lisa Norris, and she was pregnant again with their first girl. His kids, she said, 'loved every bone in his body'. He had resolved to change for them, to concentrate on being a good dad, on being a husband, since getting out of jail a few months back.

He had not been the specific target of the shooting at the wake, even though the Gooch had been looking for him. They had opened fire indiscriminately. In fact Gilbert had only returned to the estate, a witness told the *Manchester Evening News*, to attend the funeral. 'It took Tyrone a few years to get over Marcus's death,' she said. 'But he had moved away from the area and was trying to sort himself out. He was only down here for the funeral of his friend. He didn't come down here armed because he wasn't like that. I have known him all my life. His family are decent and now they have lost two sons. He grew up here and some of the boys down here have got a name. But everybody had been trying to get Tyrone away from that lifestyle, everybody liked him.'

Another woman gave reporters their first glimpse of the evening's horror. 'I was in my car with some little kids I was about to take home and my car got hit by bullets,' she told them. 'The women and kids that were outside were screaming and threw themselves on the floor. Other people were running. Tyrone was one of them, but he got caught in the stomach and ran before sinking to the floor.'

Firethorn Avenue, the other south Manchester street significant to the enquiry, was soon cordoned off and milling with forensics officers. A balaclava was recovered hanging from a fence. It had been left there by Aeeron Campbell, one of the men who had run from the car and braved the barbed wire in flight from the police. He was linked to the shooting because his DNA was found on it along with a particle of firearms residue and microscopic fibres which matched samples recovered from the Honda Legend. A discarded pair of gloves found by a local on his way home from a boozy session had also been worn by Campbell.

Examination of the Honda revealed that one of the gunmen was a front seat passenger, as he had left four areas of bullet damage to the nearside front door window. In all, twelve shots had been fired from three weapons: two revolvers, including a .357 Smith and Wesson revolver linked to six other shootings, and a 9mm semi-automatic. Campbell was in the drug business, and although his IQ was rated as low as sixty-seven, he commanded grafters in his own street dealing operation. He was known to go about with the Williams brothers, although their association was not based on any great friendship but shared criminal interests. He was also a member of the Gooch gang.

Campbell was arrested on August 28, a month and a day later. When he was taken into custody, an eye-watering quantity of heroin was found plugged up his anus, a common hiding place for drug dealers. He denied involvement in the shooting. At the time, he said, he was probably at a party in Fallowfield. He said he had never been on Firethorn Avenue, and if his DNA were on the gloves and balaclava then he must have worn them at some point, but he and his mates swapped clothes all the time. He made no comment after that, but police and the CPS were satisfied they had enough. On September 1, he was charged with the murder of Tyrone Gilbert.

THINGS BEGAN FALLING apart for the rest of the gang when Stefan 'Tricks' Melia turned on them. For a good while Tricks, one of the grafters employed by the gang in Tameside, had enjoyed the favour of Narada Williams, who gave him a place to stay and a job as a dealer, and went out chasing girls with him. However, by the end of 2007, Tricks's stock had fallen. Ricardo and Chucky had never quite taken to him and suspicions were growing that he was a grass, that he smoked the crack he was supposed to be selling and that he was setting up his own dealing enterprise. When some of Yardie's money went missing, Tricks was suspected.

He found himself waking from unconsciousness one night, unable to move, surrounded by darkness. He had been tied to a tree, and felt the point of a gun in his face. Disembodied voices threatened his life. He thought he recognised one of his masked captors, a familiar crackle: Chucky had a certain timbre to his voice, like a Scouser. When they finally let him go, he noticed a lattice of knife marks on his belly. Chucky had cut him while he was unconscious, he was sure of it.

Stefan Melia was no angel. He enforced drug debts with a craft knife and threatened to petrol bomb the home of one hapless user. But he was alone. His family had turned their backs on him after he sided with the Gooch. His uncle Carlos had friends on the 'other' side, and had driven Tyrone Gilbert to the hospital on the night he was shot. Tricks became convinced he was a dead man walking.

About a week after his ordeal tied to the tree, he went to the police. Tricks said he did not want to be part of it anymore. He would later testify that his conscience had bothered him, that he did not like what he had been doing and had become fearful for his own safety. Big hints had been dropped by

Ricardo and Chucky that the L$$ were responsible for the deaths of Chin and Gilbert. He told police about a time when he was in the car with Hassan Shah and Ricardo Williams, driving past Anson Road, and one of them said in a meaningful way, 'That's where my man got licked down.' Another time, Tricks was with Yardie and some of the girls when a news item came on the TV about the Gilbert shooting and Yardie said the same thing, 'My man got licked down.'

There was more, a lot of guns being passed around, like the time when he and his best mate, Aaron Alexander, had been given one each by Yardie on a visit to the Legends nightclub in Ashton under Lyne. There had been no trouble until they were driving back to Moston, when two men pulled out in front of them. Yardie put on a pair of gloves, took a revolver from Tricks and shot four times at the men. Later, Tricks was asked by Ricardo and Chucky to hide two handguns for them. These, they said, were 'hot'. Tricks stashed them under a bed at a friend's house, and later Ricardo picked one up, returning it hours later. Chucky used the other gun to protect Colin Joyce on a night out when Yardie was also armed and ready. Eventually Yardie took possession of one of the handguns and Joyce the other.

Michael Wilkinson also came forward. He told police that in the days following the Ucal Chin murder, he had been ordered, along with Aaron Alexander, to go to discount sports outfitter Decathlon for some 'riding gear', meaning waterproof, flammable and fibreless clothes that could be worn and then destroyed. Narada had given them a chunk of the drug takings to buy the clobber and some 'cold killer gloves'.

The revelations of Melia, Wilkinson and others provided the grounds for charges of possessing firearms with intent to endanger life, and incriminated Narada Williams in the Gilbert murder. On January 14, both Williams brothers and Chucky Shah were picked up. The trio answered 'no comment' in interview. They and Gonoo Hussain were charged with conspiracy to possess firearms with intent to endanger life and conspiracy to supply drugs, after Karen Scotland and her son came forward with yet more damning revelations.

Scotland's house had been raided by police within weeks of the Gilbert murder. Almost relieved, she told them about the goings on in the attic. By then, her brother and her son Robert had removed the machine gun and dumped it. The family pointed police to the weapon, triple-wrapped in plastic, in some bushes. There was more. Just a few days after the shooting, she had read in the paper that a Honda Legend had been used. She rang Narada and told him that she still had the logbook for a Honda Legend, *the* Honda Legend. Narada told her to burn it. When she rang Robert and told him to burn it, she found out the boy had already taken the documents into some woods and set fire to them.

Bit by bit, as a series of associates, retainers, employees, spurned lovers and hangers-on came forward with nuggets of information, a picture of the L$$'s criminal lifestyle was revealed to detectives. They bought drugs in bulk from sources in the city and on Merseyside, using a fleet of hire cars, taxis, and drivers like Michael Wilkinson to make deliveries to street dealers undetected. At times, and certainly when the operation was smaller, the Williams brothers and Hassan Shah would cut, split and package the drugs themselves, but this was usually the duty of Aaron Alexander and Ricci Moss, if not the street dealers themselves. Narada was in charge of general operations, and specialised in crack cocaine. On the next tier were Chucky and Ricardo, who concentrated largely on selling heroin and keeping the dealers in line. These gophers would either pay 'rent' to the Gooch or take a £50 a day wage after handing over everything they made. If they messed with the money, they were beaten, threatened or tormented, as Tricks was. They also sold drugs in clubs and bars and to prisoners in 'throw-overs', which involved hurling a loaded tennis ball over the walls of a prison.

Rivalry in the drug trade was the source of friction with the Longsight Crew, but their mutual hatred went beyond that. Years of tit-for-tat shootings had locked both gangs into a savage enmity that was part blood feud, part deadly game. In London, *bwoidem* is what they call the police. In Manchester, they use phrase *bwoidem,* or *the boys* to describe gangland enemies. Ostensibly, it denigrates them, but also rings with a strange note of affection and respect for the old adversary, a rival player in a game for the highest stakes. Of course, they despised each other and perpetrated the most heinous violence upon one another, but they also understood one another. In many cases they had played together in the streets or been to school together.

The war defined both clans as dangerous and potent, as somebody. They were far more focused on fighting one another than they were on fighting the police, and certainly the law-abiding population. Only the enemy lived by the same code, and consequently felt the fear that they felt. And what else was there? They spent their days wading through a fug of marijuana smoke, watching DVDs, playing computer games, eating bad food, chasing girls. They spent more time with each other than they did with their families.

COLIN JOYCE AND Lee Amos were suspected, early on, of having been instrumental in both the killings and the general upsurge in violence. Neither had stuck to their prison-release licence conditions, so police were free to lock them back up even though they did not yet have the evidence to charge them with fresh offences. First, they had to find them. On August 1, an operation codenamed Silverstone was launched at a high-level police meeting. More than 100 officers were involved in the plans to arrest the men, who Dave Keller, the bluff Scouser who was then Chief Superintendent of the inner-city Metropolitan Division, dubbed 'psychopaths who shoot for fun' and consequently, 'the biggest threat to public safety in the city'. Amos was tracked down to his girlfriend's home in Mansfield in a raid involving armed officers and hostage negotiators. Joyce was dragged from a taxi on the A666 at Walkden and subdued with teargas.

'After they came out of prison it was noticeable that tensions increased and there were a lot more firearms-related incidents,' Keller later told the *Manchester Evening News*. The figures were alarming: fifty-six serious woundings force-wide between April 2006 and March 2007, and forty-one serious woundings in the three months after that. There had been 120 firearms discharges across the conurbation between April 1, 2006 and March 31, 2007, and this would increase to 145 the year after. About half of these occurred in inner-city Manchester's 'Metropolitan' division and the neighbouring Old Trafford area, which together made up just five per cent of GMP's total area. Up to seventy per cent of these shootings were gang related.

'The mere presence of these two individuals caused an increase in tensions,' said Keller. 'We made it our main aim to catch them and return them to prison. They are people with no boundaries, no morals, no rules and no regard for the law. They do what they want, when they want. They think they are above the law. Some people get sucked into gun crime when they are young and they need help to escape that way of life. But people like this are so embroiled there is no hope of redemption.'

In February 2008, hours before they were due to be re-released on completion of their earlier sentences, Joyce and Amos were formally arrested and charged with the murders of Ucal Chin and Tyrone Gilbert. Cell-site evidence clearly implicated the pair in the killings, and would prove to be one of the most effective weapons in the police's arsenal. Its use would prompt comparisons with *The Wire*, the US TV show enjoying critical acclaim at the time. The reality was more mundane. Cell sites, the mobile phone masts hidden above off-licences and behind billboards and the like, are a gift to investigators looking to place people at key locations. Since the nearest cell site typically routes the call, except at the busiest of times, evidence of this kind, ostensibly recorded by telephone companies for billing purposes, gives a fairly accurate reading of where someone is when they make a call. If a series of texts or calls are made which show up on different cell sites, this usually indicates the user is on the move. The mobile phone, even the pay-as-you-go favoured by gangsters, then becomes a tracking device. Analysis of the phones seized from Joyce and Amos revealed that they had been in contact with each other, with others linked to the murders, and in places relevant to the murders at the material times.

Phone evidence matched up Colin Joyce's 'pattern of travel' with that of the silver Audi captured on CCTV in the build-up to Ucal Chin's murder. Effectively, Joyce could be placed in the car at the moment the bullets were fired, with Amos some distance away in Radcliffe at the time, but in communication up to half an hour before. The story of their movements on the day of Tyrone Gilbert's murder was also told by phone evidence. The data revealed that Joyce and Amos met up in Prestwich at 2 p.m. They went to a Stockport garage where they got the brakes fixed on the Audi. An eyewitness saw the two men, who signed the garage's book with the initials 'C' and 'P', short for their nicknames Piggy and Cabbo, before leaving the place together. Elsewhere in the book Joyce carelessly left another clue, writing the letter P next to the word Evo. Police had surveillance footage of Joyce using a Mitsubishi Evo that summer. A call between Joyce and Amos a few seconds before 5.50 p.m. indicated that they were now apart, with the former in Levenshulme. But an hour later, they could be placed together again, with both phones up in Cheetham Hill, along with a number of their cronies. The prosecution would later describe this as 'an organised and very significant meeting', held either at the home of their mates the Hussain brothers or on playing fields nearby.

Shortly before 8 p.m on the night of Gilbert's murder, Amos and Joyce both bought phone credit. They were going to need it. Two-and-a-half hours later, Narada Williams could be placed in Fallowfield, somewhere near Wilmslow Road but not at home. The records indicate business-like chats between Narada and his brother Ricardo, who ordered a taxi from his home at Moston at around 11.20 that night, and Narada and Colin Joyce. This suggested to the prosecution that Narada was keeping Joyce updated on his brother's movements, and more, that the elder Williams was 'utilising a safe location to orchestrate, organise and manage the commission of this murderous attack'.

By twelve minutes to midnight, five minutes before the murder, Joyce's phone could be placed at the cell site that served Frobisher Close. Fourteen minutes later, he was in Burnage, less than half a mile from Firethorn Avenue, where the Honda Legend was dumped. Ricardo Williams could be placed in another car on the same route. Lee Amos's phone put him in the same car as Joyce. Unravelled, the tangle of communication revealed that Joyce and Amos had been in one of the cars used in the Frobisher Close shooting, Ricardo Williams was in another and Narada Williams was a central point of contact. Aeeron Campbell was linked by DNA on the balaclava and gloves found at Firethorn, which in turn could be linked to the Honda Legend. In the aftermath of the shooting, Joyce and Amos headed for Stockport. On the way, Joyce phoned Qadir Hussain, whose phone then moved to the Burnage area. Detectives believed Joyce was ordering Hussain to pick up the abandoned Honda, unaware that police had already seen it.

Joyce and Amos were each questioned for three days. In the documentary *Bringing Down the Gooch* Joyce was later described by the interviewing detective as 'chatty, affable, very charming to a degree'. Except when the tapes went on – and he confined himself to mumbling 'no comment' answers. The mysterious Lee Amos was even more controlled. He remained completely silent through the entirety of the interviews. He stared blankly at a piece of paper in front of him on the desk as the cops fired questions at him. Only one topic made him shift in his seat.

'There was no reaction from him at all, no physical expression from him other than at the point where I asked him to discuss with me the murder of his brother. At that point there was a reaction from him. He was clearly uncomfortable in dicussing that with me', the cop who quizzed him said.

When officers moved on from the murder of Stephen Amos – the 2002 killing that inspired the Gooch's campaign of vengeance – Amos regained his composure. For the rest of the interview Amos 'refused to communicate whatsoever and remained this disciplined person staring at the desk'.

The phone, forensic and baillistics evidence against the gang was bolstered by the defections in the Gooch ranks. The Serious Organised Crime and Police Act 2005 (SOCPA) provided law enforcement agencies with a string of gang-busting powers, of which sections 71 to 75, the 'supergrass' provisions, established a new framework for dealing with informants in big prosecutions. In the early seventies, career villain Derek 'Bertie' Smalls made legal history as Britain's first supergrass. A prominent member of London's bank robbing fraternity, he was facing at least twenty years in jail when he offered to squeal on his pals. The offer was accepted, and Smalls won a written assurance of immunity from prosecution from Director of Public Prosecutions Sir Norman Skelhorn. The arrangement resulted in a string of convictions, but the Law Lords later ruled it had been an 'unholy deal', and from then on supergrasses would receive a heavily discounted sentence following a guilty plea rather than total immunity.

SOCPA turned the clock back to the Skelhorn-Smalls deal, with bells on. Prosecutors could, if the right criteria were met, make formal agreements not to prosecute a person, or not to use their own evidence against them – so-called 'restricted use' undertakings. To benefit, a villain would have to be 'cleansed' by revealing the full extent of their crimes. They would also have to tell *everything* they knew about the matters under investigation and those involved, and had to cooperate throughout the inquiry, giving evidence in court where necessary. All the terms of the deal were laid out in writing. Prosecutors no longer had to take them at their word that they would deliver on their side of the bargain. SOCPA gave power of sanction, allowing investigators to go back to court and review the terms of the deal if an informer turned out to be a letdown.

Once the decision had been taken to pursue charges against core members of the L$$/YGC faction, the testimony of peripheral members of the crew – like Stefan 'Tricks' Melia, Karen Scotland and Michael Wilkinson – was secured with restricted use undertakings, the first time they would be used in Manchester.

Witness anonymity had first been used to tackle gun criminals after two teenage girls were shot dead outside a New Year's Eve party in Birmingham in 2003, in a bungled gang attack by the Burger Bar Boys gang on the rival Johnson Crew. Two years after the girls' deaths, four defendants were convicted on the testimony of anonymous witnesses, including a known criminal who gave evidence under a pseudonym. Concealed from view, the witness's true identity was known only to the judge and the prosecution and his voice was distorted by technology before being fed into the dock, the public gallery and the press benches. It was the reluctance of witnesses to cooperate with the authorities from the earliest stage in the investigation – all too common in gang cases, given the perpetrators' propensity for violence and the intimacy of the communities they thrive in – that prompted West Midlands Police and the Crown Prosecution Service to make the anonymity application. The precedent remained unchallenged for over three years, in which time witness anonymity was used in a number of cases involving gun criminals, raising hopes that the system finally had the tools to demolish the walls of silence that allowed killers to go unpunished.

But in June 2008, months before the trial of the L$$/YGC faction was due to begin, this cherished tool of gangbusters and anti-terrorism police was removed by the Law Lords. Coincidentally, it was the case of another New Year's Eve party shooting that led to the ruling. In a crime that was cretinous even by the already asinine standards of impulse shootings, Iain Davis shot a DJ in Hackney, east London, because he didn't want a party to stop. The bullet went through the DJ's neck, through a partition wall, and into the head of a reveller in the next room. Both men died. Witness testimony was secured in the trial using pseudonyms, voice distortion and screens, and in 2004 the gunman was given two life sentences. But, four years later, on appeal, the Law Lords ruled that 'protective measures, which ensured the anonymity of three witnesses without whose evidence the defendant could not have been convicted of murder, rendered the trial unfair and were, accordingly, unlawful'. The senior Law Lord, Lord Bingham, said it was 'a long-established principle of the English common law that, subject to certain exceptions and statutory qualifications, the defendant in a criminal trial should be confronted by his accusers in order that he might cross-examine them and challenge their evidence.' The ruling did not prevent witnesses from being shielded from publicity, but reasserted the right of the accused, enshrined in common law, to know who was pointing the finger.

Two days later, the Government announced that legislation to protect anonymous witnesses would be brought forward, amid panic from police chiefs that investigations would be jeopardised, criticism of the decision from the right-wing press, and fear that convicted gangbangers would launch fresh appeals at the taxpayer's expense. *The Times* reported that 'ministers are determined to rush through emergency laws', with around forty murder cases at risk and up to 600 applications for anonymity going through the system. Labour sought all-party backing for legislation to be rushed through both Houses of Parliament before the summer recess and on July 3, the Criminal Evidence (Witness Anonymity) Bill was introduced. An emergency measure, the Bill sought to replace the common law rules with statutory powers. A briefing by the civil rights organisation Liberty expressed concerns about such haste and warned that witness anonymity would often have 'serious fair trial implications'.

On July 21, however, the Witness Anonymity Act received Royal Assent. Manchester prosecutors pursuing the Gooch breathed a sigh of relief. But once the trial got underway the device was not as useful as might have been expected. It did lead to some revelations in the inquest into the death of Jessie James however, which opened soon after, in August of that year. The coroner took the unusual step of holding the inquest in a criminal court so that anonymity provisions could be used to protect the identity of those giving evidence. Screened from public view, witnesses were made to sound like Daleks from the TV series *Dr Who* by voice distortion technology, which made it almost impossible to identify even their sex.

One witness, identified only as 'D', told the court that Jessie had been threatened by a youth from the Gooch Close Gang, who called him 'Doddington' in front of a group of Gooch boys days before the shooting. The witness wrote the name of this youth on a piece of paper, which was handed to police at the end of his evidence. He insisted that Jessie was not a gang member but that coming from the Doddington side of the estate was enough to label him.

What he saw on the night of the murder was more telling. D described how, minutes before he died, Jessie chatted to a boy outside the Sports and Social, his friends having gone to the party at Caythorpe Street. This boy, identified as 'Z', told Jessie not to enter the park alone. The witness said he believed this was because Z knew something was going to happen. Z, apparently, had a cousin who was a member of the Gooch. And when Jessie's body was finally found, he started 'going on a bit weird'. When Barbara Reid and Rose Reid arrived at the scene, the boy began saying the shooting had 'nothing to do with his cousin'. Witness D said everybody at the scene thought the Gooch or Old Trafford Crips, who he described as 'younger Gooch', were responsible.

Later, Z himself took the stand. He admitted that his cousin was associated with gang members and that he had advised Jessie not to go into the park, but said he did so because it was dark and Jessie was alone, claiming his cousin was 'locked up' at the time of the murder in any case.

The inquest was dramatically halted on the third day after a new witness came forward. The man, who had approached a religious leader with the names of two suspects who were active members of the Old Trafford Crips, said he finally felt able to talk to police because of the witness protection measures. Senior detective Shaun Donnellan said it was 'the first time since the start of the inquiry that I have had sight of witness testimony that I believe might lead to a prosecution'. It seemed as if police might finally catch the killer, and the inquest was adjourned again to allow them time.

The CPS announced at the end of September that there was not enough evidence to charge the two suspects.

Tommy Pitt, the volatile leader of the Pitt Bulls, who even had a nickname for his favourite MAC-10 machine gun. His violent reign was cut short when gang member Joshua 'Slips' Mensah agreed to testify against him.

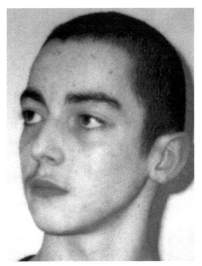

Police believed Thomas 'Little T' Ramsey, a Pitt Bull soldier, was shot dead by one of his own crew after he was blamed for a police raid on one of their safehouses, though no-one has been convicted of his murder. He was only sixteen years old years old.

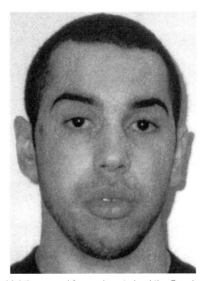

Lee 'Cabbo' Amos (left) and his friend Colin 'Piggy' Joyce (right) emerged from prison to lead the Gooch Close Gang on a murderous spree. Motivated partly by the desire to avenge the killing of Amos's brother Stephen by a rival from the Longsight Crew, they became the most feared duo in south Manchester.

The various faces of Michael Sammon, the old-school criminal who disguised his identity while on the run from a sentence for a major fraud. He switched to illegal arms dealing, bringing blank-firing and gas pressure guns from Europe and converting them to fire live ammunition. Many of them ended up in the hands of gang members.

Some of the guns seized in Operation Carbon, the Greater Manchester Police investigation into Sammon and his gang. They are believed to have imported nearly 300 weapons, which were then reactivated at a secret workshop in the Ancoats area. Sammon was subsequently jailed for thirty years. Scores of his guns have never been traced.

Ian McLeod, the Doddington 'original gangster' who once ran a drugs market on the Alexandra Park estate, Moss Side, and who survived several shootings. He later set up a security company but maintained his gangland ties and recruited two young men to carry out a hit on behalf of a Salford gangster.

Police tape surrounds the Brass Handles public house in Salford after two gunmen entered the premises to carry out the assassination organised by McLeod. They badly wounded two men but were then disarmed and shot dead with their own weapon.

Photo © Press Association

The nine millimetre self-loading Tokarev pistol used to shoot sixteen-year-old Giuseppe Gregory. Its serial number had been scratched off and it had no safety catch. Ballistics tests revealed it had also been used in an attempted murder in London and in two prior shooting incidents in Manchester. Two young men, Shadrach Phipps (right) and Michael Egerton (top right), were later jailed for handling the weapon.

Killer Njabulo Ndlovu posing in gang colours, his blue bandana representing the Old Trafford Crips, one of a number of new gangs affiliated to the bigger and more established Gooch. Their rivals in the Doddington and the Moss Side Bloods wore red, in imitation of the street gangs of Los Angeles.

Hiruy Zerihun, the former altar boy of Ethiopian descent who shot Giuseppe 'G-Sepz' Gregory outside the Robin Hood pub in Stretford. Zerihun was linked to the Fallowfield Mad Dogs, allies of the Old Trafford Crips, and the killing was believed to be revenge for the murder of his friend Louis Brathwaite.

A huge 'wanted' poster in Manchester city centre featuring Moses 'Mojo' Mathias. The fifteen-year-old, infatuated with the gang culture, had gone on the run after the Gregory murder and a £15,000 reward was offered for information leading to his capture. He was eventually arrested on a train in the Netherlands and was later jailed for life.
Photo © Press Association

Seventeen-year-old Ryan Florence makes a 'gun' sign behind Conservative Party leader David Cameron on a visit to Manchester, a picture that went around the world. Florence, who didn't even know who Cameron was, later boasted to newspapers that he was in a gang called Benchill Mad Dogs, from the Wythenshawe area of the city, and had made the 'click, bang' gesture for 'a buzz'.

Photo © Press Association

A senior GMP officer once called Salford a 'centre of excellence' for armed robbery and the city's 'blaggers' were among the most ruthless and prolific in the country. One such gang was led by Richard Walsh (left). With his brother Jonathon (middle) and accomplice William Moore (right), he planned to steal £100,000 from a cash delivery van, only to be ambushed in the act by police. Moore was Tasered to subdue him, while a fourth robber, Gavin Noakes, was shot by armed officers but survived.

Wayne McDonald, brother-in-law of one of the north-west's biggest drug importers, was another notorious robber. After shooting police dog handler Katie Johnson in the leg during a raid on at a pub near Preston, Lancs, McDonald was found guilty in April 2009 of wounding with intent to resist arrest, robbery and firearms offences, but was cleared of attempted murder. He was jailed for an indeterminate period for the public protection and was also convicted for shooting two people outside a nightclub in an impulse attack.

Cannabis dealer Faisal Aslam (left) and Asim Khan, jailed for life for the gruesome murder of university student Umair Waseem at the Angelzarke Reservoir beauty spot. Waseem had got into bad company and fell out with others over a debt he believed he was owed. Khan, posing as a friend, then lured him into the meeting that would cost him his life.

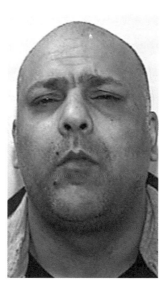

Simeon Henderson (left), the hapless hitman who shot the wrong target on behalf of his Asian associates, resulting in the death of innocent shop worker Nasar Hussain at Brookhouse Wines in Eccles. Henderson had allegedly been recruited by a gang including Mohammed 'Chach' Hafiz (centre), a convicted kidnapper and member of the Asian underworld who he met in prison. Fellow conspirator Ryan Manning (right) was originally meant to be the triggerman until a change of plan. Henderson later gave evidence against his erstwhile coleagues, securing a shorter jail sentence.

8

Life and Death

IT TOOK THREE weeks of legal argument before one of the biggest gang trials in British history began. The venue was Liverpool Crown Court, a good thirty miles from the Manchester gangs' sphere of influence. The defendants – Amos, Joyce, Campbell, the Williams brothers, 'Chucky' Shah and associates – were bussed in from Strangeways Prison under heavy security every day, to a second-floor courtroom flanked by armed police, its benches filled with twenty-two barristers.

The most compelling testimony came from witnesses who gave evidence 'with special measures', either residents who had seen things they wished they hadn't or the close associates of the Gooch who had signed restricted use agreements. Anonymity in the latter cases would have been pointless, since the nature of their evidence made it apparent who they were. They still benefited from screens, the extra comfort being that the men in the dock could not stare them out or make intimidating gestures if they were minded. Screens were among a number of special measures introduced by the Youth Justice and Criminal Evidence Act 1999. 'Bad character' evidence was another relatively new implement available to the prosecutors. The Criminal Justice Act of 2003 laid down statutory provisions by which jurors could be told of the disposition of victims, defendants and witnesses to misconduct. It meant the jury in the Gooch trial would learn about Joyce and Amos's conviction for firearms offences, as well as reasons why they might doubt the evidence of Stefan Melia, one of the most important prosecution witnesses.

Karen Scotland was one of those who testified from behind a screen, guarded by cops with machine guns and with all the courtroom TVs and monitors inverted in case they picked up her reflection. The youngest witness was her son, then just 12 years old. He told the jury he had seen 'things kids shouldn't see', as well as all the DVDs he watched with Narada Williams.

'Violent films?' asked Andrew Menary QC, prosecuting.

'No, his favourite was *Finding Nemo*,' said the boy.

Other stories were more sinister. Hassan 'Chucky' Shah was said to have forced a sixteen-year-old girl to give oral sex at gunpoint and to have shot dead a cat. Narada was alleged to have offered a twelve-year-old boy money to enforce a debt, while a girl he had upset claimed he kept wraps of heroin and cocaine stuffed under his foreskin.

In the confines of the dock, a different side to Colin Joyce and Lee Amos emerged. The wild men of the street generally listened with impassive dignity to the evidence against them. Lawyers, dock officers and prison officers who dealt with them found that both were thoughtful men, just as capable of being courteous and charming as they were of being dangerously inflexible, impulsive and manipulative. There was the odd defendants' revolt – a refusal to enter the dock until some police officers had left the courtroom, the men convinced the cops had been feeding witnesses information they shouldn't – and a refusal to enter the vans to court on a cold morning when the heating was broken. There was some gurning at witnesses and at the victims' families, and at times, snickering. None of this would have happened without the nod from Amos and Joyce, and when they insisted on order in the dock, there was order.

Joyce scoured all the papers in the case, then sacked his QC and took charge of his own defence as the case wore on. His handle on the evidence was remarkable for a rough-hewn layman who was mostly educated in crime. The judge, Mr Justice Langstaff, was patient with Joyce, extending him all the leeway the judicial system does to those with the hubris to conduct their own defence. From behind the glass, Joyce called a string of retainers to support his case. One was Amanda Marshall, a respectable looking young woman who was the daughter of Sandra Ashcroft, a good friend of Joyce's from old. Ms Marshall had been at Ruskin Avenue in April 2000 when Joyce, Amos and various others had been lifted at the 'birthday party' – the one with a .38 revolver, a Colt .45, night vision goggles, binoculars, and two scanners tuned to the police frequency. She had been arrested alongside the gangbangers but not charged with anything. Her mother was once subject to an Asbo that banned her from playing loud music and shouting near the property after she allegedly boasted of being the 'Godmother of the Gooch'.

'Do you know somebody called Junior Richards?' Joyce asked Amanda Marshall.

'He was my boyfriend for three or four years, I was still with him this year,' she said.

She went on to testify that Richards had a phone which ended with the letters 846. This was his 'sly number', the phone he used to check other girls. She got the number when he went the toilet by calling herself from this other phone. This happened on July 19, she said.

'Someone has fed you that date, haven't they?' asked Andrew Menary QC.

No, she was quite sure because it was two weeks after her friend's birthday, which they had celebrated with a night out. The 846 phone just happened to be the phone that linked Joyce to the murder of Tyrone Gilbert, and July 18 just happened to be the first date it was used.

Joyce attempted to heap more blame on Junior Richards who, while he was certainly considered by police to be a Gooch gang member at the time, had for whatever reason either fallen out of favour with Joyce or Marshall, or was considered expendable. The 'P' that had been signed in the garage visitors' book, the 'P' that apparently stood for 'Piggy', and had been signed next to the letter 'C' that apparently stood for 'Cabbo', must actually have stood for 'Peter', Joyce tried to claim. Peter was Junior Richards' nickname, because of his postures when he played football. Surely, if that were true, Richards must have had the worst nickname in gang history, trumping even his real nicknames, Smegsy, or Smigger.

Joyce also gave evidence in his own defence. He was keen to get a few things off his chest, claiming that he had been 'beat up' by police on the day of his arrest. He complained he had been left nursing 'facial injuries, black eyes, grazes on my head, cuts around my ears, lumps and stuff' – none of which were 'marks of resistance'. He denied that he had been involved in any criminal activity during his time out on licence, denied that he had been at a gang summit all those years ago at Ruskin Avenue but said he had merely been 'mucking about' with a gun in a bedroom, and denied organising the funeral of L$$ member Kelvin Taylor, the event which provided the prosecution with documentary evidence of the Gooch paying their respects to a 'fallen soldier'.

He also grumbled that a police officer had been stalking him. DC Rod Carter had known Joyce since the nineties, when as a teenager he had been a respected neutral in gang circles, present at the funeral of Orville Bell, the youth who the LSC was formed in memory of. The LSC had actually invited Joyce to join them but he chose to run with the Gooch. DC Carter was the first policeman Joyce saw when he got out of prison, he recognised him instantly. 'ACU, you,' he said. The acronym showed how long Joyce had been away – ACU stood for Armed Crime Unit, a team now absorbed by Xcalibre, the anti-gang crime operation. Back in the days of the ACU, Carter had encountered Joyce numerous times. On Joyce's release, Carter's task was not only to keep an eye on what he and Amos were up to but also to make sure they were not being put under any pressure. Amos, a self-contained character, was cagey with the detective. Joyce was evasive, ducking between addresses.

Joyce claimed in his defence that he did not have the phone that linked him to the murder of Ucal Chin on him at the time suggesting it was used by a number of people. He said he had left his coat behind at a house in Cheetham Hill and that the phone was in the pocket. Qadir Hussain had returned it to him later, also hooking him up with a few Budweisers and a bag of cannabis. Later, the court would hear that Joyce had been called ninety-five times on that phone during a fifty-five-day period by his mother. Hussain was a convenient foil for Joyce's desperate defence. Like his brothers, Amir and Nasir, he had not been charged with anything on the Operation Viola indictment, but they were labelled as 'criminal associates' closely identified with key Gooch players at critical times. Fixers and brokers mainly engaged in the car hire business, the Hussains were at Joyce's beck and call after his release. They would pick him up from wherever he was living and chauffeur him to work in one of a number of luxury cars. He had been given the grand title 'head of security' at a Salford off licence, which would later be at the centre of an entirely separate gangland investigation.

Nearly all of Joyce's retainers were young Asian men who related to him as a Muslim hardman following his conversion in the jailhouse. He would sometimes arbitrate between fighting groups of black and Asian youths. No-one who knew him called him Colin, they called him David, or Piggy. One young man, called to provide an alibi for Joyce for the day of Chin's murder, testified, 'I call him Yard, cos he talks yard to me.' Yard, the Jamaican patois word for home, was used here as shorthand for the Urdu and Punjabi dialects. Narada and Ricardo Williams fitted into this little black-Asian subculture. As Jamaican coolies, their roots were on the Indian subcontinent. However, because of the demands of the indentured labour system that brought their ancestors to the island, and the strength of the Jamaican national identity, Jamaican 'Indians' are totally integrated with the majority black population on the island, forego traditional dress and have long forgotten their old languages. It was only when they came to Manchester than anyone ever called Narada or Ricardo a 'Paki'.

Carl Edwards, a blood brother who Joyce had met for the first time during his brief period at liberty, spoke up for him in court, in between grumbling about how he had been at court all week and 'not got a penny from nobody'. The small, dark man described how he had taken his brother in after he was badly injured in a car accident but unable to go to the hospital because he had breached his bail conditions. 'There was nothing I could do but put him up and help him back on his feet. I wasn't happy with that but what could I do?' Mr Edwards joked that his brother had turned up walking like Robocop. He was about in the day, so he nursed him back to health with the Yard food his mother cooked.

On the night Tyrone Gilbert was killed, Joyce was finally back on his feet and talking about moving out, leaving the house to pick up some keys for a new flat, Edwards claimed. 'I'd been babysitting him for three or four weeks, after he's gone I just wanted a bit of "me" time,' said Mr Edwards. 'It was nice to have your woman around and have some good lovin' and that without someone peeking over you shoulder, y'know what I'm saying?' He insisted that 'David' returned between 8 and 9 p.m. and did not leave the house after that. They stayed in and watched TV. 'I was watching *Big Brother* and he was taking the mickey.' The prosecutor put it to

Edwards that Joyce had actually been living at a place called The Oaks at the time, and not with him at all. Edwards denied it.

It was a failure of the criminal justice system that Joyce was able to commit the offences he did, apparently under supervision, while on licence, and in breach of it, but it also showed that a determined man will act regardless. It was also a failure that Narada Williams was able to contact a protected witness on a supposedly secret number from a contraband mobile phone in a jail cell at Altcourse Prison during the trial. The witness had told somebody his number, and that person told Williams. Stefan 'Tricks' Melia was sitting in a hotel room with two police officers nearby when the call came through.

'Stefan, do you know who this is?'

Alarmed, Melia put down the phone. 'I jumped up and looked out the window and looked through the keyhole because I thought they might have found out where I was,' he later testified. 'I just had a call from a person I'm giving evidence against so I was a bit shocked. I had to check to make sure I wasn't under attack or anything.'

The phone rang again. Melia decided to answer it and try to record the call. But when Williams's battery kept going dead, Melia called him back via his personal phone. He changed the setting to private, then used the loudspeaker on his witness protection phone to record the conversation.

Williams pleaded with Melia to say that his uncle Carlos bullied him and had forced and bribed him to lie in court. In an attempt to curry favour, he referred back to the time Melia had been tied to a tree and tortured, saying he had known nothing about it.

Williams: 'When you said you'd been tied up and all that, none of us knew what you was talking about.'

Melia: 'I know Chucky was there. I'm telling you they had me tied me to a tree. I didn't even know it would be like that over a bit of change. I have lost everything G, my family don't want to know me.

Williams: 'I'm in prison, I only got a bit of time, bro. You know me, if them man had done something to you, wouldn't they tell me?'

Melia: 'Like I say, I don't know why Chucky …'

Williams: 'Chucky could not touch you and not tell me about it. Forget the Pakis, I'm talking about me and you, my bredrin and some other people like your bredrin Aaron.'

Melia: 'I had love for you, I was beefing with my uncle and all that for you, G, but when Chucky started doing all that to me … Do you think I don't think about all the good times, just me, you and Aaron. I remember all that G, but there's only so much man can take. Chucky abusing man …'

Williams: 'Me and you used to run through gyal and used to have pure dough, we used to have some good shit.'

Melia: 'I thought I was going to die, mate.'

Williams: 'I'm telling you from the back of my heart, if Chucky would have done that to you, Chucky wouldn't have let me know? It was them little Pakis from Ashton who done that.'

Melia: 'Chucky and that tried to lick me up all the time. I heard bare things, I'm going to get fed to dogs … I wake up in Stalybridge with cuts on my stomach, tied to a tree.'

Williams was getting nowhere, but continued to plead.

Williams: 'I remember everyt'ing, G, I remember all the gyal and everyt'ing ….I can't take this prison no more. I have been here a year and I'm never coming back on road. I'm asking you as my bredrin, I can't take this prison no more, G. I can't take it no more. I can't handle it, G. There's no need to cry, homes, because I heard your cry the other day, homes, and I felt your pain. Remember the chopper I bought one time? I swear I'll give you that. That's all I got in the world. Five-oh took everything I got. What I was going to pawn to survive in jail, I will even give you that. I got locked up on my birthday last year, November.'

Melia: 'How's Aaron [Alexander]?'

Narada: 'He's not the same. My man's not the same. Aaron knows deep tings about me … My solicitor told me thirty year. That means I'm seventy when I come out of jail, that's if I make that long in prison. Who lives to that age? Nobody. I'm asking you as my old time bredrin, forget about Chucky and them. I'm begging you, you must give help, help us out. I haven't got nuttin no more. I'm not asking you to retract your statement, all I'm saying. I'm not asking you to go to the Five-oh. I think the police have been giving you information. Our solicitors think all the witnesses have let them know what gwaan first.'

Melia: 'Yes and no G.'

Williams: 'Since Kray's death I have never swore on his grave. I tell you the truth, I want to murder [Chucky]. I'm not going to bullshit you because I knocked him out two months ago. Forget him now, I'm talking about me and you, about how you can help me and everybody … Think about me and you the way we used to roll. I want you to help us out … I'm asking you, I'm giving you my word, all I want you to do is just to help us out.'

Melia: 'What do I need to do?'

Williams: 'That's what I'm trying to work out myself, because today that was my QC talking to you, you know?'

Melia: 'How long is Azer [Aaron Alexander] looking at?'

Williams: 'My man's on the firearms and everyt'ing. When them man aren't around, my man drop tears on my shoulder you know … The only thing I can think of is when solicitors say t'ings to you, I don't know G. The only thing I can think of is just say, "I tell you the truth, I've been lying." They can't throw you in the pen. Forget about the others … What you say is, "Carlos [Melia's uncle, Carlos Aculey] put me up to say everything." '

Melia: 'We got to plan it better than this.'

Williams: 'Man's own bredrin they're using against us. Five-oh laughing at us in the dock. Two squirts and no shower gel for the next two weeks. I don't get no letters no more, everybody sold me out, nobody at all, nobody. Help me, I can't take prison ... say you never see me with drugs, say you never see me with guns, please, I'm begging you ... lies, lies, lies ... my solicitor told me thirty years, that means I'm seventy if I come out of jail, that's if I make it that long in prison ... I got liver cancer, I'm dying ... My old-time bredrin, my road-dog.'

That phone call would look bad when presented to the jury, and formed a new chunk of the case against Narada Williams.

THE TRIAL FINALLY drew to a close after six months of evidence that veered between the tedious and the shocking. There was palpable tension and nervous giggling in the dock when the jury returned from its deliberations and the verdicts were finally announced. Colin Joyce, despite his slyly constructed defence and epic three-day closing speech, was found guilty of the Chin and Gilbert murders, the attempted murder of Michael Gordon, and conspiracy to possess firearms with intent to endanger life. Lee Amos was found guilty of the murder of Tyrone Gilbert. Aeeron Campbell, Narada Williams and Ricardo Williams were found guilty of the Gilbert and Gordon shootings, conspiracy to possess firearms with intent to endanger life and conspiracy to supply class A drugs. Kayael Wint and Tyler Mullings were found guilty of possession of firearms with intent to endanger life for their part in the shootout at Wilcock Street. Ricci Moss was found guilty of conspiracy to supply class A drugs for his part in the Williams' brothers street dealing operation. Hassan 'Chucky' Shah and Aaron Alexander were found guilty of conspiracy to possess firearms with intent to endanger life and conspiracy to supply drugs.

With life sentences imminent, the snickering stopped to allow Joyce to speak. He blamed the media for his woes in what became known on the press bench as his *Braveheart* speech. 'It is drunken, hysterical media coverage. It is a circus and is not going to make any difference. I have no doubt from the outset of this case you have made up your mind but it is not going to take away the freedom I have within me or the innocence I have got.' His friends in the dock applauded.

Prior to sentencing, the families of Tyrone Gilbert and Ucal Chin had a chance to speak. They never knew their loved ones as gang members. They were sons, brothers, fathers and lovers. Ucal was Vivienne Chin's eldest boy. She had come over to England from Jamaica on her own. The young family had settled at Longsight, and she loved her son for a 'good person, kind and thoughtful'. People would tell her how polite and respectful he was. She remembered his paper round, and how he went to the church group and liked fixing bikes and cars. 'Without him, I feel empty and often cry when I'm alone,' she said. 'I ask why he was taken away from me, leaving me and his little son and daughter alone. He was a good son, always there when I needed him.'

Colin Joyce's shoulders slumped, and he blinked when the mother of Ucal's two children described how she missed him. Lisa Marie Norris, Tyrone's girl since the age of fifteen, summed up the absurdity of the conflict. 'He had friends on both sides of the gang divide. He was best mates with a brother of Lee Amos and Lee Amos's sister was best friends with Tyrone's sister. Obviously, growing up in Longsight, he knew lots of people. In my opinion if you live in the Longsight area people automatically see you as belonging to one gang or the other and that overshadows everything else.'

Passing sentence on Joyce, Mr Justice Brian Langstaff said that when he had secured release from his 2001 sentence, the gang leader had used his 'very considerable personal charm' to sway the authorities 'into not realising what you were about.' He went on, 'There's no doubt to me that you are a deeply controlling man. There's equally no doubt that you control those who are in the dock with you. I have watched all of you during the course of this trial, I have seen things from here which counsel may not see, looking towards me as they do. I accept that you are undoubtedly a leader of men.'

Minutes later, Joyce, then twenty-nine, was ordered to serve thirty-nine years before he could be considered for parole. Halved, this would still qualify as a life sentence. But this was not to be halved, with the rest of the term spent on licence. Joyce would have to serve a full thirty-nine years before he could even be considered for parole. The 'starting point' for sentencing a firearms murder is thirty years. The judge said he had 'flirted with the possibility' of giving him a whole life term, which would condemn him to die in jail, before settling for thirty-nine because, he said, 'I think it right to give you some hope that in the future you might be able to put your obvious talents to constructive use.'

Amos, aged thirty-three, was jailed for thirty-five years. Aeeron Campbell, twenty-five, was sentenced to a minimum of thirty-two years; Narada Williams, twenty-eight, was sentenced to a minimum of thirty-five years; Ricardo, twenty-six, will have to serve a minimum of thirty-four years; Aaron Alexander, twenty-three, was jailed for thirteen years; Hassan Shah, twenty-five, was jailed for a minimum of nine years for the same charges as Alexander; Kayael Wint, twenty, got five-and-a-half years; Ricci Moss, twenty-one, got six years, as did Tyler Joel Mullings, aged eighteen; Gonoo Hussain, the university dropout who drove for the gang, admitted firearms and drugs offences and was jailed for five-and-a-half years. In all, eleven gang members were convicted of twenty-seven of the twenty-eight charges against them. The jury failed to reach a verdict on one count of murder on Amos relating to Ucal Chin. As they were led down, the Williams brothers could be heard protesting that they hadn't killed anybody.

The prosecution had cost a reputed £20m, and would be the last major trial under the old, rather more generous, Legal

Aid renumeration system. It had involved 50,000 pages of evidence, a small army of cops, caseworkers and solicitors, not to mention twenty-two highly paid barristers and a High Court judge. Firearms officers had guarded the entrance to the court every single day, a metal detecting arch screened everybody who went into the room. It had involved voice distortion technology, covert routes in and out of court and witness protection. The eleven defendants had been bussed in a heavily guarded prison van, flanked by police vehicles every single day, the families of the victims taking the same route in transport provided for them by the authorities. It had been a remarkable trial, preceded by a remarkable investigation. And, in sentencing, Joyce and Amos were given longer mini-mum terms than notorious sixties gangsters Ronnie and Reg-gie Kray.

' "Modern Day Al Capone" Jailed For 39 Years,' declared Sky News that day, referring to Colin Joyce, with the rest of the British media using similarly lurid headlines. The Capone reference came from a comment by the judge, who likened what happened on the streets of Manchester to Prohibition-era Chicago. 'Manchester is not the Wild West, but many of you treated its streets as if it were,' he added, mixing his similes. The *Manchester Evening News*, which had covered events most extensively, referred to Joyce as the 'self-styled general' of a 'rag-tag army'. Joyce's mother, Kathleen, pro-tested at the portrayal, however, telling the *South Manchester Reporter*, 'Colin didn't go looking to join a gang. He didn't wake up one morning and think I'm going to be a gangster.'

The sentencing of Joyce and Amos was further celebrated by police posters which depicted them 'Ageing Behind Bars', their faces grotesquely wizened. Shortly after they were posted, relatives of the pair launched a lawsuit, backed by civil liberties campaigners Liberty, who argued that the posters breached their rights under the European Convention on Human Rights. The lawsuit was quietly dropped weeks later.

Police visited all eleven Gooch gang members to see if they had any information about the murder of Jessie James, upping the reward money to £50,000 at the same time. Some of them refused to leave their cells, and no useful information came out of the visits.

THE INQUEST INTO Jessie James's death resumed almost three years after it had begun, but it would be of little comfort to his bereft family. The two suspects, the man who identified them, and Jane Antrobus, the senior officer who had now replaced Shaun Donnellan on the investigation, gave evidence. The suspects, both gang members convicted of firearms offences, were identified only as 'ZZ' and 'YY'. Antrobus told the inquest that the men were among thirty-four individuals who had ben TIE'd – traced, interviewed and eliminated – in 2006. ZZ had been one of the first suspects and had been interviewed on September 14. He claimed that on the night in question he had been at a wake in Whalley Range and had left around at 12.45 a.m. with his father, who took him to a dwelling in Moss Side. He said he first knew of the shooting the next morning. ZZ actually backed up the family's belief that Jessie James was coming under pressure to join a gang in the days before his death, and recalled a fight between Jessie and another youth in the weeks beforehand, even claiming to have intervened in it. However, he denied any involvement in the murder.

'We could not disprove the account of witness ZZ,' admitted Antrobus.

YY's address was searched less than a month after Jessie's death, and just over a week later, he volunteered for interview. He also had an alibi: he had been at a friend's house in Old Trafford, he said, and at about 11 p.m. went out with friends, who were interviewed and confirmed his account. They went by taxi to a bar on Oxford Road, and then to a club in the

Northern Quarter of the city centre. They left the club, unhappy with the music policy, and went to a pizza parlour. This, YY claimed, was shortly before 1 a.m. The group then walked along Oxford Road, the main route through the university district, intending to catch a bus home. At that point, a marked police van stopped them and asked where they were going. YY claimed that he and two others then got onto a bus to Stretford. They got off at the Whalley pub and walked back to an address in Old Trafford, where he stayed the night. Asked about the murder, he said he had no information to help. He admitted knowing ZZ but denied being a member of any gang.

The two suspects had been arrested back in August 2008, after a man claimed that ZZ had confessed involvement in the murder to him and another inmate in Strangeways prison, walking back to different wings together after visiting time, in March 2007. His account of their conversation seemed convincing. He claimed that ZZ complained about being blamed for the shooting and that the police had come to his house and interviewed him. ZZ, the witness claimed, said he was on the scene 'but it was not me who pulled the trigger'. He mentioned that he had a particular type of gun, that YY had a different type of gun, and that it was YY who had pulled the trigger. The witness, according to his account, told ZZ to go to police but he did not respond. There then followed some discussion about where the guns came from. It was not revealed in the inquest, but the source of the guns, according to the inmate, was 'Piggy', the nickname, of course, of Gooch general Colin Joyce.

There were problems with the witness's account. Colin Joyce was in prison at the time, so it would have been difficult, if not impossible, for him to have armed the killers, at best he could have made phone calls from behind bars. The other inmate who the witness identified as party to ZZ's confession denied it had taken place. However, a second person told police that ZZ had also confessed to them, a person with no connection to the inmate. But the evidence given by this witness, known as 'C', bore little resemblance to the facts of Jessie's murder.

The fundamental problem was a lack of material evidence to back up the witness accounts. For his part, ZZ denied saying anything to implicate himself or anyone else. Jane Antrobus also said that ZZ had confessed to involvement in another murder 'when he wasn't involved in it at all'. 'Sometimes, from previous dealings with some of these people who purport to be members of these gangs, they do admit to things they haven't done in order to make themselves look good,' she said. 'Bigging themselves up.'

Antrobus did not believe that Jessie was the intended target, but did not rule out the possibility that he was murdered after refusing to join a gang. A new theory emerged, partly based on the evidence of the Strangeways inmate-witness, who claimed that ZZ said his gunman accomplice had been aiming for 'one of the twins'. Independent evidence supported the idea that one of a pair of twins was mixed up in feuding with the OT Crips at the time. 'The person in question bears a remarkable likeness in photographs to Jessie,' said Antrobus.

ZZ's alibi was challenged by the family's lawyer, Pete Weatherby QC, at the inquest, but Antrobus admitted that, with the exception of the witness accounts, 'evidence points away' from his involvement. YY's alibi could also not be verified by CCTV or other records, but there was no hard evidence to negate it either. Certainly, his phone could be placed in the Tib Street area, a good three miles from the murder scene, at the time the gunman or gunmen entered the park.

When called to give evidence, the witness who had come forward with ZZ's alleged confession stuck by his account. He said he had been on association on 'K' wing of the prison in the company of a man from the same computer class and ZZ, who he knew from Moss Side. 'He said to me he was there on the scene on the night of the shooting … He also told us that on the night of the shooting he had .57 Magnum and that this other involved had an automatic. This other person had pulled the trigger.'

The witness, who was facing deportation, was asked if he was making it up to gain favour with the police and help his case to stay in the country. He said no, that he had met Jessie at a barbecue in 2004 and wanted to 'prevent this from happening again to somebody's child, or my child'. He added, 'It was a tragedy that happened to the young teenager, that's why I come forward. The immigration matter was going a long way before this case, it had nothing to do with it. I did it for a better community, so my son and daughter can be free in this community. This young life got cut short.'

ZZ admitted that he was a gang member and had been in prison in March 2007 but denied confessing to anyone, claiming that he couldn't have met the witness because he was in segregation in the Category A area of Strangeways. This was later found to be untrue: ZZ had actually been on the Category B regime, and would have had the opportunity to mix with prisoners like the witness. By the time this was confirmed, however, it was too late: the inquest had concluded. ZZ also told the hearing he knew Jessie James and was sympathetic to the family.

YY admitted that his brother had had a 'disagreement' with Jessie weeks before his death but, when it was suggested that his brother had been trying to bully Jessie into being in a gang, he said he didn't know what it was about and 'didn't have a clue' who killed him. Asked about what he thought of Jessie's killers he said, 'Anyone who commits a murder isn't a hero.'

Returning a verdict of unlawful killing by persons unknown, the Manchester coroner said, 'Jessie suffered very serious gunshot wounds which were non-survivable even with the most prompt medical attention. Questions about delay in times of raising awareness of the incident should be viewed in that light.' Adding that there was a 'great deal of evidence' that Jessie was not in a gang, he said, 'It might simply be wrong place, wrong time, or appearing to look like another who might be involved in other activities. We still have no idea who is responsible for Jessie's death or the reasons why.

'I sincerely hope this case has evidenced that if you want to live in a society where fifteen-year-old boys get shot in a park and nobody gets caught for it, then we deserve the society we live in. I hope that things have changed and I hope if nothing else Jessie's death would mark a watershed for the community to reflect upon itself that we would never want another similar situation happening again to another family. It's still an outstanding case and you just never know what may happen. Stranger things do happen even a long time after events. I sincerely hope this is one of those cases.'

The inquest could not provide a firm answer to why Jessie was killed, but it painted a stark picture of how innocent young people could be caught in the crossfire of gun crime. It seemed Jessie had been bullied by at least one Gooch gang member in the weeks before his death, and then shot dead by another, either because he was in the wrong place at the wrong time, or because he had been mistaken for somebody else. Police actually heard an unsubstantiated claim that Lee Amos had carried out the shooting himself in an early act of revenge after getting out of jail. Certainly, there were police officers who believed the re-emergence of a totemic troublemaker like Amos contributed to the tit-for-tat surge which claimed Jessie's life. For Jessie's mum, Barbara Reid, none of this speculation is any use. She moved out of Moss Side and has not returned to the area. Police used to visit her regularly to keep her updated on the case, but as the investigation entered its fifth year, police officers wrote to say they would no longer come unless they had anything to say; they felt the visits were an intrusion. GMP say the case will never be closed, and appeal for information at every milestone. 'My life has not, cannot move on until the killer is found, and even justice will never bring my boy back,' says Mrs Reid. 'Jessie was our pride and joy, and my heart stopped on September 9, 2006.'

When Jessie James's inquest first opened, the *Manchester Evening News* had asked 'How Many More' in a special edition, its front page picturing the faces of the fifty-five people who had been killed between 1999, when there was a surge in shootings after a period of relative quiet, and the date of publication in August 2007, when the number of street shootings reached 'epidemic levels'. Many of the deaths had attracted comparatively little attention beyond their home city and no-one had been brought to justice in twenty-one of the cases. 'The victims come from all walks of life, all backgrounds and were aged from 12 to 50,' said the report. 'They are mums, dads, sons, daughters, brothers and sisters. Some begged for mercy, others were shot in the back; some were lured to their death, others died instantly; some were deliberate targets, others were victims of mistaken identity. One victim named his killer with his dying breath; another victim was 16 weeks' pregnant with her killer's child when she was gunned down.'

The spike in shootings at the time the article was published could arguably be attributed to three things. The conspiracies which smuggled converted replicas in the country and into the hands of gangs, a ripple effect, which meant that every idiot who could lay their hands on a gun began using it, thinking it would get them a 'name' like the gang members in south Manchester had, and the dangerous influence of two old faces, back to wreak havoc on the streets. It came as no surprise, to those working in and writing about criminal justice that the names of Colin Joyce and Lee Amos came up in the Jessie James investigation as they had in so many others. They had ensured the national notoriety of the gang they belonged to, wreaking havoc on the streets in a brief period of freedom, architects of a new nadir in ultra-violence.

The relative calm in the immediate aftermath of their capture would be shattered before long. A new generation was at war. While they would express their creativity with music, they would take out their frustrations and grievances with horrifying consequences.

9

Gunchester Grime

LUKE LAWRENCE HAD been caught trying to buy a gun, and the court prosecutor was using his own rap lyrics, found in the glove compartment of his car, against him. According to the prosecutor, they showed the writer was steeped in gang culture. The practice of using tidbits like web searches, rap lyrics and photographs to prove evidence of gang membership was becoming common. The prosecutor pointed out phrases in which the rapper described how he would 'murder my foes' as evidence that Lawrence had 'considerable motive' to have the gun in his car. Judge Andrew Gilbart QC, the most senior judge in Manchester, seemed concerned that the lyrics should be used in this way.

'Ever listen to hip hop?' he asked one of the barristers.

'No, my lord.'

'Do you have teenage children who make you listen to hip hop?'

'No, my lord.'

'Well, hip hop is sometimes concerned with gun crime. Robert Johnson wrote about gun crime too. As someone raised on the blues of the thirties, it's troubling.'

Perhaps not many grime MCs have songs like Johnson's '32–20 Blues' in mind when they pen violent lyrics, but there is a link with the blues tradition, in which the raw, the ugly, the painful and the personal are voiced. The raw street sound they called 'grime' clattered out of London's pirate stations in the early part of the decade. 'Riddims' were joyously dissonant, lyrics as edgy as a knifeman's mood. Garage, its elder sibling, had been much more female-friendly and fabulous, with only the harder edges of late-nineties crews like So Solid, More Fire, Pay As Go and Heartless hinting at the rugged shape of things to come.

Early grime borrowed Jamaica's slang and soundsystem culture to fuse with a British sense of humour and the DIY aesthetic of early hip hop. It took a while to catch on, except for in isolated pockets. Dizzee Rascal would go overground after going solo from pioneers Roll Deep and enjoying chart success with the 2004 album *Boy In Da Corner*, but the vast majority of his peers toiled underground, forced to sell CDs from the boots of cars and perform live PAs for small change by an unreceptive mainstream. As the decade wore on, pioneers Wiley and Tinchy Stryder would finally get the taste of chart success their efforts deserved but this was long after grime's first flourish, when tracks like DJ Wonder's 'What', Wiley's Eski riddims, Alias's 'Gladiator' and 'Hoe' were as underground as hip hop from the South Bronx had once been.

It took time to catch on in Manchester. For a while Virus Syndicate were the only local grime artists, playing on the Sidewinder shows that brought garage fans from across the provinces to Milton Keynes every quarter. Early grime events in Manchester were shut down amid 'intelligence-based' police concerns and promotional difficulties. The DJs in the classier R&B venues, like the Circle Club and Sugar Lounge, didn't know what it was. Lethal Bizzle's show at Club Havana in 2005 was among the first few club appearances by a major London grime artist. To get into the venue, a favourite of straight members and gang members alike, you had to go through two turnstiles. You handed your money to a cashier behind a two-way mirror and a seemingly disembodied hand would slide from a slit to pass you your change. Then you looked into a CCTV camera concealed in a television. Downstairs, big bouncers wore body armour under oversized, light grey jackets.

Such tight security was the legacy of the violent excesses that earned the city the name Gunchester, but by the millennium there was rarely trouble in there. Huge speakers blasted out waves of sound into an electric atmosphere, and as night turned to morning sweat would pour from the walls. It was unusual to see gang riders dressed in black tracksuits swaggering around the club, but on the night Lethal Bizzle played they were out in force. The east London MC, who had a number one hit as a boy with 'Oi!' when part of More Fire Crew, arrived very late, by which time the mood was tense. The DJ tried gamely to keep the crowd's mood up into the early hours, but the gangbangers who had got past the doors were soon hurtling around the club like pinballs, elbowing people, staring out anyone who caught their eye, even contemptuously sitting on people who were sitting down.

Bizzle, a stocky presence in a silver jacket, arrived with a young entourage in a bad mood. For about twenty minutes he ripped violently over the mic to remixes of his Forward riddim and the crowd's energy focused on the angry music. Then he started MC-ing about Gooch and Doddington and asking who was with who. The mood darkened. One lad crack-danced into people shouting, 'RIP Doddin'ton!' Quick as anything, Bizzle slipped out the back. Then the lights went on and the ravers were turfed out into the early morning. A phalanx of police had formed behind the tramlines, and the mood quieted again.

By the following year, the digital station Channel U was spreading the grime gospel by showcasing no-budget music videos. Some of the tracks were instant underground classics,

others were just about shouting out your neighbourhood or
'reppin' your ends'. Rules of the genre evolved quickly: there
were lots of moody skyline shots; shots of everybody under
thirty on the estate gathered on a roof or in a courtyard
showing their pride for their neglected patch of pebbledash;
pitbull terriers pulling at chains and chasing their own tails;
mopeds doing wheelies over concrete. Factory Records guru
Tony Wilson signed Raw-T, a group of young lads from the
tower blocks that loomed by Brooks Bar on the estate locally
known as Seven Sisters. Their single, 'Round Our Way', got on
TV and showed off Moss Side's Alexandra Park estate. Wilson
was open about the deal: it was for exposure, he didn't expect
to make a return on it and wouldn't be paying them. Videos
that couldn't get on Channel U could always go on YouTube.
Even three lads from Bacup, a small town of hilly vistas and
narrow, cobbled lanes, got together to make an internet video
repping their ends. An unintentionally hilarious attempt to
give that quiet corner of Lancashire a sprinkling of ghetto
credibility, the video was quite nicely put together. It gained
notoriety when it emerged that one of the MCs was one of the
killers of Sophie Lancaster, a young woman horrifically
stabbed and beaten to death in a park for dressing as a Goth.

By the middle of the decade, south Manchester street gangs
each had a sound system to call their own. On the Gooch side
were the Fallowfield Mad Dogs, or FMD, with MCs like Flow,
Creptor and Troopz dropping bars, and on the Longsight side
were Subliminal Criminalz, with lyricists like Riekz and Niall.
The little scene attracted an underground following of its
own, especially among teenagers. Grime, with its warts-and-
all portrayal of British estate life, was tailormade for the
Manchester street scene. It was accessible. All you needed was
a basic music-making computer program and a commitment
to your craft. A would-be MC need only perfect a few bars of
lyrics and get together with his mates to create an infectious
track. He didn't have to imitate the American millionaire

studio gangsters that were dominating hip hop, rapping about pushing yayo on the streets to easily influenced, impoverished kids while living an A-list lifestyle. He could draw inspiration from his own life, he could live the life he rapped about, blurring the lines between art and reality, street crime and street culture.

One of the first indications of FMD's more sinister side came with an anonymous phone call to the news room of the *Manchester Evening News* in 2004. 'The man was insistent, only a newspaper story could save his son's life,' said the reporter who took the call. 'Even by the standards of late night calls to news rooms, it was an odd one. The caller would leave no details, identifying himself only as an Asian resident of Fallowfield. He claimed that the area was being terrorised by a racist gang of skinheads known as FMD. One of their bikes was missing and now they were after his son.' The man put the phone down in disgust when the reporter refused to get involved, and the matter of the missing bike would be quietly resolved days later. The line about FMD being a 'racist gang of skinheads' had been entirely made up, but the man's terror was real. A missing bike was enough to get someone shot in estates where gangs were active, and the FMD – or Fallowfield Mandem to give them their original moniker – were apparently the new kids on the block.

In the early years of the gang, the FMD were known more for anti-social behaviour than anything else. One fifteen-year-old member was evicted, then banned from the area by a ten-year ASBO, after a spree of crime and intimidation. They were considered more of a neighbourhood nuisance than hardened gangbangers, and no-one outside their turf knew who they were. Then, in 2003, on an avenue on the Fallowfield estate, Shaka Kent shot dead a popular nineteen-year-old called Marcus Fullerton after an argument. It should have served as a salutary warning to any local youths. Instead a number of lads who had grown up with Marcus and who called themselves Fallowfield Mandem, patois for 'those Fallowfield men', were drawn, as too often happens, into gang culture in the years following his murder. The FMD claimed affiliation with the Gooch by friendship and family ties, and so inherited their hatred for the Doddington and its affiliates. It showed the creep of the subculture from the inner city to the inner suburbs, Fallowfield being known more for its large student population than for gangs.

Luke Lawrence's lyrics were destined for a YouTube diss track. His raps described how there would be 'another dozen bodies in the cemetery' when 'Twin B' got out of jail. Twin B – the twin brothers Marvin and Michael Berkeley – had risen from ASBO teens to shot-callers in the Fallowfield Mandem. The pair delighted in playing the gangster and in snapping pictures of themselves posing with guns. They also saw the possibilities in the dangerous but potentially lucrative area of 'taxing' – robbing drug dealers, who would never go to the police.

The FMD decided that two men seen sitting in a Mazda in a Gorton street were dealers. They were watched for a while, then one of the FMD opened a rear door of their car and threatened them with a screwdriver. When the driver tried to speed off, they were run off the road by another FMD man, who shot out the rear windscreen. They tried to run but they were caught and bound with plastic cable ties, bundled into the back of the vehicle and driven to Sale Water Park.

'You're going to work for us,' they were told.

One of the men was put on the phone to Michael Berkeley, who was in jail at the time but had a cellphone in his pad.

'Do what my mate says,' ordered Berkeley. 'Anything they need, you give them. It will be easier for you to do what they say. If I was there, I would chop you into pieces.'

The two men were kicked out on a main road. They were in fact not drug dealers, just a painter and decorator and his mate.

Three days earlier, in Hyde, two more men in a VW Golf were tailed through the streets by a Honda. It drew next to the Volkswagen and a gun was pointed through the window.

'You'd better do what we say or you're both gonna get shot.'

In a deserted Hyde town centre, they were interrogated about whether they sold drugs. They were then ordered to phone a friend, who was also taken hostage at gunpoint. When two of the victims made a break for freedom, one of them was shot in the back, kicked in the head, and bundled back into the Golf. Six hours after their ordeal began, the men were let go, minus their cash and jewellery.

Marvin was arrested with a number of others in May 2006. Michael, who by then had been released from prison, was arrested that November. Marvin was subsequently given an indeterminate sentence after pleading guilty to conspiracy to kidnap, possession of a firearm with intent to endanger life and conspiracy to commit robbery. Michael was convicted for assisting offenders and was jailed for two years and four months. Six others were jailed with them.

With the Berkeleys and their cohorts locked up, a new generation of bad lads from the area filled the void. They kept the FMD acronym but called themselves Fallowfield Mad Dogs, partly because of an interest in breeding canines. Adept at promoting themselves on YouTube, and on Facebook too until they were banned, the Mad Dogs were the quintessential Manchester gang of the period. At the heart of the action was a young MC known as Ramone 'Razor' Brown. If you weren't in gang circles, he presented as diminutive and good-natured, but by the age of twenty-three, he had what a judge called an 'appalling record' and was confined to certain areas of Manchester by 'personal safety issues' – the number of rivals who were after him. As a young offender, he had been one of six homesick Manchester lads who went on the rampage in a prison chapel at Deerbolt Young Offenders' Institution in County Durham, shouting abuse and pelting chairs at the vicar conducting Sunday service, then barricading themselves in the chapel. In a siege lasting seven hours, the group drank the communion wine, dressed in the vicar's vestments and daubed the walls in graffiti claiming Satan had sent them. Unwilling fellow inmates who were trapped with them had to smash their way out. One said they had 'gone mental'. The wardens, who left the chapel when violence broke out to get back-up, called in colleagues from other prisons, armed with stun grenades, by which time £40,000-worth of damage had been caused. Deerbolt was too far for visits, the rebels said. The rioters included Desmond Noonan, one of the younger members of the Manchester crime clan.

Back in 2006, young MCs affiliated to both FMD and Longsight put aside their Gooch/Doddington tribal hostilities to collaborate on a track, united in their enthusiasm for the 'Manny', or Manchester, grime scene. For a brief period, it seemed as if the music might provide a creative outlet for pack rivalry. It made sense, since they all knew each other; there was even a pair of brothers, one who claimed Gooch and one who claimed Doddington, whose bunkbed punch-ups came to the attention of youth workers. Even without blood or social ties, members of both gangs have more in common than they do not, generally either being black or mixed-race, or white or Asian youths who have grown up in the same neighbourhoods, in the same challenging socio-economic circumstances.

By 2008, this had been forgotten and the FMD/Longsight truce collapsed in brutal fashion. That January, twenty-year-old Halton McCollin was shot and killed in a Chinese takeaway in Stretford. McCollin, whose murder remains unsolved, had no connection to gangs. He worked as a sales representative for Aviva and played Sunday League football. On the night he died, he was in the China Gardens with Remy McLaren-Parker, who had ties to the Haydock Crew, a Doddington-affiliated gang from the Stretford area. The Haydock Crew were avid authors of the 'Fuck Da Bwoidem' tracks that flew back and forth following the collapse of the grime truce. Unfortunately for McCollin, he also bore what one detective described as a 'strong facial resemblance' to Aaron Rouse, well-known in gang circles as a Doddington player, and it seems likely that the gunman took him for Rouse. It is also highly likely that Gooch elements were behind the shooting – the gun used to kill Halton was also used in the drive-by which claimed the life of LSC man Tyrone Gilbert some six months earlier. McLaren-Parker was later jailed after teaming up with Rouse and Gavin Donald, the son of Doddington founder Ian McLeod, to supply guns to customers in London. Donald, a veteran of the turn-of-the century's street wars, had moved to Yorkshire after his closest brush with death: a bullet had ricocheted around one of his eye sockets, leaving him half-blind. He evidently remained an influence on the younger element despite the move across the Pennines.

Just days after McCollin was killed, a gunman, almost certainly from one of the Doddington affiliates, ran into the William Hill betting shop in Withington in a revenge attack and opened fire on three local youths he took to be FMD members. One of them was Louis Brathwaite, who was sixteen years old. He was hit in the chest, leg and shoulder. An eighteen-year-old was shot in the torso. Though badly injured, Brathwaite at first seemed to be on the mend, but his condition subsequently deteriorated and he died in hospital twelve days later. The fragile peace that had followed the arrests of Amos, Joyce and the L$$ had been destroyed.

Nick Clegg, then the new leader of the Liberal Democrats, visited the little shrine that quickly appeared at the Mauldeth Road scene. There was a Manchester City shirt, and the words 'A Fallen Soldier' had been scribbled on a picture in tribute. Louis fast became a talismanic figure for the youngers, as Marcus Fullerton had years earlier. A number of his friends went out and got tattoos paying tribute to him. His heartbroken mother, however, told one journalist she didn't want him painted as 'just another Fallowfield man'.

In the months after the two killings, tensions ran high. Youth workers and police encountered youths who, living on the fault lines of gang territory, were forced to pick a side for protection, as the posses of young toughs beat up anybody perceived to be from the wrong area. By and large, these new gangs enjoyed little notoriety beyond the playgrounds, college common rooms and estates they sprang from. There were small cliques like Rusholme Crips, three of whom ended up in the dock after robbing the youth club they went to, having been instantly recognised. The trio, all fatherless, were lads whose criminality was confined to minding crackhouses, low level robbery and thugging it out on the street with other cliques of immigrant youths like Dem Crazy Somalians. The Moss Side Bloods were a streetfighting offshoot of the Doddington, while the colourfully named Portuguese Mafia were a group of Angolan and Brazilian lads, all quite tasty footballers, who hung around the city centre at night. Then there were any number of robbery teams, and the gangs that local people were terrified to get on the wrong side of in insular neighbourhoods, cliques from Stockport's Brinnington estate, Gorton's Mount Road Crew, the Partington thugs, and bad boys from the vast Wythenshawe estate.

Generally it took a catastrophic event or a slew of serious crimes to catapult them to wider attention, as would happen with the Old Trafford Crips and Fallowfield Mad Dogs. Otherwise they were legends only in their own minds. Infamy of the kind the Gooch and Doddington Original Gangsters had enjoyed in their bloody heyday was far off. Since a number of the south Manchester cliques claimed allegiance to those two gangs, the crimes they committed were naturally attributed to the Gooch or the Doddington. This irritated a fair few greyhairs who felt, with a perverse sanctimony, that the youngers were bringing 'dirt on the name' with unauthorised, wanton violence. One ageing gangbanger, when he heard about the 2009 murder of Giuseppe Gregory by killers tied to the Fallowfield Mad Dogs/Old Trafford Crips, said, 'Gooch? These ain't Gooch. If I seen these pricks I'd knock 'em out myself.'

Following the shootings of Louis Brathwaite and Halton McCollin, the gang situation was declared a 'Force Level Critical Incident' by GMP for the first time in their history. They put together a 'problem profile' – an assessment of gang-related shootings which looked at where, when and why they happened. They found that gun crime committed by younger gangbangers was 'chaotic', with 'unknown males' likely to be targeted for walking through gang territories and gatherings of youths in public places at risk of drive-bys. 'Minor incidents' were said to result in a 'disproportionate escalation' in levels of violence. Most radical about the report was the change in rhetoric: gang members were described as 'extremely vulnerable'. These young men were typically aged between fifteen and twenty, of 'black African-Caribbean descent', and living within a two-mile radius of Moss Side, the historic nucleus of the scene. Anti-social behaviour and opportunistic street robberies were their stock in trade.

'The vast majority of gang members come from broken homes, living with their mothers and siblings with no paternal influence,' said the profile. 'Such is the small geographic area within which the opposing gangs operate; gang-related firearms discharges are often directed at the home address of gang members. This puts other family members, neighbours and community members in significant danger. Scientific analysis of firearms discharge patterns showed a considerable level of inexperience in handling weapons, making the likelihood of hitting the intended target remote but increasing the collateral threat to innocent persons and property in the vicinity ... unlike the fiscal focus of historic gang activity, financial gain has little influence on current membership.'

Within a fortnight of Louis Brathwaite's murder, Greater
Manchester Police had launched Operation Cougar, a new
approach to tackling the gang problem. One of Cougar's
strategies saw gang members being put in care or locked up in
the cells for their own safety under emergency police protection orders. In another new move, thirty-four parents were
written to and told that police had concerns about their child
and the company they were keeping. It was the first time the
problem had been treated as a 'child protection' issue. This
was combined, however, with a much less politically correct
mainstay of inner-city policing: stop-and-search. Between
the launch of Cougar in February 2008 and the end of June of
that year, a staggering 909 stop-and-searches were carried
out, with 148 arrests. By Christmas, the number of stops was
approaching 1500. They were carried out under Section 60 of
the Criminal Justice and Public Order Act 1995, which gave
officers the right to search people in a defined area at a
particular time, if they believed there was a risk of serious
violence or that the person was carrying a weapon. Police
maintained that they were intelligence-led, specifically targeted at known troublemakers. The routine presence of
police on the street not only made it difficult for gangs to
congregate in public, but it also enabled police to establish a
neutral dialogue with some of the more garrulous lads
involved in the scene.

Stop-and-search has always carried the whiff of racial and
class profiling and is a sensitive issue in inner city communities; it is undeniably demeaning being stopped and searched
by a police officer, to be treated as a *suspect* when you have
been minding your own business, perhaps on your way home
from work or college. But, as part of Operation Cougar, it was
successful in improving community safety and undoubtedly
saved lives. Between February 2008, when it began, and
November of that year, the number of gang-related shootings
fell by 92.7 per cent in the Metropolitan Division, which

covers Moss Side, and the neighbouring Trafford division, which covers Old Trafford, and there were no shootings at all in the first five months of the initiative. In the five years before Cougar launched there had been at least one shooting a month, every month.

The Xcalibre Task Force was given a £6.5 million funding boost in the wake of Halton and Louis' murders. To prevent a return to the bad old days, the anti-gun crime unit swarmed on clusters of youths who congregated in known trouble spots in the inner-city Metropolitan division, stopping and searching them and dispersing them. Spotters patrolled in unmarked cars, keeping an eye out for bother. Surveillance was stepped up to identify the places where the gunmen kept their weapons. CCTV, already boosted in Moss Side in the wake of Jessie James' death, was increased at what the *Times* described as 'frontier points between rival gangs' turf. 'Since the start of Operation Cougar,' reported the newspaper, 'only three shots have been fired compared with more than ten times as many in 2007.' Chief Constable Peter Fahy told them, 'I have no doubt at all that lives have been saved. There are young people walking the streets of Manchester today who would otherwise be in an early grave.'

While high-visibility policing was disrupting the gangs, Manchester Multi-Agency Gang Strategy, which had been set up in 2001, was beavering away behind the scenes. MMAGS helped gang members' families relocate from trouble-spots, sought to change seemingly entrenched thinking with cognitive behavioural and mentoring programmes, provided diversionary activities and mentoring schemes, and even engaged in some street-level mediation work. Meanwhile, projects like Reclaim took boys and girls from inner-city areas and fostered aspiration and leadership qualities in them. One of its most dedicated workers was Joe Amos, the clean-living brother of the notorious Goochie Lee Amos.

GMP were so pleased with the progress in the city they invited the Home Secretary, Jacqui Smith, to Manchester to congratulate them. Unfortunately her press conference had to be cancelled because it was at the height of the trial of Lee Amos, Joyce and the L$$ and the high court judge feared there could be an inference drawn between the massive drop in gun crime and the removal of the ten defendants from the streets.

The gangs had not gone away, however. That September, in the shadow of the Apollo theatre in Ardwick, a teenager tried to carjack a woman in a desperate bid to escape the FMD. He could hear the chains of their BMXs whirring and their curses as he ran, ten of the 'bwoidem', ballied up and bearing down on him. 'Gimme the keys, yo, gimme the keys,' he screamed, thumping on the bonnet of the car which screeched to a halt in front of him. He then ran across the roundabout in panic, risking life and limb. Someone else was watching, the drama unfolding scene by scene in a CCTV hub in the city centre. He had never been so glad to see the police. He almost ran into their arms, wrists out to be cuffed, as they pulled up at the scene. The bwoidem did not let up though. They circled the cops threatening him and shouting how lucky he was to be arrested, making shooting gestures with their hands.

On paper this was a simple affray, a bunch of young lads chasing a boy they didn't like, with not a knife pulled or a shot fired. Sentencing at Manchester Crown Court, Judge Clement Goldstone QC gave the gang a verbal roasting – 'The courts will not stand idly by while youths like yourselves maraud menacingly like packs of wild animals, trying to make the job of police more difficult in the belief and expectation that you can and will take the law into your own hands' but ultimately he was restricted in the sentences he could give. None of those involved, including Ramone 'Razor' Brown and Jerome Brathwaite, brother of the late Louis Brathwaite, got longer than eight months apiece, while most were spared jail or YOI terms. The crop-headed detective in a grey suit looked disappointed. His colleagues, the court had heard, had been intimidated by the actions of these yobs, who had left their prey in fear for his life. On top of this, images culled from the Internet showed the defendants in thuggish poses wearing blue bandanas, denoting membership of a 'Crip' set.

Passing sentence, Judge Goldstone ordered that the defendants were 'not to wear anything that covers the face', nor 'coloured headgear or symbol that indicates allegiance to any gang'. In the first order of its kind, they were banned from uploading gang pictures on Facebook by a clause which said they must not 'post or distribute on any website any photos' of themselves together. The defendants were also banned from an area of south-east Manchester identifiable as rival territory, 'save to enter Manchester Royal Infirmary for personal medical treatment, or as permitted by a supervising officer or police officer'.

The order could make no difference to the boy that had been chased. By the day of sentence, he was already dead. His name was Giuseppe Gregory. He died on May 11, 2009, eight months after the chase that night in Ardwick.

10

Old Trafford Crips

AT SCHOOL AND at home, Giuseppe Gregory was known as a 'warm, considerate and caring young man', expected to get top grades. On the street, away from his mother, his gran and his teachers, he was G-Sepz, a face known on both sides of the gang divide. He was initiated in the grim realities of inner-city street life at just thirteen years old when, late one Saturday night, a large, muscular gunman leapt from a Ford Focus and opened fire on a group of young people loitering outside a house. At least one report claimed that the gunman held on to one of the youngsters, a kid nicknamed Shak, as he unloaded five bullets into his chest, back, groin, buttock and thigh. Giuseppe, another of the youths cycling about at the time, was hit in the leg.

Despite their shared ordeal, there would be no love lost in the coming years between Shak and G-Sepz. Shak, the nephew of a murdered, top-level Young Gooch Crew figure, was one of the youths who chased Giuseppe in September 2008. By that time, G-Sepz had close friends associated with the Longsight Crew's younger faction, who called themselves L-Town, while Shak hung out with the rival Fallowfield Mad Dogs.

In November of that year, Gregory was arrested at the home of a suspected gangbanger on suspicion of possessing heroin with intent to supply. That same month, police sent his mother a letter warning that his life was at risk, one of the warnings issued under Operation Cougar. The scheme was designed for youngsters exactly like Giuseppe, those whose parents might not realise they were keeping dangerous company. When he first revealed the initiative to the press, by which time fourteen youngsters had already been referred to Social Services as being at risk, Superintendent Dave Keller, then the top cop in the Metropolitan Division, had put it bluntly: 'If a youngster is hanging around in a known gang area then as far as I'm concerned they are putting themselves at risk of being shot.' Sadly, Giuseppe's was one life Cougar couldn't save.

His death marked the end for what was, in the history of the Manchester street gang conflict, the longest period without a murder for ten years. The previous fatality, Louis Brathwaite's, had been fifteen months before. This reduction was due to Operation Cougar's intense street policing, as well as a large number of the most dangerously influential gang members, such as Amos and Joyce of the Gooch, being behind bars.

The letter Giuseppe Gregory's mother received warned that his behaviour, such as being in certain areas with certain people in certain clothes, meant he could suffer 'serious harm', and that his activities were being logged for 'future court actions'. On the night he died, Gregory was with his friend Travis, who had also been advised by a number of police officers that some of the Fallowfield Mad Dogs intended to kill him; a so-called Osman warning.

That Sunday in May 2009, Travis woke at 3 p.m. Some time later, he was picked up by what he described as 'a girlfriend' and a friend of hers. The friend dropped off Travis and his girl at a cinema, where they watched the latest movie in the *Fast and the Furious* series and munched popcorn. Then he rang his friend Anthan to see what he was up to. His girlfriend's friend picked them up again and dropped Travis back home. Anthan said he was free, so Travis jumped on his bike and pedalled over to the adventure playground where Anthan was waiting in a new, gun-metal grey VW Golf. Travis stashed his bike in a nearby garden and jumped in the car. Giuseppe Gregory was in the back in his 'going out' gear, a flat cap on his head. At sixteen he was some years younger than Anthan and Travis, but close enough to Anthan to call him his cousin, even though they were not related.

The three drove to Stretford. Anthan stopped to pick up a lad called Glynn, who lived in the Stretford area. Glynn felt rough that day, but agreed to go out. He joined the group, all of whom he had known for about two years, after giving his mum a kiss. They drove to a Chinese chip shop in Urmston and bought food. Travis would remember how when he bought noodles and prawns, Giuseppe copied him, but the food was new to him and he didn't really like it. They stood outside the shop eating for a while before getting back on the M60 and driving to Eccles, where Glynn picked up some money he was owed by a friend. It was Glynn who suggested going to the Robin Hood pub because it got busy on a Sunday and played 'our sort' of dancehall music. There was also West Indian food. As Glynn remembered it, it was the best night of the week. He had been in there the week before with Anthan and Travis, and Giuseppe had been in there as well.

When they arrived at the Robin Hood, a big boozer close to Stretford Arndale, Glynn got the idea that the others wanted to know what it was like before going in. If it was quiet, they would come back later when it was busier. He poked his head inside and saw a few girls they knew. A doorman told him that if he wanted to stay, he would have to pay £2. He returned to the car.

Travis was waiting in the car with the others. 'I wasn't really paying attention to what was going on around me,' he later told police. 'I was just on my phone in a world of my own. There were about fifteen cars on the car park. I didn't recognise any as belonging to people I would chill with. No people were on the car park, which is unusual. I was just slouched in the car on my phone. We never spoke about going into the pub, we had the engine running, the light was off, music was low, the window was wound up. We were parked for about five minutes and then we began to drive off the car park.'

Anthan spoke. 'I swear I can see someone over there,' he said, looking towards some bushes. He opened the door, and someone else said, 'Hurry up, shadows.'

Anthan could suddenly sense tension in the car and saw figures outside dressed in dark clothing. 'Sometimes when I close my eyes I can see the shadows coming out of the bush and trying to get over each other with their arms stretched out in front of them, pointing at the car,' he later said. 'It was all in one moment, as soon as the car started to go I heard, bang, bang, bang.'

Anthan put his foot down and the GTi screeched out of the car park as its windscreen shattered. Glynn ducked down in the back.

'The car was still moving but the shots had stopped. I was scared and panicked,' said Glynn. 'Then I saw Travis' head coming in front of me and I said, "Is everybody OK? Is everybody OK?" Anthan was driving as fast as he could to get away. I checked myself quick that I was OK by patting myself down. I didn't hear Giuseppe next to me saying he was OK.'

Travis looked around at the others. 'Glynn was alright but he just had blood on him. But it wasn't his blood, so I looked and saw Giuseppe. He was sat up and making noises like he was breathing blood.'

Glynn realised in the same instant what had happened. 'I turned and looked at him and his head was just back. As I looked at him, I screamed, "Oh no, he's been shot." As I've been holding him, the car has turned to get out of the car park and his body has just fell on me. I was just screaming for help.'

Anthan heard someone say, 'He's been shot, keep him awake.' He concentrated on driving to hospital as quickly as he could. 'I didn't look back as I was driving off but I looked in my mirror to see if anyone was following us. I remember looking back once en route to the hospital and I saw that Giuseppe's head was flopping.'

Glynn tried to make Giuseppe sit up, and repeated, 'Talk to me, talk to me,' over and over. They flew to hospital, screeching around corners and jumping red lights before finally pulling up outside Accident and Emergency at Trafford General. Guiseppe's friends yelled for help and the boy was lifted onto a stretcher and wheeled off. 'Our phones started ringing,' recalled Travis. 'People wanted to know what had happened. The police had arrived, the hospital must have phoned them. Nobody spoke to them. I had nothing to say to them. Then the armed response turned up.'

Anthan rang Giuseppe's mum and she arrived with his grandmother. He then tried to follow them into the room where they were treating him but ended up being arrested. Giuseppe Gregory died at 2.24 a.m. The bullet had gone through the right side of his head just above the ear, travelled through his brain and out the other side of his skull, exiting above the left ear.

Anthan would tell police, 'I'm not in a gang, neither were any of the others in the car.' For his part, Travis would claim that the car they were in was a 'low-key car, it wasn't as though it was known'. However, the reality is that the shadowy figures who emerged from the bushes to riddle the car with bullets had deliberately targeted its occupants, believing them to be L-Town. The car was a rental regularly used by Anthan and Travis. Only two things, associations and perceptions, truly define gang membership, behind the colourful names, gang colours and the bicycles. A gang member is defined by the company he keeps and how that places him in the eyes of rival criminal groups, the police and the victims of his crimes. Even the most diehard, unrepentant career villain will swear in the dock, in the interview room, or at the probation office that he does not belong to a gang, conscious of the stigma that it carries beyond their circle. All the pride, all the ride-or-die swagger vanishes in the dock, and even the most active gangland player relegates himself at best to someone who can be called a 'gang associate', or has 'friends in gangs', or often just 'knows a lot of people', 'grew up with people in gangs', or 'being from the area is labelled as a gang member'. Few will willingly admit the inconvenient truth that they have a history of gang crime behind them.

In this case, the shadows in the bush had a motive which went beyond, but was inextricably linked to, the perceived associations of the men in the car. Just a few days before the shooting, Travis had been told that he would not face charges over the murder of Louis Brathwaite.

HIRUY ZERIHUN WAS an altar boy. He helped the father at St Kentigern's Church, not far from where he grew up on the Fallowfield estate. His parents, well-educated and upright Ethiopians, raised him with the rigid expectations of aspirational families. He would read, work hard, stay out of trouble and get a white-collar job. Two siblings studied law. But Hiruy was different. In his teens he started getting into trouble with the police, and he left his Catholic comprehensive school with no GCSEs. Between the ages of fourteen and seventeen, he racked up convictions for twenty-three offences, including robbery, car theft, reckless driving, burglary and disorderly behaviour.

He spent most of his time with his friends, among them Louis Brathwaite. They had known each other since they were young boys in the same play scheme. Hiruy's mother didn't like his friends to come to the house. Where they lived was the sort of place where kids could easily congregate, kids on bikes, kids making noise, drinking, smoking weed. Hiruy smoked a lot of weed. He smoked so much that he started selling it himself, to cover his own intake. He was still a nice, helpful boy though, a respectful lad who was kind to people. All the neighbours thought so. His mother was still proud of him.

Yet a disturbing strand of self-hate runs through gang culture. Asked why he thought black boys were killing each other in south Manchester, one gang member told this author, 'Because we're niggers, innit.' Another local rudeboy, exiled to Sheffield, described how when his father gave him 'four bills', or £400, for his birthday, he bought a gun. He didn't plan to use it on a lad who crossed him at college because that was 'white boy beef' – the implication being that if one of his black peers had offended him in the same way, they would have been shot. A hostility towards Africa is also seen in the culture. The YouTube diss track 'Fuck Dem L-Town Africans', recorded by a Fallowfield Mandem MC – when there are Africans on both sides – is an illustration of some attitudes. In a Manchester scene which looked almost exclusively to the urban ghettoes of Jamaica and the US for outside inspiration, Africans were sometimes pilloried as uncool. Gang culture gave youths like Njabulo Ndlovu, who was raised in a Zimbabwean family, the chance to redefine themselves. No longer the unpronounceable immigrant kid, he became JB or J-Bizzle, the no-bullshit muscle man in the blue Cripz bandana.

At a young age, Ndlovu fell in with the Old Trafford lot who hung around the Brooks Bar crossroads. With a number of Young Gooch heads doing long stretches, and the Original Gooch greyhairs no longer actively shooting people, the Old Trafford contingent were, at one stage in the noughties, the most active Gooch soldiers in Manchester, congregating at

Arch Bar in Hulme and stirring up trouble in Moss Side while also engaging in tit-for-tats with a dwindling pack of Doddington to the east.

By the time Ndlovu came of age, the Doddington had been invigorated by new cliques: the Moss Side Bloods, L-Town and Stretford's Haydock Close. On either side these factions differed in number, influence and access to firearms, but would provide backup for one another if attacked by somebody of the other stripe. Such an event was the killing of Louis Brathwaite. Ndlovu hadn't really known Brathwaite but his tribal loyalties brought him into the revenge mission.

At 7.30 p.m. on May 10, two police officers, one of them from the Xcalibre task force, were driving down Platt Lane, Fallowfield, in an unmarked car when they spotted a group loitering outside a betting shop. Hiruy Zerihun was with Remi Sarge, the fifteen-year-old perpetrator of a string of aggravated burglaries in the area which involved horror movie style violence, Mark Taylor, victim of a shooting attempt which would prompt one Tory politician to say that Manchester was in the grip of an urban war, and Ramone Brown, who the officers were particularly interested in. The officers searched Brown and recorded the IMEA numbers of his two cellphones. They also took a note of his clothes and jewellery. The lads were surprisingly cooperative and engaged in conversation. In the twenty minutes that the two PCs talked to them, their pictures were taken covertly by intelligence gatherers.

Later that evening Zerihun called two taxis from Fallowfield. The first driver 'didn't feel right' about the job and drove off without picking him up. The second, from a different firm, took him to Stamford Street in Old Trafford.

SARA SAW ONLY a little, but it was enough to give her a bad feeling. She saw the young men meet up at Stamford Street, she saw the way Njabulo Ndlovu and his gang friends were acting, and afterwards she put everything together and realised she had witnessed the prelude to a murder. No guns or bullets changed hands, she heard no declarations of revenge, just subtle things, something in the air, enough hints for a streetwise young girl to understand. A willowy brunette, by the age of fifteen Sara was spending much of her time hanging around the streets of Old Trafford with bad lads. She had gone to primary school with some of them, been out with others and been introduced to more by them and by her girlfriends. On the day Gregory was murdered, she cycled to the home of a friend and together they went to their 'forest place', a wooded area, where they shared two bottles of wine. While there, she rang Njabulo, and the two bored girls drunkenly cycled to Old Trafford to meet him. She fancied Njabulo, but she had been out with a couple of his friends and he wasn't interested, though he sometimes used her place to smoke weed.

CCTV captured the girls cycling into an area they knew as 'the Gooch estate', as they went looking for cannabis. They got chased off the estate by a lad they knew after Sara's friend got into an argument with him, then met with Ndlovu and two other Old Trafford Crips. They stood at Norton Street. Sara noticed that Njabulo was wearing a khaki puffa jacket of a type he 'wouldn't normally wear'. She thought it looked comical. Everything else he wore was black, and he had on gloves. There was something black around his neck, like a balaclava. After about fifteen minutes, a taxi pulled up with two other lads in it. Ndlovu said he was going home and got into the taxi. The two other Crips walked off and got into another car, leaving the girls in the street. They thought about going home until they saw two other OTC lads. They weren't much interested in talking either. She thought they were acting a little bit strange, like they had 'something on their minds'. Usually they were talkative, but not tonight. She rang Ndlovu to see if he was coming back out but there was no answer. 'It was all,' Sara thought, 'a bit shady'. She stayed at her friend's home that night and did not get home until the following afternoon.

'My mum told me the next day that she'd seen the police outside the Robin Hood pub, she said there's some murder or something,' she recalled. 'I found out later on that it was Giuseppe, and he was Longsight. I assumed it was definitely them [the Old Trafford Crips] because I'd seen what I'd seen, because of how they were that night, they're normally really loud and really talkative and stuff.'

The New Moon cab Njabulo got into left Stamford Street, Old Trafford, at just past 11 p.m. The other two passengers were Hiruy Zerihun and a gang-obsessed fifteen-year-old called Moses Mathias. At the wheel was Yaseen Kholwadia, the son of one of the firm's owners. The car headed north to Crumpsall, where the passengers collected a Tokarev hand-gun from a schoolfriend Moses had leaned on to stash for him. From there, the small band of OTC/FMD gunmen headed for the Robin Hood pub in Stretford. At 11.35 p.m. three police officers left the pub after a routine check. Less than ten minutes later, the gunmen arrived, and Giuseppe Gregory was shot in the head. CCTV at the scene caught three young men – Zerihun, Ndlovu and Mathias – crossing the car park immediately after the shots were fired. All three wore balaclavas. They entered the pub.

'They came in like bouncing around, it was like they were hopping and skipping, like they were hyper about something,' said a witness. 'They were waving the guns around … with their fingers on the triggers. I thought they'd come in to shoot someone, I don't know who but it looked like that to me. They came past the doors and along the wall where the toilets are and the side door. There was one of the bouncers stood by the door … when he saw the guy with the gun I saw him slide off to the double door to get out of the way. They were looking at everyone in their faces. Then they went over to the edge of the dancefloor where a lot of girls were dancing. That's when everyone noticed there was guys in the pub with guns and people started screaming.'

Mathias carried a black gun in his left hand. Zerihun carried the silver Tokarev that fired the fatal shot. Ndlovu had his hands in his pockets. He covered the door while his accomplices swaggered around the venue, scanning the faces of the punters to see if they could recognise any bwoidem. They snatched a gold and diamond chain from a customer before swaggering out again and getting off in the cab.

THE MORNING AFTER, a sympathetic Ndlovu sat in the Whalley pub with the taxi driver, Yaseen Kholwadia. Kholwadia had spent a torrid night at Longsight police station, having been arrested within forty-five minutes of the shooting after a witness took down his number plate. Forensic examination of his vehicle showed high levels of type 1 and type 2 gunshot residue in the front passenger area, and moderate to low levels of type 3 gunshot residue, with a single particle of type 1 from the rear of the car. It was clear that at least one person or item heavily contaminated with gunshot residue had been in the car. In the eight hours he was in custody, Kholwadia learnt for the first time that somebody had been shot dead and that he was a suspect.

On his release from the cells, the cabbie had gone straight to Old Trafford looking for answers. He left his number with some Crips he found hanging around Stamford Street, and soon after, Ndlovu – the man he knew only as JB – rang back and met him. JB was making out he knew nothing of the murder beyond what he had heard on the news. Only one snippet, that the victim's car had been driving off the car park when it was hit, indicated inside knowledge to police when they interviewed Kholwadia on May 28 at Wigan police station. By then, Kholwadia was conceding that his balaclava-clad passengers had 'probably' been involved in the shooting. He identified them as 'JB', a 'Somali-looking man', and a third youth called 'Mojo', that being the street name of Moses Mathias. Kholwadia told the cops how he had agreed to delete text messages and phone calls in the aftermath of the shooting, aware that police would be coming for him. By the time of his second interview, police had a theory that the victims had been lured into the line of fire by a honeytrap, as a transcript later revealed.

Detective: 'Like I said before, I don't believe in coincidences and the timing of these gunmen getting taken to the pub by yourself, and their victims arriving at the pub, the timing is impeccable. It's like, it's almost like a military operation.'

Yaseen Kholwadia: 'Hmm.'

Detective: 'Now it's my theory, well it's not just my theory, it's a theory of the investigation, that the victims have been lured to the pub. Probably by some girls and they've been set up in that effect. It's not the first murder of this type that I've been involved in where it's the taxi driver ... in fact, it's not even the second where there's been a taxi involved. But it's a big gamble, isn't it, for them to think that the taxi driver, alright we've murdered somebody last night it's all in the papers, it's all over Facebook, people are talking about it, it's a big gamble for them to be certain that you wouldn't go to the police.'

Kholwadia: 'That's why they made me park round the corner and ... just like basically for me not to know anything. It's not even that they thought, oh, don't tell no one we've just done this, it was nothing like, like you say ... They sat back in the car, nothing like, oh, we just shot someone. Or nothing like, yeah don't tell anyone. Nothing. Even when I dropped 'em off they didn't even say nothing, just all they've done was just touch me down like that. There was nothing, we done this, don't say we done that, yeah? Nothing.'

Detective: 'Please don't think I'm trying to be awkward or anything like that. What we're investigating, Yaseen, is the murder of a sixteen-year-old kid, in a residential street when there's people out enjoying themselves, I think it was a Bank Holiday was it, a Bank Holiday weekend?'

Kholwadia: 'Yeah, it was a Bank Holiday weekend.'

Detective: 'Well there's people out there in the street you know enjoying themselves at a pub, and we've got gunmen going in and brutally murdering somebody. So although I appreciate you're saying you're innocent and it's a great inconvenience to you and it's a great discomfort to you being in a police station, but unfortunately when we balance our priorities, it's more a priority that we detect who has done this and put them in front of a court and get them the sentence they quite rightly deserve.'

The fact that he had driven Zerihun and Moses Mathias to the Robin Hood pub a week before Giuseppe was killed also brought Kholwadia under suspicion. On that occasion, Kholwadia had parked nearby at St George's Road, just as he would do a week later, while his armed, masked passengers had walked up to the pub, plainly seeking an enemy. Confronted by a punter, one of the men produced a gun and held it against the man's head before swaggering away.

The killers attempted to cover their tracks by discarding their SIM cards and buying new phones the day afterwards, but had already used numbers easily attributable to them throughout the planning and execution. A patchwork of phone calls, CCTV footage and witness testimony traced each of their paths to the Robin Hood. Zerihun was arrested in Fallowfield a month after the murder but refused to answer questions. Njabulo Ndlovu was arrested on the same day and also gave a 'no comment' interview, but provided a prepared statement denying any involvement in any incident on May 3 or May 10. The billing and cell-site evidence flew in the face of their denials, and they were charged with murder. Moses

Mathias, however, was nowhere to be found. Showing a criminal cunning way beyond his years, he had left the country.

Without the cell-site evidence, the police and the Crown Prosecution Service would have had a much more assailable case. Gregory's killers had used their phones constantly on the night in question. What that evidence did, as it had in the case of the conviction of the YGC elders Joyce and Amos, was put the killers in the right places at the right times. The weapon which fired the fatal bullet was later recovered by chance, when the residents of a Gorton street contacted police after a noisy all-night party raged well into the afternoon. When the officers arrived at a ginnel behind the offending house, they found Shadrach Phipps and a young boy, no older than nine years, lurking there. Minutes earlier a woman in the house opposite had seen what she thought was a magpie landing in her garden. It turned out to be a black bag containing a self-loading Tokarev with the serial number scratched off. It had no safety catch on it, and if the trigger had been pulled, it would have fired the first of four bullets before automatically bringing a second up into the breach.

DNA from three people was taken from the strap of the bag, including Shadrach Phipps and his pal Michael Egerton. DNA from Egerton, who had spent most of the party with the loaded gun stuffed down his tracksuit bottoms, was also found in a sample taken from the trigger, and he would later admit firearms offences. For his part, Phipps would deny having handled the gun in the face of the evidence, but a mobile phone seized from a guest at the party contained a number of photographs, taken that day, which showed Phipps with the very same bag the gun was found in slung across his shoulder.

The National Ballistics Intelligence Service (NABIS) database had been set up in April 2008, as part of the then-Labour Government's strategy to tackle gun crime. NABIS recorded

all the firearms and ballistic material police recovered nationwide, allowing officers to link firearms incidents. Checks on
the recovered Tokarev would reveal that it had been used the
previous year in an attempted murder in London. Four
months after that, the weapon had travelled north to Manchester, and most probably into the hands of Gooch-affiliated
splinter groups. It could be linked to shots fired at a group of
lads in Longsight on August 21, and then again the following
January, when a gunman on a motorbike opened fire on
another group in Longsight. The unrecovered gun, the .32,
had also turned up in a couple of shootings in the months
before Gregory's murder. On February 22, it was used in a
shooting in the Brunswick area – Longsight Crew territory –
and then on May 2, eight days before Gregory was shot, it was
fired during a 'group disturbance' in Rusholme.

THE TRIAL OF those charged with killing Giuseppe Gregory
opened without a motive. This was because the motive was
tied up with the defendants' and victim's links to gangs, and it
was argued that detailing these links could prejudice the
chance of a fair trial. Hence the prosecution opening
described how and where Gregory was killed, but not the why.
Of course, no motive is needed to prove a case, only evidence,
but juries expect one.

However, once the judge had ruled in favour of the prosecution's 'bad character' application, they were able to outline
motive and 'propensity'. Records of stop-and-searches
helped. As police had discovered back in 2001 when bringing
Joyce and Amos to justice following the raid on the YGC
safehouse at Ruskin Street, small snippets of intelligence, on
their own useless, could be combined to create a damning
picture of gangland association and activity. Police records
revealed that as far back as Christmas 2007, Zerihun had been
stopped in the company of Louis's brother Jerome and one of

their FMD pals, and that Jerome had described himself as a member of FMD. A few days after the death of Louis Brathwaite, Zerihun and Jerome had been stopped wearing body armour. This was more than enough for the prosecution to say that Zerihun was a friend of Brathwaite and had links to gang members. When this was combined with the revelation that Giuseppe's friend Travis had been suspected of the murder of Brathwaite and that Giuseppe Gregory had been shot before, facts also allowed by the bad character application, the prosecution were able to present the theory that Gregory was the victim of revenge and gang rivalry.

Ndlovu's 'bad character' consisted of a previous conviction for robbery and a letter he had written to his sister while serving that sentence in which he told her to warn another youth that 'I'm going to fuck him up for selling me out to LSC boys'. It was signed off, 'Lil bro, j bizzle, YGC, locc down, Hindley Hotel'. He had also been stopped, at Manchester's Caribbean Carnival in August 2008, wearing a hoodie that said 'RIP Martin Bennett', who was murdered in 1999 when Ndlovu was still at primary school. And there was a jacket, very similar, if not the same, to the one worn by one of the three figures who emerged from the shadows, the one who, after the shooting had stopped, stood guard at the door while his two gun-toting accomplices scoured the pub for more targets. The reversible jacket, recovered from Ndlovu's home address, had type 3 gunshot residue, which contains zinc. While this did not match the guns fired at Gregory, or the residue found in Kholwadia's car, it was evidence of what the prosecution described as 'a propensity to use or carry firearms'.

That 'propensity' was a hallmark of south Manchester's gangs. This willingness to use extreme violence over trifles gave them a notoriety far beyond the generally low-to-mid ranking reach and ambition of their aquisitive criminality during the noughties. Outside Court One, where the case would be heard for a month, was a metal detection arc and officers standing guard. This ring of steel jarred with the unthreatening appearance of the men in the dock. Zerihun, whippet-slim, fine-featured, light-skinned and lanky with an easy smile, looked more like a young jazz musician, in the shirt and tie he wore every day, than a murderous street thug. Ndlovu was much more muscular – a byproduct of working out during his stay in the 'Hindley Hotel' – but a high, perfectly combed afro and slumberous eyes, which blinked and flickered nervously now and then, gave his look a curious softness. Bespectacled Kholwadia, a slim, unprepossessing Asian youth with gel in his hair, looked more like a mobile phone salesman than a gangsters' getaway driver. Shadrach Phipps had a stocky build and the beginnings of a badman's glare, but was not much taller than 5ft 6ins.

All, except Phipps who chose not to give evidence, repeatedly protested their innocence in the defence half of the case. Zerihun insisted that he did not remember the phone calls that had passed between him and the others. He said they could have been 'about getting weed' but were definitely not plotting. He denied ever having met Kholwadia. Knowing it was his phone that incriminated him, he insisted that on the night of the murder he had lent it to Moses Mathias, who had vanished in the aftermath of the murder. It was a convoluted tale, one which he had made no mention of when entering his defence statement earlier, a story which the prosecution could easily argue had been cynically crafted to fit the evidence against him. Zerihun's story wasn't helped by the fact that the records show Mathias's phone was being used at around the same time. If Zerihun's account was to be believed, Mathias was not only switching between the two phones, but taking the time to talk to any friends of Zerihun who rang the phone expecting to find him.

A taxi had been ordered to come to Zerihun's home on the night of the murder, bound for the rendezvous at Stamford

Street. Zerihun insisted Mathias must also have been responsible for this call and that it was possible he had been trying to set him up. He claimed he had lent him the handset with a view to selling it to him for 'a grand'. It was worth that, he said, because the number was a busy weed line, and at the time Zerihun was making £50 profit on each ounce he sold. Zerihun claimed he had spent most of the night of the murder smoking weed himself at his mate Damo's house, before Mathias returned his phone at 2 a.m., giving 'no inkling' that he had been up to anything. Far from being at the scene of the murder, Zerihun claimed to have passed out stoned on the sofa at his mate's house.

'I wasn't there,' he said. 'I never took revenge for Louis Brathwaite.' He claimed that he had heard of the shooting the following morning from a worker at Manchester Multi-Agency Gangs Strategy, the team which works to divert at-risk youngsters from the gang lifestyle.

Giving evidence in a cool, collected style that, in the event of a guilty verdict, was interpreted as callous, Zerihun denied being a gang member. 'I hang around with them, I know them, they are my friends, but I don't actually call myself a gang member.' Asked to put his association with FMD on a scale, he said 'I was like on the outskirts, mainly.' Louis Brathwaite was a good friend, they had grown up together and were 'close mates'. He also described Ramone Brown, who he admitted was a 'gang member', as a 'mate'. He admitted knowing Ndlovu, but said he wasn't 'too close', just someone who bought weed off him now and again. He admitted that he had borrowed body armour from a friend and wore it 'most of the time' for three months following Louis's death, particularly in the Mauldeth Road area of Withington, which he described as 'pretty much a hotspot at the time'. The reason, he said, was caution: 'Really and truly I just thought he was in the same position as me. If someone could come along and shoot him, what's to say it couldn't happen to me?'

Even Zerihun's tattoos would form part of the case against him. One of them read 'RIP Louis never forget you Smiley', Smiley being Louis' nickname. The prosecution were particularly interested in one with the letters 'LBR'. Zerihun insisted this meant 'Love Before Revenge' because 'I don't see any good out of it … someone is going to come back and try and murder one of my friends'. He got this tattoo, he claimed, because girls were thinking he was a gang member. The prosecution was convinced that LBR stood for 'Louis Brathwaite Revenge' or more plausibly, 'LB Ryda', and supported the theory with one of FMD's grime tunes posted on YouTube under that very name.

The two people he claimed he had spent the evening with were his mate Jimmy, who had been shot when Louis Brathwaite was killed, and another lad, Damien, who turned up at the scene of Louis' murder just as the gunman was fleeing. From the witness box, Damien, one of a number of FMD members, associates and MCs depicted hanging from nooses in a YouTube grime video, insisted that on the night of the murder Zerihun had slept at his house, leaving late the next morning. Damien, who conceded he was 'associated' with a 'couple of members' of FMD, also had a tattoo in memory of Brathwaite. He answered questions in a monosyllabic, nasal monotone.

Asked about the night Louis died, he described seeing a lone gunman, 'dressed in black, just like a shadow'.

'Who was thought to be responsible for what happened that day?'

'No-one,' he told Stephen Riordan, the prosecuting QC.

'Who was it believed might have been responsible for this?'

'I'm not sure, another gang.'

'Thought to be another gang, wasn't it? Some names were flying around weren't they?'

'There was lots of names but in the end I just didn't listen to them.'

'Was there a mood for revenge, Mr White, when Louis got shot?'

'No.'

'What was the attitude of people to what had happened?'

'It was a big shock. There was a tight group of us. It was a big shock.'

Damien claimed that Jimmy had also been at his house that evening, and that Hiruy had joined the gathering later. But, yet again, mobile phone evidence would challenge the defence version of events.

'You and James Brady were not together at that time because that's his telephone phoning you for about fifty-five seconds, isn't it?'

'No, no, can't be.'

'You have come here to support your friend Hiruy by telling lies haven't you? What you have done is to describe the type of evening which no doubt has taken place many times but it didn't take place on the night of the tenth, did it?'

At least one person believed Hiruy's defence: his mother. She confronted a reporter about his coverage of the case, which she insisted was lies, and said her son's conduct while on remand had been exemplary. 'He got two gold stars at Wetherby,' she said. 'He moved to Lancaster Farms, where he was given IT duties and food. He counselled and comforted new prisoners. He is the kindest person. No-one who knows him can believe. Everyone is grieving for us. Luckily we live in a good area, we have lived there for twenty-one years. He was born in that house. I thought England was better than this. He has problems with the police, they think he is a Somalian. But they know me, they respect me. He is not in a gang. They want to tie him because of his friend. He is a good boy, you know, he has to fit in with the people in the area. We are Christian, very spiritual people.

'I used to read all about these miscarriages of justice, like Papillon and the Count of Monte Cristo. And in Ethiopia we had a friend, who was jailed for a year, you know because of the political situation, and I used to take her these books. It was like, telepathic. And now, it is happening to my son.'

Some defendants charm juries to the extent that they get smiles, waves, and even the odd thumbs-up on acquittal. From early in Ndlovu's testimony, it seemed unlikely he would be one of them. He had a sullen, stony countenance in the witness box, and a deep, no-nonsense, Mancunian patois rasped from one side of his mouth. He told court that he got into the back of Kholwadia's cab at Stamford Street simply to get some weed off his friend Moses Mathias, then got out again. Sara was being 'giddy' that night, so rather than say goodbye to her he went straight back to his friend's house, where he spent the night playing *Grand Theft Auto*, smoking weed, 'having joke and that'. He left in the early hours and went to the home of another friend, an OT Crip later jailed for firearms offences. He claimed he first learnt of the murder in the early hours after his friend read about it on Facebook, where a girl had posted, 'RIP G-Sepz.' He insisted he hadn't changed his sim card because the 357 number could be tied to the murder, it just so happened that he stopped using that number permanently after that night. And the meeting with Kholwadia the morning after? That, Ndlovu claimed, was simply to find out what had happened with Kholwadia and his three passengers – one of which he was not, he insisted. Like Zerihun, he appeared a bit too blasé about the worst aspects of street culture to courtroom observers.

'I known [Giuseppe] for time, far back when he got shot in his leg,' said Ndlovu. Speaking of Giuseppe's death some three years later, he added, 'I didn't really believe it at the time. A lot of people get shot and people say they're dead but they're not. I didn't believe he was dead, dead-dead, till next day, when I saw it on the news.'

'Louis Brathwaite and Giuseppe Gregory were on different sides, weren't they?' asked the prosecuting QC.

'I don't know, I say I know more about Giuseppe than Louis.'

'Travis [surname withheld] was on the opposite side of Louis Brathwaite.'

'If that's what you think, then yeah. I know Travis is a Longsight gang member but I don't know if Louis was a gang member or not. People think I'm a gang member.'

'That's quite dangerous for you, isn't it?'

'Yeah.'

'The danger is because gang members are prepared to use violence.'

'Most of them, yeah.'

'The violence includes shooting. That's why you are very careful to tell us that you are affiliated to a gang but not a member of a gang.'

'I'm not a gang member, I'm not prepared to use violence on anyone.'

'And shoot guns.'

'That's not true,' he said. 'Most of my mates that I chill with know that I'm not that type of person who likes people around me carrying guns. They know me as a mate, they don't class me as a gang member.'

Ndlovu was confronted about the letter in which he described himself as 'YGC' and vowed to 'fuck up' a friend for selling him out to Longsight.

'He was someone close to me, it just surprises me. He stopped coming because he was chilling with other guys. It kind of shocked me that he had started chilling with gang members. That was something I wrote just for him. Just to piss him off as he has turned Longsight gang member, which he has.'

And what about the Dunlop jacket? The one recovered from his home that was remarkably similar to the one worn by one of the revenge squad?

'Jackets get swapped around. I tend to borrow a jacket and then borrow my jacket out ....I borrowed it from a mate.'

'Do you like Dunlop jackets?'

'It's kind of a low make. I don't go out of my way to buy Dunlop jackets.'

Taxi driver Kholwadia's defence case hinged on the idea that he was naïve and anxious to please. No evidence of any gang associations was found beyond the fact that he had counted Gooch gang members as regular customers. In the end, the jury acquitted him of murder.

Zerihun, just seventeen at the time of the murder, and Ndlovu, who never carried a gun or fired a shot on the fateful night, were not so lucky. As 'guilty' verdicts were returned, Zerihun ripped off the tie he had worn every day and tossed it to the floor, while Ndlovu slumped blinking in the dock as if he had been punched. Both turned to hide their tears.

Sentencing, Mr Justice Holroyde said a 'bleak and dispiriting' picture had emerged during the trial of 'young men engaged in wholly pointless inter-gang violence, based on nothing more than the unfounded assertion by each of the rival gangs of a right to claim a certain small area of south Manchester as its own'.

He went on, 'There has been in recent years a cycle of violence and revenge. The waste of young lives is dreadful in this case. One teenage boy has been killed, two others will spend in prison what should have been the most productive years of adulthood. Whilst those growing up in the relevant area are no doubt exposed to the gang and firearms culture, there's nothing in the evidence in this trial to suggest there's any measure of compulsion to join it. Those who do join are volunteers.'

Despite their youth, he added, the defendants seemed 'precocious' in their street wisdom, and in their actions that night showed 'a calmness and an arrogance beyond your years'. A number of aggravating features worsened the murderers' position in the eyes of the law: premeditation, the gang element and the apparent motivation of revenge. The use of two guns, the firing at close range of eight live rounds, a number of which were aimed at head height through the rear window of a slow moving car, and the continued firing of shots as it passed out of range, all left the judge satisfied that both men shared an intention to kill.

Hiruy Zerihun returned to the dock to be sentenced in his black track gear. He was detained for a minimum term of twenty-three years. Ndlovu was jailed for a minimum term of twenty-one years. Shadrach Phipps, nineteen, was found guilty of handling the murder weapon and was jailed for ten years, while Michael Egerton, twenty-one, admitted the same charge and was jailed for five years and four months. As the judge wound up his sentencing remarks Mrs Zerihun pressed her anguished face up against the glass screening the public gallery. 'This is not justice, this trial is a joke,' she said. 'You are not a judge.'

AT CHRISTMAS 2011, Moses 'Mojo' Mathias became the third person jailed for the murder of Giuseppe Gregory. Barely fifteen at the time of the killing, Mathias had escaped trial at the same time as Ndlovu and Zerihun by skipping to the continent, where he was aided by underworld connections. When police raided his home in his absence, they found some telling lyrics in his journal: 'Its Mojo Meister tings ghan, kill 1 nigga den den me gone, move 2 Spain away anotha home land ... I cant handle 25 25, I think I might die.' In August of 2009, a couple of months after he vanished, GMP controversially identified the boy as prime suspect in the case, beaming Wild West style 'Wanted' posters from electronic billboards at Piccadilly Station and Piccadilly Gardens, with a £15,000 reward for information on his whereabouts.

Spain, where a relative had a holiday home, was one of a number of European countries he may have passed through, until he was caught by chance in the Netherlands in June 2011, as he travelled on a high-speed train to Germany. His ID card raised suspicions in a spot-check, as the name on it, 'Pawel Patelski', and nationality were Polish. Mathias was arrested and charged with passport offences, which he later admitted. He was serving a four-month sentence in a detention centre when an officer from the Serious Organised Crime Agency, there on other business, recognised him as a wanted man. Mathias was stunned when this officer visited him and called him by his real name. He was returned to the UK on a European Arrest Warrant.

Despite his youth, Mathias had organised the murder along with Zerihun. He supplied the murder weapon, the Tokarev he had hidden at a friend's house. Zerihun used that gun to fire the lethal bullet while the left-handed Mathias also opened fire with a .32 handgun. Detectives also believed, but were unable to prove, that a female friend of Mathias had acted as a mole inside the pub, keeping the Gooch gunmen updated on the whereabouts of their target, Travis Bailey, and his pals.

Unlike Zerihun, Mathias was not a friend of Louis Brathwaite, the boy whose murder was to be avenged. Mathias's motivation was blind hatred of the Gooch's enemies. A good-looking Rusholme kid who bore a passing resemblance to a young, pre-dread Bob Marley, Mathias had been getting in trouble since his early teens, when he began socialising with gang members. His descent into murderous crime could be traced from summer 2007, when Tyrone Gilbert was shot dead at Ucal Chin's wake. Gunmen from either the Longsight Crew or the Doddington hit back quickly. Within hours, a drive-by gunman had licked off some shots in a park in Gooch territory at a group of young people who had attended a party at the nearby Zion Centre. Moses Mathias was among them and was wounded in the leg.

'In those days he was not a gang member, but after he had been shot he became an angry young man and talked about gangs all the time,' said Njabulo Ndlovu, who had known Mathias since 2006. 'From what I've heard, it was the Doddington who shot him. After that, he made no secret of the fact he was a Gooch gang member.' In fact Mathias told anyone who would listen, including cops he encountered, that he was 'running with the OT Crips', and aspired to be a gangster like his Gooch friends. He got a tattoo on his arm saying 'Loc', derived from 'Loco', the LA slang term for 'crazy', took to carrying around a balaclava and a blue bandana, and filled his Myspace pages with pictures of himself in the company of older gang members.

By January 2008, police had issued Mathias with an Osman notice warning that his life was at risk. His family moved to Prestwich, north Manchester, away from the gang scene, yet he continued to socialise with gang members, to the point where police began to keep an eye on any less-involved youngsters who associated with him. These facts, and his rap lyrics, would be used as evidence that he was entrenched in the gang culture at the trial of Zerihun and Ndlovu, who found themselves condemned by their association with him.

Mathias pleaded guilty to the murder 'on a basis'. At his sentencing hearing a few months later, that spurious basis was aired. In lawyer-speak, it was 'calculated to minimise his culpability' about as much as was humanly possible, and was patently tailored to fit the evidence against him. The week before Giuseppe Gregory was killed, Mathias had gone to the Robin Hood with Zerihun on what the prosecution insisted was reconnaissance. Mathias, however, claimed that this visit and the later one were both connected with an ill-organised plan they had to rob the pub. On the first occasion, he claimed, they had been frustrated because the pub had closed before they got there. Second time around, they had been about to go in and do the job when they were distracted by the arrival of the car carrying Gregory, and had ended up shooting him by accident. Called to give evidence, Mathias claimed that he and Zerihun had been preparing for the job by readying their weapons in a nearby bush when they saw some headlights approaching them. 'It's the bwoidem,' Zerihun was said to have shouted. Mathias understood this to mean gangland rivals, he claimed. He heard a 'bang' and opened fire, taking Zerihun's lead, he insisted.

'We murdered but we didn't mean to,' he said.

Mr Justice Holroyde said his account, riddled with contradictions, was 'simply incredible'. As he walked from the witness box back to the dock, the teenager passed within inches of Giuseppe Gregory's family, who averted their gaze. He was jailed for life, and cannot apply for parole until he has served eighteen years.

11

Police and Thieves

ARMED ROBBERY IS something of a specialism in the Salford underworld. The city's highly active 'blaggers' have carried out some of the most audacious crimes of recent times, and have frequently paid the penalty. In the nineties, one of the most active earned a whopping twenty-three-year jail sentence after his heavily armed gang stole hundreds of thousands of pounds in a violent spree. The twenty-first century saw an influx of new 'talent' that was equally as prolific.

Iain Parkinson employed the blaggers' equivalent of shock and awe tactics before he was nailed by a fleck of his own spittle. Picture the scene; a bank manageress is pootling to work in her Micra with a colleague when suddenly the parcel shelf pops up and a screaming, crop-headed thug appears from the boot. Shrieking hysterically, the woman, seconds away from losing control of her car, slams on the brakes at the barked orders of the sinister jack-in-the-box. When the car stops, the party is greeted by a gunman and the women are kidnapped and forced to drive to the bank in Bolton. There, manager Janet Wild is forced to hand over £302,000 before she, the cashier and another employee are bundled into the gang's stolen people carrier, trussed up, driven away and dumped at a country park.

That terrifying robbery was the third Parkinson's gang had perpetrated. Two earlier raids, at a Post Office and branch of the Royal Bank of Scotland, saw a member of the gang similarly pop a car boot, curl up inside and pop out as the target drove to work. Kidnapped at gunpoint, the workers were ordered to open safes, netting the robbers £372,000 in cash. In 2002, at the age of twenty-seven, Parkinson was convicted of robbery, kidnap and possession of an imitation firearm while committing an offence. The tiniest of gobbets of saliva, recovered from the carpet in the bank manager's boot, told on him. David Cullen, then twenty-two, was cleared, but would become locally notorious within a few years.

In April 2006, Cullen drove for a gang of Salford heads, led by Peter Anderson, a professional robber, to a branch of the Lloyds TSB in Preston, Lancashire. Anderson and the hot-headed McClenan twins, who had been recruited hours earlier, stormed the bank. They shoved a gun in the face of a terrified worker and ordered the manager to kneel in the strong-room and give up the keys to cash dispensers. They fled with £130,000, but ran into armed police nearby. Bradley McClenan fired a shot at them, then dropped his gun seconds before they returned fire.

It was the second time the gang had been thwarted. Two weeks earlier, observed by police, they got stuck in traffic on their way to raid the bank, arriving only after it was closed. Following the second attempt, the four who had been active in the robbery were locked up after pleading guilty to robbery and firearms offences, alongside two others who had plotted in the earlier, foiled bid. Anderson was jailed indeterminately for the public protection, with a minimum term of six years, as was Bradley McClenan. Aaron McClenan admitted robbery, possessing a firearm and possessing a prohibited weapon and was also jailed indeterminately for the public protection, with a minimum term of five years. Cullen was jailed for ten years.

The Proceeds of Crime Act became law in 2002. Designed to hit criminals in the pocket, the act codified the guidance on money laundering into one comprehensive package, empowering the police and customs officials to seize cash they believed had been garnered by crime and to secure its forfeiture in magistrates' proceedings. Villains' assets could be seized at the outset of an investigation, suspects were forced to prove that their assets were not the proceeds of crime, and the authorities no longer had to prove what crimes the money or goods had come from. Greater Manchester Police had raised £2.3 million from POCA proceedings by 2010, with a generous proportion of the cash being distributed among community groups. On one day alone in December 2010, there were seven POCA hearings at Manchester Magistrates' Court, raising nearly £40,000. POCA would come to be nicknamed 'Gangster Tax.'

David Cullen and Peter Anderson had gone to some lengths to disguise their loot, using loved ones to help them. As a result, the families of Cullen and Anderson would become the first-ever criminals' relatives to be pursued in asset confiscation proceedings. Investigations into their affairs began shortly after the Preston raid that took them off the street. The authorities would learn that Cullen had begun spending big soon after his 2002 acquittal. He bought his first home in Prestwich for £100,000, £40,000 of which he paid upfront. He then spent another £30,000 on renovations. To disguise his connection with the property, Cullen used his younger brother Arron, a joiner, to obtain the mortgage and register the house. His girlfriend, Natasha Smyth, paid the mortgage using housing benefit she fraudulently claimed. Laundering the proceeds of crime would become a family affair for the Cullens.

Within a year, the Prestwich house had been sold at a profit and David Cullen moved to Swinton in Salford. Again, his brother and girlfriend acted as fronts for him. Cullen, a man with no official income, also began spending big on cars. He bought a Ford Harley Davidson special edition pick-up truck for £23,000, and an £8,000 Fiat Stilo as a runaround for Natasha, who enjoyed what police dubbed a 'WAG lifestyle', including holidays in Dubai and Florida, and expensive jewellery.

Police had been watching David Cullen since March 2005, observing his reconnaissance missions to banks, where he would memorise the opening procedures. They got an insight into just how extravagant he was. He bought a £28,000 VW Touareg, a £22,000 convertible Porsche 996, a £25,000 BMW 7 series and a £30,000 M3 BMW. He wrote off the 7 series in a crash but didn't claim on the insurance he had paid £3,000 for, replacing it with the M3 a couple of weeks later. Yet in the previous six years, he had declared less than £2,000 to the taxman.

Weeks before he was caught red-handed at the 2006 Preston job, Cullen sold the house at Swinton. The £74,000 profit was placed in Arron's bank account, ready for the next acquisition. Arron was David's main banker, effectively cleaning the money as it passed through his hands, but other relatives played their part too, opening bank accounts under false names to filter the cash through. When Cullen was nicked at Preston, older brother Tony stepped into the breach, divvying up the £74,000 to a number of others in an attempt to wash it. Tony Cullen, a former professional footballer and at one stage coach for rebel club FC United, had his own hustle: an illegal money-lending business earning £8,000 a month in interest. Naturally he kept no records and had no bank accounts. His partner, Christina Williamson, provided him with £35,000 of capital by lying to her mortgage provider and letting him launder the profits through her bank accounts. A crooked book-keeper provided Tony Cullen with false wage slips which he used as evidence of low-income employment. Then he and Williamson defrauded thousands of pounds in working family tax credits and housing benefit. Meanwhile, Tony drove a £30,000 Range Rover Vogue previously owned by footballer Ryan Giggs, while Williamson swanned about in a £26,000 Touareg. A collection of designer watches, including a £30,000 Franck Muller, was found in a jewellery box at their home. Tony had also conspired in a benefits scam with David and their mother, Bernadette. She had been on the take since the early nineties, which meant she had been at it for fifteen years by the time she was caught out in 2007. She invented a false identity to buy two properties in Salford and Prestwich, before using her real name to rack up benefits by claiming she was a tenant. She also splashed out £76,000 on a holiday home in Florida.

In March 2010, the Cullens were described as 'determinedly wedded to crime' by a judge, who sentenced them for a string of offences. David Cullen got an extra three years for money laundering and conspiracy to defraud. The money had been filtered through the family so successfully Proceeds of Crime Act investigations could only link £13,000 of realisable assets to him. He was ordered to sell what he had and repay the money. Tony Cullen was jailed for two years after admitting housing benefit fraud, conspiracy to defraud and operating as an unlicensed moneylender. He was told to pay £160,000. Arron Cullen admitted money laundering, got two years and was later ordered to sell his home and pay back £217,000. Bernadette Cullen was labelled a 'prime mover' in the family's criminality and got fifteen months after pleading guilty to conspiracy to defraud, dishonestly making false statements and concealing criminal property. She would also have to sell her home to raise the £115,000 the authorities demanded. Christina Williamson admitted money laundering and got a twelve-month suspended jail term and 250 hours unpaid work, with a £16,000 POCA bill, while Natasha Smyth got a twelve-month suspended prison sentence and 150 hours unpaid work after admitting benefit fraud and money laundering, and was later ordered to pay £11,525 under the Proceeds of Crime Act. In total, the Cullens were thought to have made £1.6 million from crime.

Cullen's old bank robbing associate, Peter Anderson, had been just as blatant with his ill-gotten gains. While claiming £14,000 in incapacity benefit for 'depression and anxiety', claiming that his parents were his 'carers', he enjoyed holidays in Thailand and wore a £2,000 watch. When police raided the family home near Wigan, £28,000 in banknotes was found on top of a wardrobe. While his sister and mother-in-law helped him wash the money, his girlfriend, Danielle Bardsley, enjoyed a similarly extravagant lifestyle, benefiting to the tune of £112,000. The *Manchester Evening News*, where the tanned brunette was pictured in black lycra, reported, 'She wore Prada designer clothes and jewellery, went to a private gym and lived behind wrought iron gates in a comfortable semi-detached house equipped with the latest mod cons, including a Bang & Olufsen flat-screen TV. Bardsley boasted a permanent tan thanks to holidays in Mexico, Florida and Tenerife and had access to a fleet of cars including a Porsche Cayenne, Range Rover Sport and Audi A4. Despite all that, for nearly ten years the mum-of-two claimed she was unemployed and sponged £30,000 from the state in income support as a "single mother". She also claimed free school meals for her two children.'

Bardsley admitted money laundering and the mum-of-two was spared jail. But when POCA payback time arrived, only a Volkswagen Golf and a few pounds in a bank account were found by police. She was supposed to sell the Golf and pay back over £5,000. But she failed to cough up more than £2,000 and flouted the terms of her suspended sentence, resulting in seventy-two days behind bars.

RICHARD WALSH revealed his violent streak early on in life, when he and his little gang attacked a fourteen-year-old boy fishing on a towpath. Walsh grabbed the boy's rod and tackle before others set about him with a rounders bat and a screwdriver. The bullies fled with his fishing gear, a bracelet, a watch and two rings, leaving their victim bruised and bloodied, with a puncture wound in his cheek.

A decade and a couple of stretches later, Walsh was chasing bigger prey. He was now an armed robber, honing his techniques with every raid. In one, security guards had to lock themselves in a toilet to escape his gang's clutches. Undaunted, Walsh, who had been back on the streets for only four months since his last jail sentence, began preparations for a job he hoped would net at least £100,000 for him and his experienced, four-strong team. His target was a G4S cash delivery van, and he recruited Gavin Noakes, who was on bail for an armed robbery in Leeds, to assist.

Noakes, like the rest of the gang, had grown up around Salford blaggers and grafters, but had left the city for a new start. He had returned because his wife missed her family, and for a time found work as a builder. But, when the credit crunch hit, work dried up, and Noakes fell in with old associates. William Moore, from the Ordsall estate, was the next recruit. He and Richard Walsh had worked together before. Back in 2001, they had targeted post offices, banks and cash vans, delighting in their prowess in a series of poems and letters to each other; one memorable line being, 'Shotguns, ballys were all ready to play – sicko armed robbers, it's giro day!' Like Noakes, Moore was a master of evasive driving. His criminal career had begun as a youngster, when he stole copper pipe from old houses and sold it to scrapyards. Now broke, hounded by bailiffs for an £800 phone bill and apparently unable to get work as a painter and decorator, he had come in on the job after asking Noakes if he knew of anything going. Jonathon Walsh, Richard's kid brother, was the last to join the conspiracy. Life had not gone so badly for him since his release from a sentence for an earlier cash-snatch bid; he had a job at a waste management company. Still, much like his partners in crime, he was used to living beyond his means and was looking for what he considered easy money.

Their plan required detailed surveillance of the target. A particular van left a depot at Agecroft in Salford every Friday, replenishing cash machines on a route through east Lanca-shire before arriving at its final destination late in the evening. A week before the raid, set for the evening of September 25, 2009, the elder Walsh, Noakes and Moore trailed the vehicle from Salford to Bolton, then on to the towns of Darwen, Blackburn, Accrington, Haslingden, Padiham, Colne and Burnley. They planned to lie in wait for the van at the Abbey National in Haslingden before striking. Hard experience had taught them that it was best to wait until the cash had been unloaded at the branch before charging in and intimidating the guards into handing it over. Smashing the cassettes at the scene was not only time-consuming but risked spoiling the haul, and staining the robbers with red security dye.

A couple of days after the reconnaissance mission, Richard Walsh turned to his brother Jonathon for help. A mooted fourth member of the gang had dropped out and a replace-ment was needed. Richard wanted Jonathon to procure two cars for the job, at least one of them fast. The keys to a Mini Cooper and a BMW 320 were burgled from a house in Stock-port and the cars were driven off and hidden. Three days later, the gang staked out another cash van, in readiness for another strike. This one belonged to a smaller company, Lumis, and was dropping off at a Spar convenience store on the Wythen-shawe estate when Richard Walsh, Moore and Noakes were spotted eyeing it from their black Audi. A suspicious witness called the police, who kept an eye on them until the van went on its way.

That evening, Jonathon Walsh was seen filling up the tank of a Ford Focus, a car hired for the job, as preparations got fully underway. The Focus was then seen driving in convoy with the stolen cars to Oldham. There, the gang sought a safe place to leave the two stolen cars, settling for two quiet streets in Failsworth, before leaving in the Focus. The next day the men zigzagged about Salford and north Manchester, doing errands and completing their preparation. By 6.30 p.m., with hours to go, the black Audi travelled over to Failsworth, where the Walsh brothers checked the two hot cars had been undisturbed and were still fit for use. At a nearby petrol station, they filled up the vehicles and loaded up fuel cans, useful if any of the cars needed burning out, before returning them to their parking spaces. A legit Mondeo, with Moore behind the wheel, had its tyres pumped at the same time. All four of the conspirators then returned to Failsworth before two of them picked up the stolen BMW and Mini Cooper. At a car park in the neighbourhood, they were fitted with new number plates, clones of legitimate plates from cars of the same make and colour.

All four men, now in four cars, headed off to Haslingden. The G4S cash services van had left its base and the gang expected it to arrive at Abbey National some time before midnight, when they would be waiting. Gavin Noakes was to be the getaway driver from the scene in a stolen car, which would most likely be dumped before the robbers got into one or both of the legitimate cars for the trip home. Moore's role was probably to use the Mondeo as a barrier between police and his pals if things went wrong. The gang wore black waterproof clothing over their regular clothes to prevent the shedding of fibres, which could be stripped off on the return journey so they looked like ordinary motorists. By 8.24 p.m., Moore was off on patrol in the Mondeo. His three partners-in-crime waited in the car park of a Co-op close to the bank.

The adrenaline was pumping, the moment of the cash van's arrival minutes away, when police officers hared onto the car park. Police vehicles blocked in Gavin Noakes and Richard Walsh in the Mini Cooper, and the younger Walsh in the Ford Focus. Officers leapt from the blockading vehicles, shouting, 'Armed police!' But, the gang had not come this far to bend over. Both cars tried to ram their way out, grinding against the cop cars. The wheel of the Focus ground furiously into the gravel, the car's engine whinnying, as Jonathon Walsh bore down on the accelerator. The rear of the car was lifting off the ground, with officers close to being run down, when Walsh was zapped with a Taser and dragged from the vehicle. He continued struggling, volts charging through his muscular frame, and had to be punched before he calmed down. Meanwhile, Noakes was ignoring police commands and trying to reverse his way out of the corral in such a violent manner, switching quickly into forward gear and back to get more purchase, that the cops feared some of their number would be killed, and shot him. No more willing to accept defeat than his cohorts, Richard Walsh had to be dragged from the vehicle and punched.

White, well-built, crop-headed lads with solid jaws, gravelly accents and well-groomed girlfriends in the public gallery, they were the archetypal Salford robbery team. Like most of the heist outfits to trouble the courts, they mixed family members with recruited professionals, their approach to robberies combined meticulous planning, guile and brute force, and their appearance in the dock was owed to a police surveillance operation. What marked the three men out was the fact that they were standing trial at all. Jonathon and Richard Walsh, and William Moore, all admitted conspiring to commit robbery. The only thing they denied was knowing that their accomplice, Gavin Noakes, was armed with a gun. For his part, Noakes took responsibility for the gun, admitting possessing a prohibited firearm and possessing a firearm with intent to commit robbery. He supported the innocence of the others, insisting he had brought the gun to the raid without their knowledge. However, a tenacious prosecution team had rejected the pleas as they were, handed to them on a plate. The lawyers pressed ahead with the trial, resting their case on the premise that the raid had been so well-planned the men must have known about the firearm.

The Walsh brothers and Moore had good reason to deny knowing about the gun, beyond any presumption of innocence. The weapon, a 9mm Reck Miami with silencer, represented a significant difference in jail time. They, just like the prosecutors, were taking a gamble, although the stakes were much higher for the robbers. Losing the gamble meant losing the one-third sentencing credit that a guilty plea would automatically attract. It also made it more likely that they would get an indeterminate sentence for the public protection. IPPs, as they were known, were introduced by the Criminal Justice Act 2003, and first came into use in 2005. The provisions empowered judges to class a defendant as 'dangerous', typically because they were a persistently violent offender or robber, and then set a minimum time behind bars that they should serve before their release could be considered. An ordinary offender would be given a jail-term, of which they would normally serve no more than half, before being released on licence. But an inmate serving an IPP had to serve the entirety of the minimum period specified behind bars. On top of that, their release was not guaranteed when the period had elapsed, the authorities were only obliged to 'consider' setting them free. To get out of jail, an inmate on an IPP had to prove that they no longer posed a 'significant risk of serious harm to the public by the commission of specified offences'. In short, they had to show that they had reformed, namely through a process of rehabilitative classes and intensive supervision. In theory, this meant unrepentant villains could spend many more years than the period specified in

jail. Naturally, civil liberties campaigners disliked this innovation of the Labour government. One major concern, shared
by the prisons watchdog, was that inmates would languish in
jail longer than necessary because over-crowding prevented
them from getting on the courses they needed to do for the
Parole Board to approve their release. Judges in Greater Manchester's courts were not shy about passing IPPs, however,
and hardened criminals and their defence counsel fought
tooth and nail to avoid them.

Having taken his fate on the chin, Noakes was willing to
give evidence that he alone had known of the gun. He owed
the others a favour. The Walsh brothers and Noakes had
planned to plead guilty to conspiracy to burgle, because it
carried a lesser sentence. The plan was to pretend that they
were merely attempting to break into the bank and steal the
cash once it had been delivered, rather than robbing it from
the security van crew. However, Noakes had broken ranks and
pleaded guilty to robbery, a move which implicated his
partners-in-crime in the more serious offence.

The story Noakes told at trial in July 2010 was that, while
the promise of the money had been too good to refuse, he had
brought the gun to the scene in case he was double-crossed by
the others, who he didn't trust. This 'paranoiac' fear stemmed
from the murder of his brother, who had been lured to his
death, believing he was about to carry out a job, in 2003. But
the prosecution, led by Peter Cadwallader, argued that 'they
were so meticulous in the planning of that enterprise, it's not
credible that any of them did not know that a gun was part of
the equipment'. The prosecution were believed, and the gang
was found guilty. Each classed as a dangerous offender, they
were jailed indeterminately, for the public protection.

HAD THE JURY heard the fate of Gavin Noakes's brother,
they might have been more sympathetic to his version of

events. Philip Noakes was tortured, slashed and hacked before being shot in the head, set on fire and dumped in a shallow grave. His killer, Stephen McColl, was known as 'Boom Boom Magoo', the jokey nickname belying his maniacal reputation while pointing to his most distinctive characteristics: his willingness to shoot and the thick 'Mr Magoo' spectacles that he wore. Noakes, a big, handy villain, had at some point humiliated Boom Boom in public and so sealed his fate. He was McColl's second victim. Before he went into the funeral trade, an interesting choice of career for a double-killer, McColl was a prolific armed robber and burglar. He was also a police informant.

Years earlier, in 1997, McColl's name had come up in the trial of John Ferrier and James Dunn, two men accused of murdering a firefighter called Ralph Sprott in Scotland. It was alleged that Ferrier had paid Dunn £10,000 to kill Sprott, who had been his business partner until they fell out. Sprott, a tall martial arts expert, was murdered as he walked to work at the fire station one morning. His killer arrived on a motorbike, then joined a queue at a bus shelter, where he waited for Sprott to walk past before shooting him in the back of the head. Dunn said he had merely supplied the motorbike to a criminal, named in court as Stephen 'Magoo' McColl. Dunn and Ferrier walked on a 'not proven' verdict. McColl was questioned over the murder but not charged, and moved from his native Scotland to Salford.

In May 2001, he was recruited as an informant by Greater Manchester detectives trying to bring down Salford's cash-van robbery teams. McColl was more than willing to inform on his rivals – by that stage he had apparently been turned down as an informant by three police forces in Scotland, who were well aware of his volatile reputation. Unbeknown to his new GMP handlers, he had already plotted a murder on their patch, just two months before. Twenty-two-year-old Michael Doran, a petty criminal, had looked up to Boom Boom, but he made the mistake of informing on him – and paid with his life. Suspecting the kid of tipping police off about jobs he had planned, he falsely told him he was going to shoot someone. When McColl was arrested he knew Doran must have been the grass. A week later he took him to Scotland, with the promise of a nice little earner. Michael Doran has not been seen since.

When they put him on the payroll, Greater Manchester Police were warned of Boom Boom's sinister potential by their peers in Glasgow, and a detective reportedly travelled south to tell them in person that he was a dangerous man, not to be trusted. The warnings went unheeded. In 2003, McColl secured as a job as funeral director – a lifelong ambition – through an agency for the long-term unemployed. He secretly organised a string of armed robberies across the north-west while working there, tipping off police about rivals at the same time.

Roger Holt, a fellow employee at the Salford undertakers, later claimed that McColl orchestrated a terror campaign against him after he had a word with him about his attitude to the job. Mr Holt told the *Manchester Evening News* that his problems began after he told off McColl for banging on the windows of one of the funeral offices because grieving families might be inside. The Scotsman had also dumped a coffin in a workshop instead of taking it into the chapel with paperwork identifying the body. McColl reacted very badly to being chastised. Over the next six months, Holt was terrorised by firebombs, tyre-slashings, bricks thrown at windows, menacing phone calls and a gang attack in which three men pounced on him and stamped on his neck. He claimed that police were not prepared to arrest McColl. GMP said they did investigate the complaints, which were withdrawn, but Holt said his complaint was only dropped after he was told McColl had been charged with murder. 'I believe I was very close to getting a bullet,' he said. 'I wanted McColl charged with attempting to murder me. The police could have prevented Philip Noakes's murder and protected shopkeepers and innocent members of the public who were subjected to a horrendous series of robberies, if they had only taken me seriously.'

It was while working at the undertakers that McColl found the secluded copse at Worsley Woods, near St Mark's Church, Worsley, where he would bury the naked, mutilated body of Philip Noakes in November 2003. Noakes had belittled McColl, an occasional partner in crime, one too many times. McColl's henchman, Daniel Henson, lured Noakes away from his home with the promise of a job. Two months later, his body was found by a dog-walker.

In 2006, the thirty-eight-year-old McColl was convicted of the two murders and sentenced to a whole life term, putting him in the same bracket as the Yorkshire Ripper. At that stage he had already been sentenced to fifteen years for a string of violent robberies that had seen guns pointed in women's faces. Daniel Henson, aged twenty-three, was sentenced to life.

In a statement, GMP acknowledged that mistakes had been made, while defending the informant system. 'Informants are often involved in criminality themselves and a careful balance must be struck as to whether the information they provide is reliable. In this instance, and with the benefit of hindsight, it is clear McColl was not reliable and should not have been used. We did continue to use McColl as an informant, despite the warning given to us by police in Scotland. The balance taken at the time was that potential information McColl could provide outweighed the dangers of his reliability. In this instance, we got it wrong and should not have used him. Policing is never perfect.'

An internal review outlined the mistakes made by police in the McColl affair. Guidelines on the use of informers had not been followed and checks had not been made on McColl through the National Criminal Intelligence Service. When

Michael Doran vanished, police trying to trace him were not told at the earliest stage that he was an informant, a revelation which could have implicated McColl before he went on to kill again. The IPCC would later highlight failings in the way GMP handled informants. While its investigation found no evidence of 'criminal conduct by officers', the watchdog found fault with the systems GMP had in place for handling Covert Human Intelligence Sources. Four officers were given words of advice, and a number of recommendations were made aimed at improving the force's 'management of covert law enforcement techniques'.

12

The Man from Atlantis

AN EYEWITNESS SAW the 'wild glare' in Wayne McDonald's eyes as he rummaged in the boot of his BMW. Minutes later, in a murderous fury, he raked a crowd of clubbers with bullets from a semi-automatic handgun. The impulse shooting was sparked by an incident that had little to do with McDonald and even less to do with its innocent victims. Bryan Kemp and Wayne Howarth narrowly escaped death after being gunned down in a shocking climax to what had begun as an ordinary Saturday night on the town.

As the brother-in-law and enforcer for high-level drug importer Gerald Deaffern, McDonald was a man who liked to make his presence felt. Deaffern himself was dubbed a 'Mr Big' of the north-west underworld when he was locked up for life in 2005, at the age of thirty-nine, for conspiring to import drugs. Major league importers like Deaffern kept their distance from the havoc their trade wreaked on the streets. A highly intelligent man, he lived in east Lancashire, far from the ghetto dealers and addicts that kept him in business. By his thirties he was driving a Maserati, and could afford to commission a yacht to be custom built for £665,000.

His operation smuggled multi-million pound consignments of cocaine, ecstasy and heroin from the Continent under the floors of lorries bearing loads like washing powder. The drugs would be unloaded at a warehouse in Blackburn and the proceeds of the wholesale distribution network were laundered through plant machinery and companies controlled by Deaffern or his associates. The downfall of the organisation came after Lancashire Constabulary's Serious and Organised Crime Unit launched an investigation following the seizure of £25 million of drugs stopped on arrival in the UK.

An insider would later turn informant and testify anonymously that he had been involved in four trips for Deaffern after being introduced to him in Amsterdam in 2000. That man was richly rewarded for turning Queen's Evidence – seven years in jail instead of the twenty-eight he could have got. Another man would tell jurors of another seven importations. Deaffern told the jury that he 'was no angel' and had smoked a bit of weed in the past, but would not get involved with class A 'filth'. He stood trial twice in 2004 – the first time he was cleared after the panel failed to reach a verdict – before being convicted at Liverpool Crown Court. He was ordered to serve twenty-five years. An appeal against his conviction and sentence would fail.

'I am convinced I am taking out of circulation a big player,' said Judge Denis Clark, in sentencing. 'You were a mainline dealer in drugs, a Mr Big in the North West. You were very heavily involved in the distribution of drugs and very cleverly covered your tracks and limited your exposure but were at the top of the echelon.'

A key member of the organisation, David Scattergood, admitted conspiring to import drugs before deciding, a few weeks later, that he didn't fancy going down after all. He fled to Cyprus, taunting the police by text about life in the sun. Officers secured an international arrest warrant and he was returned to the UK following the success of a second extradition bid. He was jailed for eight-and-a-half years. An Assets

Recovery Agency investigation into the lifestyles of the outfit ran alongside the police job. Scattergood was found to have made £1,500,000, of which £339,000 was confiscated. Another lieutenant of Deaffern's was found to have earned £350,000 from his crimes, of which the authorities clawed back £248,000. Deaffern had benefited by a whopping £10,849,805, of which just £456,663 was recoverable. He was given a year to pay up at risk of an extra two years in jail. When the going had been good, Deaffern drove a £50,000 BMW and a £40,000 model for his wife. He also bought his brother-in-law and bodyguard Wayne McDonald a top-of-the-range 5 series, a car which would play a vital role in his conviction for attempting to murder two innocent people, a decade on from the crime.

Back in 2000, when McDonald spectacularly lost his temper outside Bolton's Atlantis nightclub, Deaffern's operation was at its height, and the boss was away in Amsterdam. It was after 2 a.m., and as clubbers milled outside the Atlantis nightclub in Bolton, a lad called Kevin told his friend Michael, 'Watch this, it's going to kick off.' The two men were with friends waiting for a taxi on the edge of the car park. They saw an argument between two groups of lads, and one man punching another and asking, 'Do you want some?' Across the road there was a commotion – a white girl with a slapped face was calling a huddle of Asian men 'Pakis'. Witnesses remember a group of five walked over to help the lad who had been hit and to confront the other group. Someone among this group of five said, 'Let's one-time him.'

Into this drunken confusion of late-night scuffles walked Wayne McDonald. He wasn't dressed for clubbing, unshaven in a scruffy waterproof jacket, a big stocky fellow who looked younger than his thirty-nine years, despite the receding hairline. Kevin and Michael noticed a silver BMW with the boot up. 'Someone was almost in the boot which was open', Kevin said. 'He was there four or five minutes. I saw him stand up with right arm against his jacket, at the time I thought he must have a concealed weapon - he moved away from the car. I remember his shaved head, he was quite well-built, fairly tall, he looked pretty hard.' As McDonald strode purposefully toward the club another witness noticed the 'wild glare' in his eyes. Kevin said to Michael: 'He's got something in his pocket – just watch this.'

The head doorman had locked the club after a punter told him he had been hit in the face by a man with a knuckleduster. Other customers told him that a girl had been slapped, and there was a group of five or six people across the road who he did not feel comfortable about. He saw two men walking aggressively across the road, then one produced a gun from his pocket and there was a flash.

'He walked with purpose,' Kevin added. 'As he passed into the crowd I saw him pull his arm out and stick it out as if he was pointing. I heard four, five bangs that sounded like fire-crackers going off. I saw a lad in an orange shirt fall to the floor.' The doorman activated a panic alarm as the gunman fired 'indiscriminately'. 'The scene was chaotic', said Michael. 'I saw one person being dragged inside the club by the door-staff.' This person, Bryan Kemp, had been with Lee Howarth moments before they were both gunned down. Bryan remembered only 'a blurry image of a white man pointing ...I heard a loud bang and the revving of a car,' he later testified. He was shot through the right hand, the left wrist and his right hip. Lee Howarth was also riddled with bullets – one even lodged in his phone after hitting his left-hand pocket – others broke his finger, pierced his sides, and shot straight through his left forearm. McDonald had fled on foot in the aftermath of the shooting with his pal Nasar Ahmed.

CCTV would later reveal that McDonald had gone into the club shortly after midnight, leaving two hours later with Nasar Ahmed and a man identified only as Anwar. A fight had then taken place beside a sports car that had pulled up outside the club. Anwar had driven away in this but Ahmed, the man accused of slapping the woman seen screaming racial abuse, had stayed behind. After the shooting, Ahmed fled along with McDonald, only to return less than an hour later. In his frenzy McDonald had made a schoolboy error, locking the keys to the BMW in the boot of the car after reaching into it for his gun.

Nasar Ahmed was on his way back with a spare set of keys when he was captured on CCTV by the side of the club, first running, then stopping and hiding himself from view. The operator told police what she had seen and officers caught up with him as he approached the BMW, key in hand. At that very early stage of the investigation police already had a good idea that the BMW was linked to the shooting because of what witnesses had described. John, one of Kevin and Michael's mates, had even written down the licence number of the vehicle using his girlfriend's lipstick in the aftermath of the shooting. Ahmed, later jailed for two years for assisting an offender, was arrested at 3.20 a.m. as he casually approached the car and clicked off the central locking. He was also in possession of a phone which, it was quickly established, belonged to McDonald. A search of the car revealed a Czech Ceska pistol wrapped in a sock – not the one used in the shooting – ninety-two rounds of .22 Minimag bullets, and a big bag of amphetamines. There was also an Asda carrier bag containing three more carrier bags, two of which were empty, one of which contained a tissue, which at the time, did not have enough material for DNA profiling.

Nevertheless, there was plenty to link McDonald to the car and to Ahmed, and in turn, the shooting. Eight shells, matching the eight missing from the box found in the boot of the car, were recovered by forensics from the scene. McDonald had even phoned Ahmed while he opened up the car. The car had been custom fitted with a telephone, and this had been used to call McDonald's girlfriend eight times before the night of the shooting. Hours after, McDonald called her again and told her 'something bad has happened'. She said they could talk about it in the morning.

McDonald left his home in the affluent south Manchester suburb of Didsbury and vanished – for the next seven years. Rumours placed him in Amsterdam at times, and just down the road in Stockport.

ON NEW YEAR'S Eve, 2007 McDonald dramatically reappeared. Alison Moores, the landlady of a pub in Bamber Bridge, near Preston, was in bed when her fiancé, Tony Gornall, came upstairs and told her that there were two men in the building wearing balaclavas. 'I was half-asleep,' she later told the *Bolton Evening News*, 'and I thought, why have the cleaners got balaclavas on?' McDonald and his accomplice, David Tyrell, had burst through the back door moments after staff arrived for the day's work. They had inside information from a kitchen worker and were expecting to get away with £12,000. The couple locked the entrance to their living quarters above the pub, and by the time the robbers had kicked the door in the police had been called. There was still, however, enough time for McDonald's gang to threaten to shoot the cleaners and subject the licensees to a terrifying ordeal. Tony Gornall, was pistol-whipped by the gang as his partner cowered naked under the bed. She was dragged out by one of the robbers shouting, 'Get out, bitch.' The couple were then bundled into their bathroom, tied up and told they would be shot if they called the police—but the cops were already on their way. With the blaring of sirens drawing nearer, the gang abandoned the job and fled.

It was Katie Johnson's first day as a police dog handler and she had the misfortune to bump into McDonald on the street outside. She later told the *Ormskirk Advertiser*: 'When I arrived at the pub I was with my colleague PC Tinsley. I got out the car and we were met by a colleague who informed us of what he believed was going on inside the pub. All we knew at the time was that there had been a phone call from someone in the pub saying that some people had broken in. The back door of the pub was open and a set of step ladders were by it. I got my dog out of the car and went towards the pub. As I got past the side door, my colleague walked to the front.

'I heard the door rattling, turned around and was faced with a man in the doorway, pointing a gun straight at me. He was shouting something at me like, "Get on the ground." I thought, he's going to shoot me, I'm going to die. But I still had to try and stop him doing what I thought he was going to do. He didn't give me a chance to get on the ground and I didn't have time to react before he discharged his firearm and shot me. I immediately felt an awful pain in my left thigh … and felt complete and utter fear. But still in my own mind I knew I had to try and detain him. I knew I'd been shot because of the bang and the force of something hitting me in the leg. I was thinking, I've got to stop him and try to do something. I was also thinking, don't look at your leg, because I imagined that half was missing or that it had a big hole in it, and [if I looked at it] I knew I would pass out there and then and didn't know what he would do next.'

The officer gave her dog, Chaos, the order to detain McDonald. Instead, the bewildered Alsatian nipped her on the arm and let the gunman run off. Describing the incident in a report published in the *Daily Mail*, the officer said: 'I was slumped on the floor and Chaos had been upset by the bang and I was unsure where he was. Chaos was really disturbed by the incident and there's a strong possibility he didn't see his target because he didn't train for that. He wasn't trained to attack offenders that weren't shouting and screaming. Chaos mouthed my arm but didn't penetrate the skin.'

Katie Johnson suffered wounds to her leg from the shotgun pellets as well as minor bruising on her arm from Chaos's nip. She had twelve pellet holes in her left thigh and feared she would lose her leg and that her career was over. As it turned out she was not seriously injured.

The game up, McDonald handed himself in at a police station, telling officers, 'I just shot one of your women.' Tyrell had fled the scene and spent more than twelve hours hiding in a hole he dug near a timber merchant's, sheltered by a piece of tarpaulin. He was arrested after being spotted on the railway line.

McDonald and Tyrell stood trial at Preston. In April 2009, McDonald was found guilty of wounding with intent to resist arrest, robbery and firearms offences, but cleared of attempted murder. He was jailed for life, a sentence reduced to an indeterminate length for the public protection on appeal. The IPP was, in reality, virtually indistinguishable from a life sentence as far as the courts were concerned, and if he failed to prove that he was no longer a danger to the authorities, he might never be released. Tyrell was convicted of wounding and was jailed for an indeterminate period, while two other men, including a former kitchen worker at the pub, Peter Plaskowski, were convicted of robbery.

As McDonald began serving his sentence, police began looking at the Atlantis shooting again. DNA technology had advanced, and a sample of tissue, kept all these years in a secure deep-freeze, could be positively linked to him. The trial finally got underway at Manchester Crown Court in November 2010, some ten years after the shooting. Armed officers guarded the courtroom, inside and out. The appearance of the man in the dock belied the trigger-happy gunman persona. McDonald, now forty-nine, wore glasses, dressed smartly, and assiduously read his copy of the jury bundle as his case wore on. His defence consisted of little more than a vain hope that the prosecution, led by Andrew Menary QC – a veteran of major gun and gang trials – hadn't proved their case, and the suggestion that the DNA was a plant, an 'old fashioned fitting up …like [the TV series] *Life on Mars*.'

McDonald was convicted and jailed for life in his absence after refusing to come up from the cells for sentence. Had he done so, he would have heard the judge say it was unlikely he would be released until he was an 'elderly man, if at all'. The judge added, 'He is, in my judgement, a ruthless, professional criminal who regards firearms as one of the tools of his trade. He has shown not a glimmer of remorse for the damage done to his innocent victims. I'm convinced that the defendant presents a very real danger to the public. There's no sign that his willingness to use firearms is in any way dimmed by the passage of time.'

13

The
Angelzarke Murder

BILLY WEBB WAS the Mr Big of Bolton. He ran his drugs business like a corporation, with a small army of salaried workers and a board of directors creaming off the profits. He had started out as an enforcer for fellow druglord John Barber, but when Barber was banged up in the mid-nineties, Webb took his place and transformed his operation, which brought in heroin and cocaine from Liverpool, into a multi-million pound outfit. Following Barber's release, the pair became partners. Barber was considered to be the brains behind the operation but his former henchman, a violent, sadistic character, would come to eclipse him in influence. Most shockingly, Webb was believed to have been behind the 1998 killing of Dillon Hull, a five-year-old boy shot dead by a bungling hitman as he walked home hand in hand with his stepfather, John Bates. Bates, a drug dealer who had refused to work for Webb, was the intended target of the shooting but survived after being blasted in the stomach. There was not enough evidence to arrest Webb for the horrific crime, but an undercover operation would bring down his drugs business. Before he could stand trial he was murdered; shot dead as he slept beside his girlfriend by assassins who let themselves into his flat with a key. Barber was subsequently jailed for twenty-two years for drugs offences.

The demise of the Webb-Barber organisation left a vacuum in Bolton. Rival gangs of crooks of Pakistani heritage were among those who filled the vacuum. This coincided with the rise of similar groups in other northern, post-industrial towns with deprived Asian and white communities, such as Oldham, north-east of Manchester, and Bradford and Keighley in Yorkshire. In 2000, the *Independent* reported, 'A power struggle has broken out for control of Britain's £1bn heroin market, with a new breed of Pakistani drugs syndicates emerging to challenge the supremacy of the Turkish crime gangs. Customs chiefs and the National Criminal Intelligence Service (NCIS) are alarmed at the rise in smuggling direct from Pakistan, and fear growing levels of violence as rival gangs fight for control of the trade. Heroin from Pakistan is already wreaking havoc in cities in Yorkshire, Lancashire and the Midlands, which are being saturated with the drug. An NCIS officer said: "The impact this is having on local communities is quite scary." '

In 2002, the *Guardian* also highlighted the issue. 'Experts say the reasons for the problem are obvious,' it reported. 'Drug gangs emerge wherever there is poverty, unemployment and social exclusion. It has been the rule on white sink estates for decades and describes deprived Asian – mainly Pakistani – communities across the north of England and in London ... Asian communities have also been hit by the phenomenon of successful young men and women moving away as soon as they get jobs and degrees. What they are leaving behind are poor, vulnerable and isolated communities: places that have been invaded by gangs. They have brought with them a culture of extreme violence and ostentatious wealth ... The culture of "saving face" among drug gangs can lead to the slightest perceived insult being punished with horrific violence.'

The new Asian criminals exploited their heritage for criminal gain. A family holiday to Pakistan might involve a detour to a region notorious for heroin production where a deal could be set up. Drugs could be brought over by a mule looking for a ticket to Britain, smuggled in a shipment of commercial goods, or even sent through the post. Kinship ties and the links between Asian communities in different towns made for strong criminal networks, and the burgeoning underworld even attracted university types and young men with business acumen looking for extra cash, as well as back-street kids from poor and uneducated immigrant backgrounds. In 2001, rioting had erupted in Oldham. Apart from highlighting the issue of racial division in the former mill towns, the riots showed that a new generation of Asian youths were as capable of putting a 'handy mob' together as their black or white counterparts. Far from shrinking at the first sign of a 'paki-bashing', the Asian lads were taking over.

Trafficker Fazal Hussain came to be known as 'The Godfather' in his Oldham stomping ground. But when a series of police seizures ate into his profits, he made the mistake of delivering a consignment personally. He was busted at a motorway service station with £200,000 of heroin, en route to the delivery point with his driver, Mohammed Akeem. The ensuing investigation led officers to a house in the heart of Werneth's Pakistani community and gave a new meaning to the phrase 'crimes of fashion'. Innocuous from the outside, the two-up, two-down was at the heart of a multi-national drug dealing conspiracy. Eight kilos of heroin and equipment for bashing the gear were found alongside two packages posted from Pakistan. Torn open, they contained saris, the luminescent, gold-trimmed, brightly coloured dresses worn by Asian ladies. Heroin had been sewn into the linings. Two of the gang, Mohammed Iqbal and Manir Khan, were caught at the scene.

Ijaz Ahmed, one of the operation's more senior players, bolted as the cops arrived. He left behind three mobile phones, one of which contained video footage which told of the scale and chutzpah of the plot. Ahmed could be heard giving a running commentary as workers in Pakistan beavered at the production line's decrepit sewing machines, preparing the dresses for their special purpose. Manir Khan could be seen stitching in the heroin and gesturing to the camera. The film then cuts to a package marked with an Oldham address. Once a package had been sent to one of the gang's safehouses it was taken to the house at Werneth, where the drugs would be processed before distribution. A courier firm was paid to deliver the parcels, and by contacting them, the investigators were able to stop five more which were headed for the streets. An industrial cleaning company spent two days cleaning up the Werneth terrace, so thick was the heroin dust coating every surface. In total, police, who spent nearly two years tracking the gang, believe about £1.5 million of the addictive opiate was brought into the country by the sari smugglers. Ahmed got nine-and-a-half years, Khan got eight years, Iqbal seven, Askeem, who had already done an eight-year term for importing heroin through Heathrow in the late nineties, got six years.

An unrepentant Hussain emerged from the prison gates in 2009 after serving only half of his six-year sentence. Far from returning to his old, straight life as a market trader, he threw himself into a new drug-dealing scheme involving his teenage son, Faisal. Taxi drivers were employed as couriers to buy drugs in Birmingham, Luton and Bristol and drive them north. Insiders would pose as passengers to make the runs look legitimate. In an eight month surveillance operation police seized heroin worth £700,000, cocaine worth £600,000 and cannabis worth £150,000, according to the *Manchester Evening News*. Hussain was back in jail, for nine years and eleven months, by May 2011.

Although race relations in Bolton were not quite as uneasy as in Oldham, the gangsters which emerged from the town in the noughties were cut from the same cloth as their counterparts down the road. They too had grown up scrapping on the terraced streets, had watched their fathers stooped by low-paid factory labour or six-and-a-half day weeks behind a counter, and were not prepared to do the same. Groups battling for a slice of the cake in the wake of Billy Webb's demise included Deane's Gilnow Road mob and their rivals in the Castle Street crew. Street fights between them involving an array of pool cues, hammers and knuckledusters became common. Umair Waseem forged his criminal reputation in this climate. He had come over from Pakistan at seventeen, settling in Deane with his mother and siblings. He was a straight-A electronic engineering student at Bolton University, but behind the academic façade had become a face among the local badmen, a drug dealer and underworld enforcer. Umair liked the money and lifestyle, quickly acquiring the accoutrements of an up-and-coming badman: the BMW 7 Series, the high-powered motorbike, the designer clothes, the compliant girlfriend. On a winter's day in 2009, he was offered the biggest prize of his criminal career by far: £500,000, for a job that needed a gun. It was an offer too good to refuse.

On the afternoon of February 1, he picked up his girlfriend, Khadija, from her home in Bolton. He drove her to a dead end street, left the car for a matter of seconds, came back and told her about the half a million and the gun he would be using to get it. He said that he would give her a SIM card later that night. She was to use it to text him between 10 and 11.30 p.m., and he would text her back, saying he was in Birmingham. He was vague about where he was actually headed – London and Birmingham were both suggested – but he told her that she might not see him again.

Waseem's farewell to Khadija was prophetic, but not in the way he expected. His black-and-blue body was found the next morning lying in snow at a lonely spot at Angelzarke Reservoir in Lancashire. Nearby foliage was spattered with his blood. Black duct tape bound his ankles and knees, while his hands were tied behind his back with pink nylon twine. His head had been bashed in so badly that his face was contorted. He wore two sets of clothes, unfastened cheap black jeans over blue designer ones, and a dark hoodie over other layers. There were two sets of gloves on his hands, a clear plastic disposable pair under a black, outdoor set.

A reading of the scene by detectives revealed more about the manner of his death. It had snowed heavily overnight, beginning before 10.30 p.m. The snow around the body was pristine, suggesting he had met his fate before it had stopped falling. The hem of the blue jeans and the wrists of the plastic gloves had been secured with a similar tape of the kind used to restrain him. This unusual dress would corroborate his girlfriend's account that Umair had set out to commit a crime on the night he died. What would emerge, thanks to a combination of good detective work and technology, was a story of greed, betrayal and bloody violence.

Waseem's family might not have known of his secret life, but his more law-abiding friends had long had concerns for him. They had noticed a change in his attitude, 'like he had gone up in the world'. When pressed, he bragged about making £700 a week selling drugs. His friends, who hailed from the same part of Pakistan, were aware that he had been working as a strong-arm man for a gun-toting dealer with a 'proper violent' reputation. In the week before his death, Waseem got a first-hand taste of this, according to courtoom testimony, after falling out with his former paymaster. The out-of-favour henchman was lured to a meeting, where he was set upon by a waiting gang as his former boss watched. Waseem was not seriously injured but he was angry, and frightened by a growing list of enemies that now included his former mentor. He began asking if he could get a gun through contacts in Bradford, the West Yorkshire town considered by many Pakistani underworld figures as the centre of organised crime in their community. He also told a friend he was in 'serious trouble', running out of people he could trust.

It was against this backdrop that he was offered the opportunity to make some serious money by another man, Asim Khan. Khan was a law student at Bolton University but had links to organised crime, like Umair. Khan promised Umair that he could make £500,000. He didn't reveal what the job was, but it could only have been a contract killing or an extremely lucrative robbery or extortion. Blinded by pound signs and fearful for his future, Waseem went for it.

In the months leading up the offer, Waseem had been badgering Khan for cash he believed he was owed. It stemmed from activities in his violent past. Before Waseem had fallen out with the dealer who had employed him as an enforcer, he had been involved in at least ten street fights. In August 2008, Waseem had been riding his green Kawasaki when he was ambushed by a gang from Farnworth, including two thugs who went by the streetnames Pobs and Kaka. Waseem and his bike were set about with a hammer. Pobs, Kaka and others were quickly arrested and charged with assault. Kaka's mother learnt of this, and arrangements were made for Waseem to visit her at her home, where he showed her his bruises and she pleaded with him to forgive her son. Another meeting was set up when Kaka was released on bail. By then, it had been agreed that Waseem would be paid £7,000 as 'compensation' for the damaged bike. Asim Khan, who was known to both sides, was to act as a go-between and guarantor. He was handed the cash with the understanding that he would hold onto it until the 'matter had been resolved', when he would hand it to Umair Waseem.

As a result of this agreement, Waseem walked into Astley Bridge police station and gave a new account of the attack. He now claimed that he had fallen off his bike, lost his memory and then given a false story to police because the bike wasn't insured. He said he did not want to pursue the complaint he had made or take part in an identity parade. His 'retraction' made not a jot of difference, however: the attack had been captured on CCTV, had been seen by a number of eyewitnesses, and the hammer had been recovered. Pobs and Kaka were kept in custody pending trial. But, as far as Waseem was concerned, he had done his bit and was still owed the money. Khan had other ideas, and held onto it.

The police investigation into Umair's subsequent murder would uncover an exchange of texts between Umair Waseem and Asim Khan concerning money sent in the days before he was killed. By noon on the day he died, the two men were frequently in contact with each other, and by 2.30 p.m. both their phones were using a cell site at Moses Gate, suggesting that they had met up. Detectives would later conclude that it was at this meeting that Khan proposed a serious criminal enterprise which would earn Waseem a great deal more than the £7,000 of hush money he felt was his due. But there never was any lucrative robbery or hit job. The only crime in the offing was the murder of Waseem, who had become an irritant to too many people. The promised £500,000 was bait to lure him to a violent death.

After the meeting, Waseem went to a car hire premises where he picked out a Vauxhall Vectra. Then he took Khadija for that final spin. His driving was faster than usual, he spoke in a whisper and seemed to be thinking aloud, she would remember. She did not take him seriously when he told her about the money and made a 'gunfingers' gesture to indicate what the job involved, but she did agree to help him set up an alibi by sending texts from the SIM card he promised he would drop through her door.

Faisal Aslam, a cannabis dealer who Umair also thought to be a friend, had been staying with Asim Khan at Bolton University's Hollins halls of residence. By 6.30 that evening, the room-mates were both at Angelzarke reservoir with Waseem. It was a beauty spot he knew well and loved, as he would often go there with Khadija and other friends. Khan and Aslam told him to return there later that night. An hour and fifteen minutes later, Waseem went home to Deane and told his family that he was going away. He had previously told his sister that he was going to Dover, and on another occasion had told his mother he was going to London. He was still alive at 8.50 p.m., when he was captured on CCTV at a takeaway ordering a pizza.

Exactly what happened between then and the discovery of his body the next morning is not known. What was clear was that he had been subjected to a brutal attack. His killers had used a variety of weapons to shatter his skull and facial bones. There were no injuries to the rest of his body, nor were there any defence injuries, as he had been tied up at the time. His body was found on the lower car park by litter-pickers. In the upper car park, about fifty yards away, was his BMW 7 Series.

Once police had spoken to witnesses who had seen him on the day before he died, it became clear that the hired Vauxhall was central to the enquiry. The breakthrough came when police received a tip-off that the car was parked in Crumpsall, north Manchester. An Asian man had been seen trying to start the car unsuccessfully. The car was seized in the early hours of February 6, and a forensic examination revealed it was splattered with the dead man's blood. Samples recovered from the driver's door showed that somebody stained by his blood had brushed against it. There was also blood on the bodywork below the boot, suggesting it had been very close to the victim when he was attacked. Waseem had not only gone willingly to the lonely spot where he was murdered, but had also hired his killers' getaway car.

The man seen trying to start the car at Crumpsall, Aroon Asad, was quickly arrested. He told police that Faisal Aslam had given him the car to sell, dropping it off between 11 and 11.45 p.m. on February 1. Aslam, who was wearing gloves at the time, had also handed him a phone. Although the phone contained no SIM card, it could be established by the IMEA number that it was the phone Waseem had been using on the night of his death.

Faisal Aslam had already fled when police executed a search warrant at his home a week after the murder. The next day, he rang police from Leeds, before handing himself in at a police station, where he was arrested on suspicion of murder. His initial account was that the victim had asked him to get rid of a car on February 1. He said he had taken the car off Waseem's hands before passing it on to the man seen driving it in Crumpsall. He said he had last seen the victim, well and uninjured, at 8.30 p.m., and denied taking possession of the phone or visiting Angelzarke. Since Aslam suggested that Asim Khan could verify some of his movements, Khan was tracked down by police. At the time he was spoken to, police had no reason to suspect he was involved, but he gave a contradictory account to Aslam's which implicated them both, while leaving out key details betrayed by the phone evidence.

Khan told the detectives that he and Aslam left the university halls and travelled in his Lexus to meet Umair Waseem near an Asda store in Bolton. He claimed that in an earlier conversation they had discussed a night out at the Trafford Centre and that all three men had a friendly chat in the Vauxhall Vectra Waseem was driving, in which he revealed plans to go to the Lake District. After fifteen minutes, he claimed, he and Aslam had gone back to halls. Like Aslam, his account excluded any visit to Angelzarke Reservoir, and failed to tally with the mobile phone evidence.

Meanwhile, after speaking to the man from whom they had recovered the blood-spattered Vectra, police traced a second-hand car dealer from Chorlton with some telling information. He said that on the night of the murder he had been offered the Vectra 'cheap, cheap, cheap'. Three hours later, Aslam and an associate had turned up at his house and talked him into getting into the car. He had been driven around in it and offered the £4,000 vehicle for just £300, then told not to worry about the money, to just take the car. Phone analysis would later reveal Aslam had rung the car dealer's phone three times after midnight on the night of the murder. He was certainly not at home and in bed by 10.30 that night, as he had claimed.

Three months after the murder, with Asad and Aslam on bail, police visited the town's mosques in a search for clues, handing out leaflets at Friday prayers. They hoped Waseem might have mentioned something to a fellow worshipper that might lead them to the killer. Weeks later, Waseem's mother, Foozya Shakir, made a direct appeal for information about the killing. 'We are an honest family. I've worked hard raising my children,' she said. 'Whoever has done this has ripped my family apart and destroyed my whole world. Umair was a fun-loving, normal lad who was enjoying university and was an A-plus student. I am and will always be proud of him and love him very much.'

By October 2009, police had enough for the CPS to authorise charging Aslam and Khan with conspiracy to murder. The prosecution, which alleged that the men had arranged for Waseem to be killed, depended on circumstantial evidence. Aslam was linked to the Vectra by witness testimony, and since it was spattered with the victim's blood, it was put that he was at the murder scene, even if he hadn't dealt any of the fatal blows. Asim Khan could not be placed at the murder scene at the time, but was linked to the hiring of the Vectra by phone evidence, and like Aslam, could be placed in the victim's company earlier that day. He also had a motive in the £7,000 that the victim had been pestering him for.

In a 2010 Manchester Crown Court trial, the pair denied the charge. They claimed they had a quiet spliff with the victim in the area of the murder, although not in the car park, earlier that day, where they chatted about a night out at the Trafford Centre. They said they had then parted, leaving Waseem alive. The jury did not buy it, and the pair were both found guilty of conspiring to murder him. The man from whom police had recovered the Vectra, Aroon Asad, was cleared of conspiracy to murder.

Aslam, aged twenty-six at the time, and Khan, then twenty-seven, had only relatively minor previous convictions. Mr Justice Parker jailed them for thirty years each, a stiff sentence for murder excluding the use of firearms, in Britain. Sentencing, he said Umair Waseem's family were 'respectable and well-educated', but 'he was naïve, seduced by glamour and fell in with the wrong kind of people'. Referring to the £7,000 that lay at the heart of the murder, the judge speculated on the involvement of others.

'It may be that Kaka or Pobs also did not wish Umair Waseem to receive that money as they had a sense of grievance that they had gone to prison, he had been involved in putting them there and still wanted the money. It may be that it had always been intended that he should not receive the money and that you, from the beginning, had been party to the deception. Deliberately posing as his friend and confidant, you, Asim Khan, tricked Umair Waseem that there was another way of receiving money, a great deal of money.'

Describing Khan as the 'principal architect' of the murder, he said, 'The killing itself was brutal, the site was a lonely, remote spot, especially late, in the dead of winter. He was tied up and then savagely attacked with fists or feet with a blunt instrument about the head, these attacks in fact destroying that part of him. A number of people must have been involved in what was in effect an execution. This was a cold-blooded, premeditated, carefully planned and savage murder.'

In July 2010, just four months after his conviction, Asim Khan failed in a bid to get his thirty-year tariff reduced. His lawyers told the Court of Appeal that at the time of the attack he was a student who 'had not settled down in life'. They argued that this 'immaturity' meant he should have been given a shorter minimum term. The court disagreed.

GUN-RUNNER KALEEM Akhtar was another young Asian criminal driven by thrill-seeking rather than financial necessity. But, unlike Umair Waseem, he did not come from a modest background with aspirational values. Akhtar was genuinely well-off. Like Faisal Aslam, he hailed from the borders of Chorlton and Whalley Range, in south Manchester. The area is favoured by some of Manchester's most affluent Asian business and professional families, and Wilbraham Road, which cuts through it, is bordered with large, custom-built houses. While the inner suburban postcode and proximity to more deprived areas of south Manchester keep things relatively discreet, Landcruisers on driveways, extravagant extensions and pedigree dogs strongly hint at the wealth concentrated there. In 2005, hundreds of thousands of pounds was stolen in cash and jewellery from houses here. The raids were carried out by street thugs, understood to have been paid by a middleman acting on the instructions of someone described by the *Asian News* as an 'Asian Fagin'. The belief that the 'Mr Big' was a community insider was based on the fact that the raiders knew exactly when to strike and where. None of the homes would be particularly obvious targets to someone who wasn't in the know.

Akhtar's family made their money from a chain of clothing stores, including Storm in Liverpool. Away from his job in the family business and his £350,000 home, a gift from his wife's family on the occasion of their traditionally arranged marriage, he was involved in one of the country's biggest gun-running networks. The outfit Akhtar belonged to sold 'assassins kits' of self-loading Baikals and bullets. Akhtar, who called himself 'Big K', enjoyed the company of two girlfriends, and big nights out in clubs. He had the key role in the operation, arranging for the guns to be brought from a Lithuanian connection in Essex before being distributed up North and in Scotland. The gang's undoing came courtesy of a police surveillance operation which observed a series of secret handovers. Undeterred by seizures and the arrest of couriers, the gang carried on, knowing police were on to them, ordering fresh batches and recruiting new couriers. Fifty-six guns were seized, identifiable by handcarved Roman numerals. Since guns are passed from hand to hand, or even rented out by their owners for specific jobs, those seized had probably been used in hundreds of shootings. Reydell Waite, the Old Trafford Crip targeted by the Doddington, ended up in jail after he was seen buying one.

In Manchester, it was relatively uncommon for Asian people to fall victim to gun violence, and certainly gang-related gun violence. Of the 55 gun murder victims counted by a *Manchester Evening News* special report, only a handful were Asian. They included Arif Iqbal, who was shot dead in an unsolved murder, locally said to be connected to a family feud, in Cheetham Hill on New Year's Eve 2008.

In 2005, Mohammed Shaheen, boss of Olympic Taxis, a well-established firm in the south Manchester suburb of Chorlton, was gunned down. He was suspected of having sexually assaulted a number of women over a period of nine years, and in the build-up to his murder, his behaviour was said to have spiralled out of control, with allegations that he had made threats against the parents of one alleged victim. His brother-in-law, Khyber Khan, decided to sort out the

problem once and for all. He got a flight from Lahore, Pakistan, and within a few days of being in Manchester had
acquired a shotgun. After a curt phone conversation in which
Shaheen told him where to go, the gunman calmly walked
into the taxi rank and 'without a word blasted Mr Shaheen in
the chest with a single barrelled shotgun', according to the
Manchester Evening News. Khan was jailed for thirty years.
The murder fitted the stereotype of the 'honour killing', while
highlighting the ease with which a gun could be obtained in
Manchester. A couple of years before that, in 2003, cabbie
Mohammed Ahmed had been shot in the head by the Pitt Bull
Crew. But, it was not until a rash of shootings at the end of the
decade that it could truly be said that a gun culture had fully
taken hold among the Asian community's criminals.

In August 2009, the *Bolton News* reported that 'feuding
gangs are firing guns on the streets of Bolton in a turf war.'
These gangs, described as 'Pakistani-Asian organised crime
groups', had evidently moved on from the street fights Umair
Waseem had cut his teeth in. At the time of the report there
had been three shootings in three months: one at a house in
The Haulgh said by sources to be 'a revenge attack' against an
Asian gang calling themselves 'the Castle Street Crew', and
two earlier ones in Daubhill, attributed to the same Castle
Street Crew attempting to intimidate Kurdish rivals. A keema
naan shop, described as a 'known hub' for local Kurds, was
among the premises targeted.

In a report later that month, Chief Constable Peter Fahy
identified the 'emerging firearms threat' to Greater Manchester Police and local communities as 'identified Asian organised crime groups, with parallels being drawn with the
historic activity of drugs gangs from the south Manchester
area in the use of firearms to secure fiscal outcomes to their
organised criminality'. His choice of words was interesting,
not only for its frankness but also for the tacit acknowledge-
ment that with south Manchester's gangs the link between

'the use of firearms' and 'fiscal outcomes' had withered in recent years. A *Manchester Evening News* report on the chief's words said police had identified Asian crime groups in Bolton, Oldham and other parts of Greater Manchester.

The chief's warning followed two fatal shootings in five days. The murders of Nasar Hussain at Brookhouse Wines, Eccles, and of Junaid Khan, gunned down in Chadderton, Oldham, were not connected, but were stark evidence of the growing trend among Asian criminals for using firearms. And that September, Amran Khan was murdered at the doorstep of his home at Glodwick, Oldham, prompting the town's *Chronicle* newspaper to speculate over 'a deadly gang war being waged on the streets'.

As it turned out, Amran Khan's murder was not part of a gang war. Like the two killings that preceded it, however, it would lift the lid on the secretive world of the emergent Asian gangs and underworld politics in Greater Manchester.

14

The Hitman

SIMEON Henderson, a bulky, bearded black man known as 'Simmo', settled in Oldham in 2008 after serving more than three years in jail for robbery. On his release, he roomed at a hostel in Wakefield, but moved on after someone shot at him, an occupational hazard for someone with Henderson's lifestyle. He drifted around, spending time in Doncaster and Liverpool, until he met a girl called Carla on a night out clubbing. She lived in Oldham, and as she and Simmo grew closer, she invited him to stay at her grandfather's house. Oldham was as good a place as any for the ex-convict to settle. He needed only a mosque – he was a Muslim convert – and a good skunk connection to feel at home.

Henderson had been born and raised on the other side of the Pennines, in Huddersfield, but was no longer safe there. Five years earlier, his friend Michael Francois had been blasted in the head outside Dreamers bar in the town's Far-town district in a gang feud. Henderson, a prominent member of Francois' circle, was at his side at the time. Yet he refused to help police or give evidence in court, upsetting his former cohorts. He had plenty of enemies on the other side of the feud as well, and after being shot at in the street several times, he left the Yorkshire town for good in 2004.

During his last jail stretch, Henderson had met Moham-med 'Chach' Hafiz in Armley Prison, and the two had become fast friends. Chach, short for *Chacha*, which means 'uncle' in Urdu, was a Cheetham Hill man and a reasonably well-known figure in the Asian criminal underworld, with convictions for kidnapping. He was also involved with a business called Pennine Vehicle Services (PVS), in the Asian neighbourhood of Glodwick, Oldham. Henderson couldn't stay at Carla's grandfather's while she wasn't there, so he started spending his days at PVS, becoming part of the circle that worked and played computer games there. He had no money, but in his way Chach, the closest person to him at the time, looked after him. Henderson would wash cars and his patron would make sure he got a bag of weed, a takeaway dinner and cars to drive.

Chach was among a handful of men with links to the car hire trade who were active in the criminal underworld. Many drug dealers change vehicles often to avoid detection, and they also like flash cars, so brokers who don't ask too many questions quickly become popular. It is not unheard of for criminals to launder cash through dodgy car hire businesses and launch investments with the proprietors. In lean periods, career criminals borrow money from these men or work for them as debt collectors or odd-job men.

Another Asian, Mohammed Farid, was also part of this world. He ran Oldham Car Hire, as well as a major drugs ring which supplied heroin, cocaine and cannabis. He swanned about in a fleet of luxury motors including a Ferrari and a Lamborghini. In late 2008, a couple of weeks after the Muslim festival of Eid, Farid became the first target of a shooting perpetrated by Simeon 'Simmo' Henderson.

Farid and an associate had agreed to guarantee a £30,000 loan for a businessman in financial trouble. The debtor was to pay back £2,000 a month, but reneged on the deal after a few payments. This left Farid, as the guarantor, in a difficult position. A delegation went to his home with an ultimatum: pay the cash or lure the debtor and the other guarantor into the clutches of kidnappers, who would extract the debt by force. Days later, Farid was told by a Bradford-based heavy that unless he coughed up, his mother's house would get shot up.

Farid was forced to summon the other guarantor and the debtor to his home for a meeting. A stocky bruiser in a balaclava turned up carrying a crossbow. He shoved his way past Farid in the hallway and barged into the front room, where he slapped the other guarantor and demanded, 'Where's my money?' Assurances were given and the man left, still issuing threats.

A few days later, Farid was out and about in the Glodwick area. The district has a close-knit community, many hailing from deprived areas of Mirpur in Pakistan, but its backstreets were also a breeding ground for the new breed of Asian bad boy, men like Amran 'Manny' Khan. Manny was the younger brother of Gulfan 'Gogo' Khan, and benefited from his reputation. Close to seven-feet and bald with a Van Dyke beard, Gulfan owned Pennine Vehicle Hire and was an influential character in Oldham's Asian community. Farid had known both brothers for years, but sentimentality disappeared when it came to money. Manny was now enforcing the debt and he wanted Farid's prized cars.

When Manny spotted Farid that day in Glodwick, he coaxed him into a car and gave him the bluntest of ultimatums. 'Who's going to pay?' he demanded, implying that dangerous men from Manchester were behind the loan and wanted their money back. 'He wasn't giving me a choice,' Farid later testified. 'He was asking for my cars ... He reached in the back and then he pulled a bag out and showed me a gun and said, "This is it what you're gonna get if you don't pay this money." I started crying and getting upset. I explained to him,

"I will pay you." At one stage I managed to get out the car and he chased me and said don't be stupid or he's gonna shoot me, and I got back in his car.'

When a delegation later drove to Oldham Car Hire seeking collection, however, the receptionist panicked and called police. This was the final straw. After a failed bid to attack Farid at his house, Simmo Henderson stuck his head through the serving hatch at Oldham Car Hire, aimed a gun at the floor, and let off three warning shots before running off. Henderson had no personal beef with Farid, who escaped unhurt. But he was penniless in a strange town, hunted by police for breaching his licence conditions, and was eager to ingratiate himself with his new allies at Pennine Vehicle Services. The only thing he had to offer them was his willingness to shoot.

The second time he shot at somebody, he found it easier. According to Henderson, Chach was apoplectic when a local kid called Imran 'Immy' Khadam called him an 'old-timer', adding mysteriously, 'Money talks.' Chach perceived this as a threat. The Colt .22 that had been used for the Farid shooting was still knocking around. 'I did it for a favour kind of thing,' Henderson later recalled. 'The idea was to shoot him and then demand money off him.'

Henderson lay in wait for Immy outside his home. When he spotted him pulling up, he leapt from his car, cocked the weapon and pulled the trigger. The bullet jammed. Henderson released it from the chamber and reloaded as Immy bolted down the street. He squeezed the trigger again as his target ran into the distance, diving behind a wall for cover. Henderson could see someone else hiding behind a car a few feet away. When the figure tried to make a break for it, Henderson let loose with the pistol. 'I aimed at him and shot him in the bum.'

The victim turned out to be Immy's brother.

If the second time had been easier, the third time felt like nothing – until afterwards, when the realisation of what he had done hit him, when he learned he had been double-crossed and that the life he was leading was incompatible with his Islamic faith. The apparently trigger-happy gunman kneeled to the east five times, every day, without fail.

Henderson was arrested for breach of licence and driving offences and spent most of the spring behind bars. By the time he got out, his girlfriend Carla was fed up with him. A petite, black-haired girl, she was a law-abiding person, some-one who travelled to work every day. She had taken Henderson into her grandfather's home but it wasn't working out. He never had any money to contribute and he had smashed up her car. She also found texts from other women on his phone. He needed a little money, enough to show her he was serious.

Few opportunities presented themselves. He fell back into the old routine of lurking around Pennine Vehicle Services and smoking weed with Chach. It was on one of these days that a jailhouse acquaintance of both men turned up at the lot. This man had close links with the PVS crowd and with Bolton's Castle Street Gang. The Castle Street outfit had been implicated by informants, locals and courtroom testimony in high-level drug dealing, but the leadership had managed to stay out of the courts. They were a close-knit gang with many members related to each other. Most of them lived and had family in the BL2 postcode area. The acquaintance said shots had been fired at an address linked to the Castle Street crew. He wanted Henderson to do something about it, namely striking back at a shop run by some brothers who Castle Street blamed. These men were linked to another Bolton faction from the Gilnow Road area. 'He wanted me to go and fire shots into a shop, either hit the shutter outside or go inside and shoot in the shop,' Henderson later testified. 'The shop was the target. It wasn't the original plan that anybody should get hurt.'

Chach was keen for Henderson to do the job, which would strengthen links between the PVS clique and the Castle Street crew. And Henderson needed money, as he owed Carla for the smashed up car, which Chach had arranged to be repaired. 'He was saying it cost more than it's supposed to have cost and he charged Carla two grand', he later recalled. 'She had to loan to pay for her car, because they were saying they would get the car and rent it out. It was her personal car and people who rented from that place were people selling drugs and that, and she didn't want her car being rented by people selling drugs. She had to borrow two grand from her boss, I had to pay her back. That caused complications and we had no money.'

THE SQUARE, A tiny shopping parade in the heart of Glodwick, is busy in the summer. On a warm July night, Henderson was there with Chach, Gogo, Manny, and a number of others from the circle. A couple of young men came down and exchanged Islamic greetings with everyone, except Henderson. Chach took umbrage at his friend being snubbed.

'If you greet me, you greet him,' he said. 'He's a Muslim. You should greet him.'

'We didn't know, you dick,' said one of the lads.

'Who are you calling a dick?'

'You, you dick.'

Chach punched the lad in the face and a fight erupted. Henderson jumped into the fray and found himself surrounded by the loudmouth's cousins. When he broke free, Chach was on the floor being kicked in the head, while Gogo stood by and watched. Henderson chased off the kicker and left the scene with Chach. The scuffle, though it had nothing to do with the shooting about to take place, would become inextricably linked with it. As it was, the shooting at the shop was supposed to take place that night, but Chach told Henderson it was off because there were too many police about.

The day after was a Saturday. Henderson spent all day in the house when Chach rang him out of the blue to say he would be there in ten minutes.

'The job's on, get some clothes,' he said.

Chach had already given Henderson a tracksuit to wear for the 'job'. When Chach arrived, he had it on over his own clothes. They set off for Pennine Vehicle Services in Chach's black Mercedes. There, Chach busied himself with final preparations while Henderson waited in the car. From there they went to a nearby Esso garage, where the Mazda that was to be used in the job was waiting, along with the driver, Ryan 'T' Manning.

Manning, a young mixed race lad, had been messing with the wrong crowd in Longsight and had moved to Wigan for a new start. He held down a job as a concierge at the Bauhaus Apartments on Little John Street, at the heart of Manchester's legal district, while running a little cannabis hustle on the side. It was through his drug contacts that he became mixed up in the Bolton underworld. Manning would later boast that he was the Castle Street gang's star signing: the Pakistani gangs liked to have a black guy on the firm to intimidate their rivals, and were often not interested in engaging in violence – a distraction from the main business of making money – themselves.

The shop targeted was on the Brookhouse council estate in Salford. Unusually for a small, family-run off-licence, it had once boasted a 'head of security': none other than Colin Joyce, the formidable Gooch gang enforcer and Muslim convert who had led a murderous campaign against the Longsight Crew. Manning did not have Joyce's underworld pedigree but he was no stranger to the thug life. His father, George Lynch, had been shot dead in Longsight in 2001. Manning was usually tasked with destroying 'hot' cars by his Castle Street paymasters, but had been willing to carry out the shooting at the shop himself. He justified it by telling himself he would only fire at the shutters. But at the last minute, the plan changed. The less than discreet lime green Maserati designated for the job vanished and he was told that 'another black kid' would be the triggerman. It was Simeon Henderson.

The men set off for Wall Street, where Chach waited for the gun to arrive. They munched samosas and drank pop, courtesy of Chach, in the forty-five minutes until a pal arrived with the weapon, concealed in a white cardboard bag with string handles. It was a Czech-made Parabellum machine gun with a folding shoulder stack, and weighed around five kilos. It could fire at a rate of 600 rounds a minute, with just the tiniest amount of pressure on the trigger switching it between single shot mode and fully automatic. Machine guns being scarce these days in the criminal underworld, it could fetch anything up to £10,000.

Manning's job was to drive Henderson to the scene in a Mazda bought for the task, then leave him there and destroy the car. Someone else would collect Henderson, and Chach started ringing around to find a getaway driver. The fixer who had first suggested the attack on Castle Street's behalf suggested that Henderson get a taxi back from the shooting. Henderson was unhappy. 'I wanted fast transport to get away,' he said. 'Plus I didn't want a taxi driver knowing what I was doing … There was some conversation about calling it off, but I was desperate. I wanted to get it out of the way. I wanted to pay my rent.'

Henderson and Chach had been surprised to learn from Manning that the shop was in Salford, and not Bolton as they had believed. The fixer, who was doing his best to reassure Henderson that a trustworthy cabbie could be found, then dropped another bombshell. He now wanted 'the guy' shot in the legs. Chach snatched the phone off Henderson and told him, 'If you want him shot in the legs it's gonna be more change.'

Henderson took the phone off Chach and told the fixer, 'I want more change.'

'I'll give you more change,' said the fixer.

It was settled: Henderson was to go into the shop and lick off some shots. The instructions were, 'If it's an old man, leave him alone. If it's a young man, put something in his legs.'

Henderson was happy. 'I wouldn't shoot an old man anyway,' he said.

The conspirators moved on to a garage owned by an associate to check out the gun. Chach wanted to take out some bullets 'for later on', according to Henderson. Then Henderson and Manning set off down the M60 motorway to Brookhouse Wines, in Eccles. Manning gave Henderson some advice. 'If you squeeze on the trigger once, it shoots once. If you keep your finger on it will keep shooting until you release your finger.'

Manning knew that because he had tested the weapon. Just a few nights before, he had fired it into the air at Queen's Park, a recreation ground in the territory of their rivals, in a Castle Street show of strength. Now Henderson was about to find out first-hand what the gun was capable of.

Manning pulled up outside the shop and Henderson got out with the bag. It was just before 8.50 p.m. His adrenaline was pumping. His face was hidden by a bandana beneath his black hoodie. In his gloved hands was the sub-machine gun, designed for maximum kill at close quarters on the battlefield, capable of unleashing six bullets in less than a second.

He stuck his head in the doorway and saw a young guy behind the counter. According to his own account, Henderson had one thought in his mind: hit him once, in the legs, and get off. 'I seen the guy, so I cocked and aimed the gun and pointed at the lowest part of his body. I have pointed the gun as far down as I could because the counter was quite high. When I pressed the trigger it didn't go off. It went forward and one bullet jumped out. I re-cocked it, squeezed it a bit, emphasised. Make sure the gun went off, squeezed it harder. It just went crazy. It went off, it shot the whole clip out, I thought. I froze for a second. I thought I'd killed him.'

A customer dove to the floor. CCTV captured Henderson, hooded, in black, pointing the gun, wrapped in its white bag, before seeming, in the time-lapsed footage, to dash back out again as the victim crumpled to his death, two bullets in his right upper arm, blistered by burn marks, another in his chest. That victim, Nasar Hussain, had come to Greater Manchester for a new start in life. Frustrated by his failure to get in the police force in his native Pakistan, the unmarried thirty-year-old had decided to try his luck in Britain. His father, farm supervisor Mohammed Riaz, did not want his eldest son to go, but seeing how determined he was, he gave his blessing and agreed to pay the people smugglers who arranged his illegal passage.

Eccles, where Nasar found work and accommodation, could not have been more different from his small village on the rural outskirts of Islamabad. But in a phone conversation, Nasar, who adopted the surname Shazad, told his dad that he was happy where he was working and that his bosses 'looked after him well'.

Just a month after that conversation, he was dead, riddled with bullets as he neared the end of his eight-hour shift. The real targets of the shooting, brothers Rafaqat, Shafaqat and Asif Khan, who the Castle Street faction perceived as rivals linked to their Gilnow Road enemies, escaped unhurt.

Asif Khan, the owner of the shop, had been reading a newspaper on his break at the time of the attack, otherwise he would have been behind the till where Nasar Hussain was stood. 'I'm very sure that I was the intended target,' he told police the following day. 'I heard the front door open. I didn't look or think anything of it, as people always come in the shop. Almost as soon as the door opened, I heard a burst of noise that sounded like somebody had let off fireworks in the shop. I could see smoke as well. The burst lasted six, seven seconds. I looked across at Nasar, who was a couple of feet away to my right. He was clutching his chest with both hands. I could see a patch of blood on his tee-shirt.' Khan ducked down behind the counter. He could hear Hussain moaning and saw him slump backwards to the floor.

Khan and another shop worker called Ali crept into the storeroom and hid until they were sure the gunman had gone. When they emerged, Hussain was on the floor behind the counter with his head propped on some boxes. 'I seen a number of patches of blood on the right hand side of his body,' said Khan. 'His eyes were beginning to roll into the back of his head.'

Khan confirmed to police that there had been 'quite a lot of trouble recently in Bolton with other shootings', including one the previous Monday close to his home. 'I think this is all linked to three males who I've heard from other people are after causing harm to my brothers and myself as well as friends of ours,' he said. 'These males are drug dealers in the Bolton area', he said, identifying members of the Castle Street crew's leadership. 'I have given evidence against these males in the past and my other brother, Rafaqat Khan, has served time in prison for a large-scale fight involving these males. There's definite bad blood going back a number of years. I can think of no other reason for somebody to come into the shop and fire a gun. I have heard these males have gone on holiday and are out of the country.'

STRAIGHT AFTER THE shooting, Henderson was met by cab driver Akmal Afzal, general ferryman for the Castle Street crew. Henderson then realised that he didn't know where he was supposed to go and neither did the driver. 'I started to panic. I wanted to get out of the area and out of the car. I just kept telling him to drive fast.'

The cabbie took a phone call at the wheel and headed to Wall Street, Oldham. A police helicopter circled above. On the back seat, a sweating Henderson wriggled out of his clothes. He discarded his gloves and bandana, peeled off the contaminated tracksuit and wrapped it around the machine gun. When they got to Wall Street, a police armed response unit was waiting outside Pennine Vehicle Services. Henderson began to think he had been set up. He told the cabbie to keep driving.

They finished up at a dead end. Henderson got out of the car. The police helicopter was still in the sky and, fearing he would get shot by police marksmen, he left the murder weapon on the backseat and ran into a Matalan store, then out onto some train tracks, which he crossed. He climbed a high wall and ducked behind trees on a grass bank. 'I was running through the trees and looking at the helicopter. I ended up coming out onto a road that I recognised. I'm in different clothing now so I'm trying to look like a normal person, trying not to look like I'm panicking. I'm walking down towards the bridge as the helicopter is over, the bridge is covering me. I've walked underneath the bridge towards the town centre.'

In town, he walked to a taxi rank and ordered a cab home. When he got there, there was an unforeseen obstacle. Chantel, a friend of Carla's, had come to see her in a taxi, but she had no money to pay him. The cabbie was getting agitated and threatening to call police, the last thing Henderson needed.

'I've been set up,' Henderson told Chach on the phone. 'And I need you to pay for a taxi.' Chach arrived ten minutes later and dealt with the irate cabbie.

Carla, a petite, blackhaired girl, would later recall how Henderson had wanted her to go out that night. She refused. She was spending the night with Chantel, and anyway was annoyed he wanted to go raving while she was working to pay for the car that he had crashed. He was not insistent, and she didn't think he appeared any different than normal, except he was wearing jeans that were so tight that she and Chantel had a laugh about it. He certainly didn't mention that he had shot someone. 'We wasn't communicating on the best terms because of what happened,' she said. 'I wasn't paying as much attention to him as normally I would have done, and once Chantel was there I didn't stay in the same room with him.'

While the two women were together, Henderson bagged up his clothes, showered and changed. Chach's number flashed up on Carla's phone and he went out to take the call. Then he left, setting off for a friend's garage. 'I've been set up', he repeated on the way there. Chach showed little reaction until Henderson said, 'I think I killed him.' Straight away, the older man got on the phone. 'Yo, someone's dead, yo,' he said. Henderson wondered what he was bragging for. At the garage, they picked up the keys to a safehouse where they watched TV and chilled out. 'I want some weed to smoke, to relax me, and some food,' Henderson told his friend. Chach went out and got some food but forgot to bring the skunk weed. He left Henderson alone in the house, arranging for someone to drop off a phone for him so they could stay in contact.

'I stayed there overnight. I couldn't get hold of Chach the whole night. I thought something was wrong. I tried to phone him all night and all morning. I didn't feel safe in the house. So I thought, you know what, I'm not staying here. I phoned my cousin and said, "Come and pick me up." '

Armed police had turned up at Henderson's home minutes after he fled. Unbeknown to them, the gunman was now on his way to a hideout in Leeds, after being picked up in a car. Greater Manchester Police dedicated a team of detectives to tracking him down while the net closed in on the conspirators. GMP had actually been seconds away from averting the killing after receiving information from the Serious Organised Crime Agency. Unfortunately, they were told that the job afoot was a robbery and were given the wrong location. By the time an armed response unit got there, Hussain was dying. Police have never disclosed how they knew to go to PVS in the moments after the killing, although rumours abounded that the premises had been bugged.

BY JULY 6, MOHAMMED 'Chach' Hafiz had been arrested and interviewed. He admitted that he knew Henderson and had been in contact with him, but denied any involvement in the killing. The murder weapon had also been found, spotted by a passer-by beneath a car in Hinton Street, Oldham. It had been dumped there by Akmal Afzal in the moments after he dropped off Henderson, whose discarded tracksuit it was wrapped in. The gun was linked to the murder by spent cartridges at the scene, while a tiny speck of blood on the trigger linked it to Ryan Manning, who had tested it out in Bolton's Queen's Park. Phone evidence would later reveal the journey Manning took after dropping Henderson off around the corner from the murder scene. Manning was back in Wigan within twenty minutes, burning out the Mazda a short distance from his own home. He then whizzed back to town and was behind the counter in the foyer of Manchester's Bauhaus Apartments, just a few minutes late for his night shift.

Chach was also working hard to find Henderson, since both men had stopped using their previous phones. He contacted a number of Henderson's associates but for days no-one would deal with him because Henderson was now convinced he had been set up to take the rap for the murder and suspected Chach might be in on it. Henderson's fears were fuelled by newspaper reports he read on the internet. He knew the gun had been found, and was troubled to learn that the formidable Colin Joyce had been linked to the shop he had shot up.

In the end, Henderson went to see an associate in Birmingham, who brokered a meeting between him and Chach. Chach arrived wearing a bulletproof vest, with his eight-year-old son in tow. Henderson thought the boy was giving him the evil eye, convinced the nasty man wanted to hurt daddy. Chach gave him £200 to tide him over, and some surprising advice.

'Hand yourself in,' he said. 'I reckon you can beat this case.'

'How come they [armed police] came to my house straight away?' asked Henderson. 'I've been set up. I'm not going to hand myself in if I'm wanted for a murder, no-one does.'

Chach then offered him a hiding place in the Beeston area of Leeds, promising he would later move him to another safehouse in Milton Keynes, then out of the country. Henderson agreed because he had no rent money and no longer felt safe where he was. Chach promised that once Henderson had been moved to a safe location down south he would contact Carla. But after leaving him at a new Leeds house, Chach failed to return the next day with the essentials that he had been promised. This was the final straw for the gunman on the run.

'I thought he was taking me for an idiot. I was there the whole day; no change of clothes, no food, no nothing. He bought me some weed and that's about it.' Henderson returned to the house he had just left. He was in the kitchen when he heard police kicking the door in. He ran to the back, vaulted the balcony and hurled his phone into the distance. His flight came to a swift end when a firearms squad closed in. Surrounded by men with guns, Henderson was forced to surrender. He was arrested and soon charged with murder.

CAB DRIVER AKMAL Afzal came to the attention of detectives in a different way. Twenty-four hours after the murder, he called the incident room. He did not give his name but said he had seen on the news that there had been a murder in Eccles and thought he might have some useful information. He said that he was used to driving Asians from the Castle Street area about, and that on the night of the murder he had received a phone call from a man he often drove around. The man had asked him to get to Eccles roundabout, but when he got to the pick-up point this man was not there. Instead, a lad who he knew as Ryan was at the scene, at the wheel of the Mazda.

He gave a detailed description of 'Ryan', right down to the tattoo he had commemorating his late father. And he went further, saying how Ryan had a passenger he didn't like the look of, a 'big black male' in a hoodie. He claimed to have driven off without this man. Afzal's account implicated Manning and Henderson while minimising his own role. At that stage, police did not know quite how involved he had been.

Afzal said he was very frightened but agreed he would meet an officer. A meeting was arranged the following day with DC Chris Barnes, of the Xcalibre task force. It will probably never be known whether Afzal came forward because of a genuine attack of conscience or whether he had been ordered to come forward by forces in the Castle Street gang, who were looking to shift the blame to the bungling Henderson, his Oldham patrons, or even the outfit's own leader.

On July 6, an extremely nervous Afzal met DC Barnes at the Premier Travel Inn at the Trafford Centre and revealed more key details. He now elaborated that the man in the hoodie at the scene of the pick-up had been carrying something wrapped in tracksuit bottoms. And it seemed that the man who had called and asked him to go to Eccles Island was the leader of the Castle Street gang. It was noted that Afzal actually quaked and looked at the floor when this man's name was mentioned. He also implicated an influential member of the Asian underworld in Oldham, saying that if he were to go to court he would need special measures to protect his identity.

For a while it seemed as if Afzal might be the prosecution's star turn. The day after the meeting at the Trafford Centre he was already offering police a theory for the shooting. 'The owner of the shop had arranged for his cousins in France to come over and shoot the leader of the Castle Street gang,' he told detectives. 'He found out and organised the shooting and the wrong man was shot.' The theory was wrong in the detail – no evidence was found of any gunmen from across the Channel – but the police would be left in little doubt that the murder was the unfortunate result of a feud between the Castle Street gang and the owners of the shop, with the Oldham connection supplying the hitman and Nasar Hussain being tragically caught in the crossfire.

Afzal had been arrested at an early stage, but in light of what he had told police they decided not to charge him and instead treat him as a witness. In each conversation, more details emerged. By the time he came to make a formal statement, he said he had been offered a £50 fee for the pick-up in Salford, was naming the 'big black man' as Simeon, and was admitting driving him to Oldham at his bidding. There, they had seen two police cars, so Simeon had fled the vehicle without paying the fare, carrying with him an item wrapped in black material, claimed Afzal. Later that evening, he heard from other taxi drivers about a shooting in Salford and at that point thought that Simeon may have been involved and that the mystery item may have been a gun. He hadn't mentioned Simeon's name before, he claimed, because he was afraid of what might happen if people thought he was a grass. Afzal was painting a picture of himself as an innocent cabbie who got sucked into being a murderer's getaway driver.

About three weeks after the murder Afzal attended an identity parade at Ashton under Lyne police station and pointed out Simeon Henderson. 'I seen him come out of a blue Mazda with a gun,' he said.

Until then, Henderson had giving the standard 'no comment' answer to detectives. He now changed his solicitor and
began to open up, knowing that he had to look after number
one. The shooting hadn't even been his squabble, but he was
being lined up to take the fall. Chach had been no use when he
was on the run, and had even told him to hand himself in. The
driver they had got him had not only dumped the gun,
wrapped as it was in his trackies with telltale DNA all over
them, but he had also tied him in with the getaway car and
placed him a few feet from the scene. It seemed like the Asians
weren't his Muslim brothers after all. They had used him as
their triggerman and then dashed him aside.

'I kept silent until the taxi driver picked me out at the ID
parade, then I knew, there's something fishy going on here', he
later said. 'I had agreement with a group of people, and the
taxi driver's picking me out in an ID parade? Then there's
something going on, isn't there? You're part of a crime and
you're the driver of the car and you have got knowledge of
shooting, why would you put the gun under the car wrapped
in clothing? It's obvious: to plant evidence, isn't it? These
people here, they have put me to go to this job and then set me
up to get caught at the end of it. They have got rid of me so
they don't have to pay me, get me out of the way, whatever'.

With these thoughts running through his mind Henderson
gave detectives his first account of the moment he shot dead
an innocent man.

'I have gone to the shop, opened the door. I had the gun
pointed. I seen some customer in front of me so I turned and
squeezed the trigger. At first nothing happened, I have had to
cock it back again. Then I'm thinking, shit, is this thing going
to go off, so I squeezed it again, then when I've squeezed it, it's
just gone mad, brrrrrr, all over the place, you get me? Fucking
hell, I think I've killed him, twenty-five or fifteen [shots] in
him. I thought, he can't live through that, he must be dead. I
was kind of shocked.'

Henderson decided to strike a deal with police and prosecutors while holding out for a lesser manslaughter charge.
Letters written by him to family and to fellow remand pris-
oner Ryan Manning revealed his anger, desperation and deep
suspicion of the three people who had put him up to it:
Chach, the Asian fixer who had come to him with the job in
the first place, and a senior member of the Pennine Vehicle
Services clique who wanted to curry favour with Castle Street.
All three men had been arrested and released without charge
at that stage.

Henderson had met Ryan Manning, who had been arrested
near his home on July 8, on a wing at Strangeways Prison
before being transferred to Wakefield. The two men had
things in common – they were both outsiders, black men who
could be easily frozen out of the close-knit Asian underworld
of Greater Manchester's Pennine towns. Both had been implicated and identified by taxi driver Akmal Afzal, and both
faced murder charges, with compelling forensic evidence to
tie them in.

In September 2009, after the two men had appeared in
court for preliminary hearings, Henderson penned a letter to
Manning in a bid to forge an alliance.

'The po-po [police] heard me say to you when I was in
court that I weren't giving evidence against you and they said
if I don't tell them all I breach contract but I only know Ryan
Manning since we met in Strangeways,' he wrote. 'I don't
recognise you as the driver of the Mazda. Them man are dirty
horrible bastards. I ain't prepared to lie and put someone
innocent in jail so they got their wires crossed. All I know is
that certain people wanted to get rid of certain people, for
what reason I don't know.'

By now he believed that the Asians had recruited him to
carry out the shooting before tipping off police. Their plan,
he thought, had been for him to be shot dead while fleeing the

armed response unit, machine gun in hand. Except the wrong man had been shot and the hitman had escaped unhurt.

In his next letter to Manning, he wrote, 'Things happened that words can't explain, people can't judge unless they have been in the position. I'm going to be named a grass if I go QE, even though I was set up. I'm going to do thirty years, maybe never get out again, that's not good. My girl's gone, though she said she'll visit. They have got her as a witness ... yeah those man done me like this ... but then such is life. Depending on what benefits me is depending on what I do. I may even bite the bullet, this a road ting and the roads are not what they seem. I'm not going to put my life in danger and do all that for nothing.'

By the end of July, Mohammed 'Chach' Hafiz had been picked up on a separate allegation of kidnap and blackmail after getting involved in a violent dispute between feuding businessmen in Birmingham. He was remanded to Winson Green Prison. Behind bars, where Henderson had plenty of friends, the power balance shifted. Henderson had a stark message for him: 'I'm going to get a long time in jail, so you owe me money.' The price of his woes and his silence was £1 million.

A senior member of Birmingham's Burger Bar Boys gang was among Henderson's allies in the joint. Chach had been introduced to the man, who had been locked up for firearms offences, on an earlier occasion at PVS.

'He was pretty influential in Birmingham and on the wing he had a lot of lads around him,' Chach recalled. 'He must have told the other lads this guy's got my cousin in trouble or whatever, there was a lot of bad vibes on the wing. Most of the time I refused to go on association. I just came out for my shower, that's it.'

The Burger Bar Boy approached Chach directly and told him that he needed to contact Subbs, one of Henderson's boys outside in the free world, about how he could help him.

Chach wasn't keen. He stalled for time, hoping that either he or the Burger Bar Boy would be shipped out of the prison. The Burger Bar Boy knew he was being fobbed off.

'If you don't fucking sort it you're gonna end up getting hurt,' he threatened.

He summoned Chach to his cell and told him to 'ring Subbs now, while I'm here'. Chach had no choice but to call Subbs on the Burger Bar Boy's contraband mobile. The message from Subbs was blunt, 'You need to look after Simeon. We have got you now, you're in our town, our neighbourhood, our prison. We don't care what you say, we want ten thousand pounds. If you don't get the money sorted soon, you're gonna end up done in.'

Chach still wasn't keen, even though the price of Simeon's woes seemed to have dropped to a more realistic level. The threats continued for over a fortnight. Chach was also going through bail proceedings and the surety wanted for his release was £175,000. He had pals who were putting up their houses to raise the cash but they were struggling to reach the target. 'I'm due out in two weeks, I'll sort it when I get out,' he lied. As it turned out, Chach's bail was refused. But the pressure eased when the Burger Bar Boy copped a twelve-year sentence and was moved to another jail.

Henderson was still determined to exact revenge. He drew maps and directions to the homes of Chach and two other members of the PVS clique in a letter addressed to 'Fam', having decided the time had come to 'take it to the street'. In that letter he said, 'Need to catch the man and get the ps [papers, meaning cash] because it's not a cheap ride dread, regardless.' He later explained what he meant by this in court, saying, 'I have done a lot of things for them and they have not paid me money. They have taken the mickey. I put my life on the line and I got nothing back.'

Almost two months to the day that Nasar Hussain was killed, Amran Khan, Gogo's brother, was shot dead. His killing was connected to an internal dispute: a PVS clerk, Jordan Francis, and his twin brother, Brett, were responsible (see Chapter 15). A bug recording prisoners' phone calls reveals Henderson's thoughts on the matter. He could be heard laughing out loud, saying, 'It was my man, it was Jordan and his brother, weren't it? Smoked him dead, Jordan and his brother Brett. They smoked him … they just had enough.'

A different side to Henderson's personality emerged in the letters he wrote to Carla, where he poured out his heart and apologised for the life he had exposed her to. The letters also revealed that he had made up his mind about how to get revenge. He would turn supergrass. 'I have been speaking to my Queen's Counsel barrister', he wrote, 'and he said I could get my sentence halved to sixteen years, depending on what I say. If I can give them enough to get eight years I'd be more than grateful, only Allah can help me.'

MEANWHILE, POLICE IN Bolton had launched an operation to try to ease tensions between Castle Street and the Gilnow Road faction associated with the owners of the shop, amid concerns of a revenge attack and intelligence that Castle Street's leader was a marked man. The tensions did ease, but police knew that it was optimistic to think they would go away for good. Unsurprisingly, Henderson never received the £1 million nor even the £10,000 he demanded. In November 2009, he entered a not guilty plea to murder, apparently looking for some kind of loophole which would bring down the charge. 'I followed my solicitor's advice,' he later said. 'He said he was a top-notch whatnot.'

By the end of January 2010, he had changed his plea to guilty on the basis that he had only intended to shoot the victim in the legs. He asked his solicitor to indicate to police he was willing to help with the prosecution, and signed a 'supergrass' agreement under the Serious Organised Crime and Police Act soon afterwards. This triggered an exhaustive process of 'scoping' interviews, which assessed exactly what he knew, and debriefing interviews, in which he was required to tell all about his life of crime so that there were no nasty surprises at court.

The interviews traced his path from troubled kid to violent outlaw. He had begun smoking cannabis at ten years old, at thirteen he had been kicked out by his single mother. That same year, he earned his first serious conviction, for actual bodily harm, after punching a schoolteacher in the face. He ended up in a secure unit at Newton Aycliffe, the first of many stints in the system. Years later, bouncing between adult prisons, he would often bump into old faces he had known from his institutionalised boyhood, part of a network of criminals across the country who had apprenticed in the young offenders' system before ending up in jail. In 1996, he burgled his mother's home, stealing items that belonged to a boyfriend he had never got on with. According to him, he was bailed to the home of Huddersfield face Michael Francois, where a new phase in his criminal career began.

'Whilst I was there, he made me do crimes to survive, I didn't get food or nothing,' Henderson claimed. He robbed a man who he claimed had been pointed out to him by Michael Francois as having lots of money, coshing him on a stairway. Then he started turning over businesses as well, apparently under pressure from another prominent member of the Fartown crew. 'I was under pressure because I owed him money and I was having a kid at the same time,' he would later explain.

He remembered the details of that first Post Office robbery quite precisely. He smashed the glass screen with a brick, then hit it with a hammer, then pulled a knife on a female member of staff. A few days later, he fled the scene of a similar robbery empty-handed after attacking a postmaster. After doing time, he turned his hand to selling crack cocaine, heroin and cannabis in Huddersfield. He would do 'crack runs' to London, sourcing cheaper product to maximise profits. Handy with his fists, he beat up a female friend's boyfriend after he laid his hands on her. Another man he battered into a coma.

'I didn't mean to and I didn't know he was going to go into a coma. He pulled a knife on me, so what do you expect me to do? He was alright when I left him.'

He was charged with a drive-by shooting on a member of a rival outfit, although no conviction followed, and he was there when Michael Francois was shot dead. A lifetime of constant cannabis smoking had left him burnt out with 'memory loss, depression, psychosis. Sometimes I didn't care what day it was. I smoke it to feel better, I thought that it made me better but it made it worse.'

By 2004, when he was jailed for robbery, he felt safer in prison than out. 'It's lonely place, but I'm used to it,' he reasoned.

By the time of his release in 2006 he was flirting with Islam, but continued his life of crime, justifying it to himself by targeting other villains. He robbed Yorkshire-based yardies of tens of thousands of pounds.

'It was drug money, not money someone had to work hard for,' he explained. 'We're not dealing with people who are law-abiding citizens.'

Henderson's only experience of legit work was as a machine operative in a Yorkshire pudding factory. Money was easy come, easy go in his world. Within weeks of a big score he would be broke again, to the delight of envious criminal peers.

'Basically being extravagant, being a show-off. People don't like that do they?'

Ripping off drug dealers was something of a specialty. He once made £40,000 by burgling a fellow villain. Later, whilst living in Oldham, a girl 'gave' him £15,000 she had been given to look after by another criminal; it was frittered away within weeks on trinkets and flashy hire cars. On another occasion, Chach was tipped off by a landlord in Leeds that his tenants – 'Chinese geezers' – were running a cannabis farm with five rooms of thickly budded plants for the taking. Chach brought down a van for the job. There was talk of camping outside all night to wait for the 'Triads' to come back and then demanding money and seizing their plants. In the end, they broke in and settled for the weed.

Much of what Henderson talked about was news to the police. They had not known that he was behind the shootings of Farid and Immy, nor that he had set fire to a house in Cheadle, apparently because the owner had upset a pair of brothers, said to be the overlords of Greater Manchester's Asian underworld, whose permission had to be sought before any serious crime in case it 'brought too much heat on the circle'. Henderson also told police some of his wilder theories about being set up, developed in the long hours on lockdown. He now reckoned his downfall had been cooked up by Pennine Vehicle Services owner Gulfan 'Gogo' Khan, who wanted him out of the way because being Chach's enforcer made him a danger. He believed it stemmed back to the scuffle in the Square at Glodwick the night before the murder. He said he had called Gogo on his failure to back up Chach in the skirmish, telling him there was 'going to be a revolution' in Oldham.

'Gogo lost his footing after he showed his true colours,' claimed Henderson. 'Chach was saying, "I don't feel I can get any support from you. There's no point me being up here, I might as well come back and get the guns, get the ballies, come back and rob everybody." That's what Chach was saying to everybody.'

'In this circle, these guys call a meeting, say everything's OK, [then] when everyone's back's turned they start shooting each other and robbing each other. From that little bit of mistrust, everybody is on a snakebite. I'm Chach's bredrin, so anybody smoke anybody, it's me who do the job. I was Chach's best friend, I would have done anything for Chach. After I blew [Gogo] up, his attitude changed towards me, all of a sudden there's this job … Gogo didn't like the way Chach took to me. That caused jealousy. Gogo didn't want to mess with me, because I was a black guy.

'They give me a machine gun knowing it would go out of control. The police was phoned before I got there to tell them I was at the shop. When I left the scene, police were waiting for me. That was all set because of what I said about Gogo and that was all to get rid because I said there's going to be like a revolution in Oldham.'

While he believed Gogo had wanted him out of the way because of his friendship with Chach, he also believed that Chach wanted to 'smoke' him in the aftermath of the murder, as 'I'm the only one who can finger him'. These theories, although aired in court, have never been proved, and sources close to the PVS clique dismiss them as the paranoid fantasies of a weed-addicted jailbird with too much time on his hands.

'There was no plot to take out Simmo,' an associate told this author. 'The whole thing was nothing to do with Glodwick really. They were doing a favour for Bolton. They got involved in someone else's war and the whole thing got fucked up and went wrong when the wrong man got shot.'

IN NOVEMBER 2010, a number of men went on trial at Manchester Crown Court for offences connected with the murder of Nasar Hussain. They included Ryan 'T' Manning, the stocky mixed race lad with a 'fade' hairstyle who had driven Henderson part-way from the scene, and Akmal 'Aki' Afzal, who had driven his taxi for the bulk of the escape. Shaggy-haired, bearded Afzal, who had given himself up to police before implicating others, had gone from hero to zero. He became a defendant at a late stage, after his final interviews, when it became clear he knew more about the crime than he was letting on. Henderson had stolen his spot as star witness, and dashed the idea of the cabbie as an innocent dupe in his own account. Mohammed 'Chach' Hafiz, the bald, rotund, bespectacled man seething in the dock, was the oldest at forty-three; the others were all in their twenties.

Henderson's appearance belied his outlaw lifestyle; he was softly spoken and well turned out in a black suit. He testified to his experience of Glodwick's emergent gangsters, the conflict he become embroiled in, and the crimes he had been recruited to carry out. He admitted that he had used guns four times before coming to Oldham. Only handguns, he said, his knowledge of machine guns coming from what he picked up on the street and the computer game *Call of Duty*. Far from being 'exhilarated' by the kill, he insisted he had been 'gutted'. When, however, it was put to him by Akmal's defence counsel, Joseph Stone QC, that he was 'a man who doesn't hesitate to pull the trigger when the money's right,' he answered, 'It depends if they deserve it, then I'll do it.' It was put to him that he was a 'cool customer under pressure, even with a gun pointed at your head.'

'I've had a lot of practice,' he answered.

It was put to him that when he had 'executed' Nasar Hussain, he had been high on 'good gear' – drugs.

'I was always on good gear,' he said.

Unlike other villains, conscious of the ramifications of the term 'dangerous' in the legal system, he willingly conceded he was no altar boy. 'I am dangerous, yeah. My actions were dangerous.'

He was challenged by each of the defendants' barristers about every aspect of his evidence. Stuart Denney QC, representing Hafiz, put it to Henderson that he was a dishonest witness who had falsely implicated his client in a bid to reduce his sentence. The silk presented a picture of a man who had graduated from 'scavenging money and cannabis' from Hafiz to trying to extort £1 million from him.

'I don't scavenge, that's not my style,' replied Henderson. He claimed that he had 'put a lot of money' into PVS and that Chach had 'ripped me off a lot of money for rentals'.

On the extortion bid, he said, 'I didn't think I was committing a crime. I was asking for what I was owed. I'm doing this because he's put me in a situation and left me to hang out to dry and I'm looking out for myself now, I have got no loyalty to that guy.'

Chach admitted that he had been with Henderson in the build-up to the shooting at Brookhouse Wines but claimed his former friend had 'never breathed a word' about the job to him. He had been arrested within hours of the murder and had given 500 pages and nine tapes worth of interviews yet somehow, despite all the talking, he had managed to remain vague about his movements on that night. Phone evidence presented a clearer picture. He could be placed in all the locations that Henderson referred to in his testimony where preparations were made for the job at hand.

In court, Chach claimed that he had parted company with Henderson after dropping him off on Ashton Road in Oldham. Phone evidence putting them together was mere coincidence, Chach said, they just frequented the same places. He did not deny that he was a criminal, but he made out that shootings were not his thing.

'I don't think Simeon would tell me he was going to do something like that because he knows I would try to talk him out of it,' he said. He was able to call evidence of a friendship between himself and Shafaqat Khan, one of the owners of Brookhouse Wines. Shafaqat, Shafiq for short, had frequented the same Leigh nightspots as Chach. Leigh, on the western outskirts of Greater Manchester, was a town where a handful of Muslim men from Oldham and Bolton would go to party away from the prying eyes of their community. A member of the doorstaff at Barbarella's, the main place where they went clubbing, testified to seeing Chach there with Shafaqat Khan, and Henderson himself had lent credence to this aspect of the defence, telling police in interviews that Chach had told him he had had 'good times' with the Bolton Khans, and that they were friends of his. If they were to be targeted, argued Chach, it would have been kept from him.

The fixer said to have approached Chach and Henderson with the Castle Street gang's problem was arrested but skipped bail, so the prosecution case that he was instrumental in organising the murder went unchallenged in court. In this context, any phone contact with this man looked incriminating. There was no phone contact between this man and Chach for the first four weeks of June, but after that the pair were in frequent contact. This was significant, because June 29 was the night that Ryan Manning fired the machine gun in Queen's Park in Bolton, in what was said to be a Castle Street show of strength. Between that day and July 1, the fixer and Chach were in contact no less than twenty times. Chach attempted to explain this by saying that the calls were all to do with a van he had rented to the man. Later conversations, according to Chach, concerned the argument with Gogo following the fight on the Square at Glodwick.

On July 4, the night Nasar Hussain was killed, there were twenty-four calls or attempted calls between Chach and the shadowy fixer. The prosecution case was that many of these concerned the final preparations, the frantic search for someone who would drive Henderson back from the shooting, and the aftermath. During this apparent search for a driver, Chach had rung a taxi driver no less than nine times in twelve minutes. Chach attempted to explain this by saying that the fixer had asked him to call him a cab and he had accidentally pressed the repeat button on his phone. The other calls – well, they were rants about Gogo, or banter about prostitutes. 'Them conversations on my phone are about bitches,' he testified. 'They've all have been to Thailand, fucking bitches there. I felt a little embarrassed to speak about bitches, there was a female officer interviewing.'

Chach insisted that not only he, but also the others in the dock with him, were innocent. 'If I thought for one moment any of those people was involved, I would not hesitate to say they are involved', he ventured magnanimously.

That night, after returning to jail, Chach was beaten up by another inmate.

Ryan Manning had been offered what he called 'a get out of jail free card' by Henderson. The gunman had promised in a prison letter that he would not implicate Manning, and when the trial began he remained true to his word. Henderson claimed he had not looked at the driver of the vehicle and did not recognise him as Manning. Despite this, Manning dramatically admitted being involved in the murder when his defence case began, admitting that the version he had previously put forward, a convoluted story about stolen cars and a mysterious light-skinned black man who was the 'real' driver, was a tissue of lies. He revealed for the first time that he had originally been tasked with the shooting by the leader of the Castle Street gang. Since his own father had been gunned down, he intended only to aim at the shutters, he said. But at the last minute the plan changed and events were taken out of his control; he was going to be the driver. Manning also admitted having fired the machine gun later used in the murder in Queen's Park, rather than spin a yarn about the speck of his blood that had been recovered on the trigger. And, in another blow to the defence of Akmal Afzal, he claimed that the gun had been supplied to him by the cabbie in a clandestine handover at Winter Hill, a Lancashire beauty spot.

Until then, things had been going quite well for 'Aki' Afzal. Taxi drivers can be difficult to convict in such cases and he was the least criminally hardened of those in the dock. But the picture that Ryan Manning presented was not of someone who simply had the misfortune to grow up and work as a driver in the same community as the Castle Street gang, but of someone who was active in their criminality. Police records seemed to back this up; Afzal had mentioned to an officer some years earlier that he was associated with the outfit. Manning said that in the fifteen times or so a month he frequented the Castle Street area, Aki was often around, that he was a 'ferry' for the gang, moving dodgy commodities about the town. Manning described himself as the 'new player' in the gang, comparing the shooting at Queen's Park to a run-out on the pitch.

For his part, Afzal alleged that Manning had threatened him part-way through the trial, saying, 'I'm going to have you taken out in the dispersal.'

'That's a lie', Manning told the jury. 'He's not going to the dispersals, he's got a nice cushy jail. He's on a protection wing at Strangeways.'

Afzal's barrister had put it to Simeon Henderson that he had been trying to implicate Afzal to get his own sentence slashed and get revenge for having been identified by him. Now, the QC had to fight off Manning as well. He accused him of also being motivated by revenge, but Manning said he would have been arrested anyway, even without Afzal coming forward.

When it was his turn to take the stand, Akmal told the jury that, far from being a gang member, he had worked hard all his life. He was the type of son who switched off his mobile phone in the house to avoid bothering his elderly parents, someone who strove to better himself.

'I have got friends in that area, I have grown up in that area, but I educated myself. I went to college. I went to university but I had to drop out, pay the bills, stuff like that,' he said.

Afzal told the court that he had been 'tricked' by Castle Street figures into going to Eccles, that Henderson had jumped into his vehicle straightaway and that, lumbered with a 'madman' in his cab, he had no choice but to do what he said. It was put to him that he must have known Henderson was involved in 'some criminal activity'. After all, by Afzal's own account, Henderson was agitated, panicking, looking out for helicopters, hiding his face from traffic cameras and demanding he switch off the sat-nav.

Surely, the prosecution said, he should have known he wasn't on his way to the pub or a party.

'While he was in my car, the only thing I was doing was driving,' replied Afzal. 'I had to drive, I couldn't say, "Scuse me, Mr Henderson, you have to get out of my car." '

Whatever the legal definition of duress, if Afzal was indeed an ordinary cabbie, it was easy to see why he had simply done as he was told. But there was evidence which suggested he wasn't just an ordinary cabbie – incriminating phone contact with a local Asian gangster on the course of the journey – and evidence that placed him in Oldham two days before the murder, at a time when calls were bouncing between him and the top tier of the conspiracy.

Afzal's claims of innocence were rejected by the jury, as were those of his co-defendants. The driver was found guilty of possessing a firearm and assisting an offender, and was jailed for seven years. Mohammed 'Chach' Hafiz was jailed for life for murder but cleared of conspiring with Henderson in the two shootings targeting Farid and Immy. Another man was convicted of the murder but cleared of firearm possession. His conviction was later overturned on appeal and, at the time of writing, he was facing retrial. Ryan Manning beat the murder rap but was found guilty of manslaughter and was jailed indeterminately for the public protection. Henderson copped the best deal by far. Had he not helped the prosecution, he would have been jailed for thirty-two years, but his testimony and guilty pleas, including to crimes which police might not otherwise have solved, bartered his time down to fifteen years. The judge told him he would 'forever be marked out' in the prison system as an informer.

A year before his son's killers were jailed, Mohammed Riaz, a tall dignified man, was flown over from Pakistan by Greater Manchester Police. He dropped tears at the place where his son died, collected his few belongings, and had the investigation explained to him.

'I still find it hard to accept Nasar is no more with us,' he said. 'He was a happy child, always respectful to everybody, and he will be in our hearts forever. Nasar left home to make a life for himself – we could not imagine that such an incident can take place in Britain, that an innocent and decent person who had no enemy and was working at the shop to make a living would be shot dead in this cruel and merciless manner.'

15

The Twins

THE INTRIGUING STORY behind the murder of Amran Khan emerged after a man turned up, dripping wet, on the doorstep of a house in Runcorn, Cheshire. He leant on a windowsill, retching, as pools gathered at his feet, his ripped trousers dragged from his waist by the weight of water. It was about 11 a.m. on a Sunday morning, and until he heard a knock at the door the householder had been playing computer games. At first he saw only the caller's reflection and assumed it was his cousin back from work, but then the brown eyes of a mixed race man peeped through the letterbox.

'Can I have an ambulance, please?'

The stranger, who spoke in a slow, faint, stuttering voice, said his brother was 'lying down across the road'. The man seemed in a 'bad way', thought the witness. He called an ambulance.

Paramedic Joanne Taylor arrived within minutes of being told that someone had jumped into the River Mersey. She found the man doubled over, clutching a cup of water. As she wrapped him in a blanket, he told her that somebody else was in the water, and so her colleague Paula Rimmer went off to look.

Inside the ambulance, Taylor asked the patient his name and how old he was.

'Jordan Francis, twenty-six,' he said.

'Have you taken anything?'

'Two boxes of paracetamol, last night.'

'Any alcohol?'

'No, but I have done this,' he said, pulling up his sleeves. Cuts, carved with a piece of a broken hotel cup, circled both of his wrists so deeply that you could see right down to the tendons. The paramedic laid him down on a stretcher and asked him why he had done what he had done.

'We killed somebody, on Friday night,' he said, as Mrs Taylor prepared dressings for his wounds.

'How long have you been in the water?'

'About ten minutes,' said Jordan.

'Who else is in the water?'

'My brother, his name is Brett. B, R, E, T, T. We're twins. Born fifteen minutes apart.'

After Mrs Taylor had dressed his wrists and put an oxygen mask on his face she asked him, 'Who have you killed?'

'Our friend … but it wasn't me.'

'Was it your brother, Brett?'

Jordan nodded his head. 'Yes, but we stick together. Do you think my mum will hate us for what we've done?'

THIRTY-SIX HOURS EARLIER, on the evening of September 18, someone had thrown a large stone onto the bonnet of a Peugeot parked in the driveway of a house in Glodwick, Oldham. When Amran 'Manny' Khan, the owner of the car, opened his front door to see what was going on, a gunman fired three times at him. One bullet hit him in the chest, the second lodged in the brickwork. As he turned, slumping to the floor, the third bullet entered his lower back.

His neighbours heard the bangs and went outside. They saw Shamilah, Amran's wife, screaming at him to stay alive for the sake of the kids. Mrs Begum, one of the neighbours, told her to calm down, while nearby the Khans' two children were crying. Amran was breathing as they moved him into the recovery position, blood trickling from a wound in the left side of his chest. Mrs Begum tried to stem the bleeding with her hand. He was still alive, trying to roll onto his back as his breathing grew calmer and shallower. Meanwhile, a getaway car accelerated away from the area.

Amran Khan died from his injuries. He was a man known among the denizens of Oldham's Asian underworld as the younger brother and business partner of Gulfan 'Gogo' Khan, boss of Pennine Vehicle Services, which was then at the centre of the investigation into the murder of shopworker Nasir Hussain.

MINUTES BEFORE MANNY'S shooting, identical twins Brett and Jordan Francis collected a car from the home of John Butterworth, who was on curfew after serving half of his sentence for possessing cocaine with intent to supply. Butterworth had been released early for good behaviour and, after becoming a father, had applied to university and resolved to go straight. His best mate, Lee Cameron, was spending the week with him after splitting up with his girlfriend. That day, Cameron had asked Butterworth if he could drop by the Francis twins' house. Butterworth remembered them from school and had been to their house once before. He agreed.

When he and Cameron got to the maisonette, the twins were talking to two men – a stocky white lad with a shaved head and a black guy – who within seconds had jumped into a BMW M3 and driven off. Cameron talked to the twins before asking Butterworth if he could give them a lift to pick up a car. On the way, they continued talking as Butterworth listened silently at the wheel. Their conversation, according to Butterworth, was highly indiscreet.

'There was a fallout over a drug debt, somewhere around the sum of twelve thousand pounds,' Butterworth would later testify. 'They were saying how there had been a fallout between Manny, Gogo, and Brett and Jordan over the sum of money. It was over two boxes of "nasty", which is heroin. They was then talking about how the debt wasn't too important but they do have to go and sort out Manny. They have to duff him up, that was the impression I was under, that they was going to give him a bit of a kicking. They were also talking about a lad who was going to provide them with weapons, which was a MAC-10, a nine-millimetre, and "pineapples", which is a slang term for grenades.'

They collected a BMW from a housing estate and it was agreed that Butterworth would allow it to be parked on his drive. It stayed there until about ten o'clock, when Butterworth saw the lights flash as it was unlocked and two men approached. One gave him a thumbs-up, the other got into the driver's side.

In text messages to his girlfriend, Jordan Francis complained that he was skint 'because of them fucking Pakis', and had to 'give everything he had'. She asked him why this was so when it wasn't his fault, and he texted her back saying that was the 'way it works'. Francis was well-versed in the grafters' code. He had done a two-and-a-half year stretch for possessing class A with intent after being caught with a dealer's stash of cocaine, scales and debtors' lists for drug-dealing and money lending. He admitted some part in the operation – spending the proceeds on designer clothes – but never named his business partner. He took a job at Pennine Vehicle Services in November 2007, around eighteen months after his release. Jordan didn't know the Khan brothers before he started work there, but he had heard of Gogo, whose nickname was well-known on the doors, in the gyms and on the street corners of the town, and who had connections across the country.

At first, Jordan, Gogo and Manny got on well. Affable and presentable, Jordan worked hard for his £150 a week, cleaning and hiring out the cars, and could be relied upon to run the business on his own. Jordan neatly fitted into the brothers' network of retainers, runners and gophers. He became a part of the family, Amran's kids called him 'uncle', and he was always welcome for tea. Jordan remained a trusted friend even after £1,000 went missing in a credit card transaction 'mix-up'. Gogo told him he would have to pay the money back, but then said no more about it. Jordan came to know Gogo as a man of his word. 'When the Khans say something, it gets done,' the twin would later testify.

According to that testimony, wholesale quantities of heroin and cannabis came in and out of the PVS premises. Jordan claimed that at times there would be 'boxes' – slang for kilos – of heroin in the office. Squabbles with other faces would end with Gogo shouting the odds, Jordan told a jury. 'They'd have arguments then they'd sort things out, then argue again. Gogo threatening them, you get shot, go through your door, that sort of thing.' Jordan claimed that he was asked, but refused, to hide a gun, and that shifting bags of cash was among his duties, along with cleaning and hiring the cars for the legitimate end of the business.

Shortly before the Christmas of 2008, when Jordan had been working there about a year, a wholesale amount of weed went missing from the premises. It was around the time Mohammed Farid was shot, and Gogo was away in Pakistan. The theft of the weed was an inside job and suspicion fell on Jordan, who was told it would have fetched £30,000 on the street.

'Look, it wasn't me,' he told Gogo.

Gogo said no more about it and Jordan carried on working there. He was even trusted, according to his own account, to go and pick up 'two boxes' of skunk with Manny a few months later.

Then one day Mohammed 'Chach' Hafiz, Gogo's business partner, warned Jordan that the drugs had been 'brought up again'. Soon after, Manny rang Jordan and told him he needed to pay the money back. Jordan didn't have it and so Manny suggested that he get him some 'work', by which he meant drugs that he could sell on at a profit. He wanted Jordan to arrange the supply as recompense for the stolen weed. It was an unusual request, since the Khans knew plenty of people who could supply them with drugs. Still, the tone of Manny's voice scared Jordan into taking action.

He turned to his brother Brett, who was better able to deal with 'unpleasant situations'. Within three or four days, Brett had brokered a deal between a Manchester-based drug dealer and Manny. The dealer was keen to enter the Oldham market and agreed that the heroin would be 'laid on' on credit. The twins, as middlemen, were the guarantors. It seemed the matter had been resolved.

A couple of days later, however, Brett got a phone call from Manny saying that there was a problem. It seemed the drugs had been collected but then were mysteriously 'intercepted' on their way to a hiding place. Manny suggested that the twins go and see Gogo, who was in hospital with a lung condition, and that he would 'sort it out'. In turn, Gogo promised that once he got out of hospital, everything would be OK – and by this the twins assumed the money for the missing drugs would be paid.

Jordan got a shock, then, when he spoke to Gogo on the phone and received a torrent of abuse. 'Remember when you watched me struggle when my stuff went missing?' asked Khan. 'How you left me in the shit when you took my weed? Fuck you, I'm going to leave you in the shit now and when I get out of hospital I'm going to rape you.' This, at least, was what Jordan later claimed he said.

In the aftermath of this, it was resolved by the twins and their suppliers that Manny Khan was going to pay for the drugs rip-off – with his life.

ON THE NIGHT of the murder, the Francis twins said good-bye to their parents and got a lift to the neighbourhood where the car was parked. A short while later, in Glodwick, a witness saw four men in hoodies and balaclavas in a car. They drove three times past Amran Khan's house before the final, fatal trip.

In the minutes after the shooting, a man at Hough Lane saw two men jogging along with their hoods up. 'I wouldn't go down there if I was you,' one of them turned to say as he ran past. A BMW with flames licking from it met the pedestrian twenty yards down the road.

Tracey Francis, the twins' mother, was shaken awake in bed. One of her boys stood in the doorway, the other leaned over her. They looked more frightened than she had ever seen them. They told her she had to get up and get out of the house.

'What's the matter?'

'Mum, you need to listen to us.'

She pulled on a dressing gown. The boys, their mother, Jordan's girlfriend Louise and the family dog then set off for their grandparents' house nearby. Seymour Francis, the twins' father, who had been at hospital to visit his dying mother, joined them later. The twins and Louise then left, only for Brett to return and sleep in the room with his parents and the dog.

In the morning, a police officer knocked on the grandparents' door and asked if anyone had a key for the Francis's house. Tracey Francis showed herself and told them that it was her house. When she came out into the street, police were everywhere, and she was told she would not be able to return home.

The twins, meanwhile, had slipped away with £3,200 in banknotes. They gave a taxi driver £100, intending to go to Liverpool, before deciding to stop at Runcorn. Just after 9 p.m., they booked a twin room at the Campanile Hotel. One of them asked at reception for a shop where he could buy paracetamol. When they found the nearest store closed, the twins caught a cab to a petrol station and bought two packets of Nurofen before heading back to their room.

They had decided to kill themselves.

A combination of vodka, skunk cannabis and the pills caused Brett to pass out first. The next thing he could recall, he was walking towards the railway with Jordan. They discussed throwing themselves under a train but changed their minds and headed for the river. They clambered over some gates and sat down on the bank before jumping into the freezing river. But after floating in the murky water, one of them changed his mind. 'Jordan decided he wanted to live,' Brett recalled. 'He climbed out and pulled me out.'

After Jordan had raised the alarm, Brett was found lying by the river. The ambulance crew squeezed through a gap in the railings and ran to his aid as he writhed, vomiting. His wrists were cut too. When he stopped retching, he looked up at the paramedic, Paula Rimmer, and whispered, 'You have nice eyes.' He claimed to have taken fifty paracetamol and to have been in the water for an hour.

Matt Whitaker, the other paramedic, asked him why he and his brother had tried to kill themselves.

'We've killed someone, but we didn't mean to,' Brett said. 'It's a long story.'

At Warrington hospital, the brothers were arrested on suspicion of murder.

THE POLICE WERE in the relatively unusual position of starting a murder investigation with two apparent confessions. But when they began interviewing the pair, on September 23, they got nowhere. For three days the twins answered none of the questions put to them. They kept silent when they were charged, and were locked up on remand.

The following February, when the pair entered their defence case statements, they denied any involvement in the killing of Amran Khan. Each of them said they were at home with their mother and Jordan's girlfriend at the time. Brett said he left at 11 p.m. that night because of a threat to his life, having returned a missed call to hear Gogo Khan screaming at him. 'You can do this to my brother?' he claimed Gogo had ranted. 'He's been shot twice, he's fucking dead. I have got a hundred grand on both of your heads, you're going to end up in a box, you son of a bitch.'

'Mum, I'm going back to prison,' John Butterworth said when the door was opened to the police. Upstairs in a holdall was a bag stuffed with pills, and he was still on licence from his drug dealing sentence. He was arrested on suspicion of possessing drugs and then on suspicion of murder, the car used by the twins having been parked on his drive. Butterworth wasn't too worried about the latter. 'I knew I was innocent,' he later said. 'When you know you're innocent you've got nothing to hide.' Besides, his electronic tag proved he had been in the house on the evening of the killing.

The drugs charge was another matter. 'I'll tell you what I know relating to that murder,' he said. 'I know who done it and why. Can you help me over the drugs? I've got a young baby and just started university.'

Butterworth, who said he had learnt of the murder in a text message the morning after, became a key prosecution witness when the trial began six months later. His evidence provided a motive and a statement of intent, and tied the twins to the burnt-out car, from which a bullet cartridge which matched the Luger murder weapon was recovered.

Butterworth refused to be cowed by the experienced defence QCs trying to tear holes in his story, looking right at the jury throughout his bullish testimony. Richard Marks, defending Jordan, challenged Butterworth over the likelihood of the twins having such a 'compromising conversation' in front of a relative stranger. Butterworth maintained that he had heard 'every word' and had been trusted to overhear the twins' careless chatter because of their mutual friend, Lee Cameron. 'Why they disclosed the information is unbeknown to me but they did disclose that information that day,' he said. It was put to Butterworth that he ought to have questioned why the twins were parking a £34,000 BMW on his mum's drive. 'I never knew the vehicle was going to be used for what it was used for. As far as I knew, they owned the vehicle and had nowhere to park it. No ifs or buts, that's what happened.'

'What you had told the police was a mix of what you had heard tell of, with gossip, rumour, street talk and tittle-tattle because you thought that was the best way in which you could get police to help you,' said Mr Marks.

'Wrong,' replied the witness.

There was at no time any conversation about any weapon, gun, grenade, or otherwise, insisted Mr Marks.

'Obviously you would say that because you're a defence lawyer,' said Butterworth. 'I know what I heard.'

Butterworth was given a conditional discharge for the drugs found at his house and was returned to custody to serve the rest of his existing sentence.

The evidence of the paramedics also frustrated the twins' defence cases. Joanne Taylor, the crew member who had attended to Jordan Francis, could not be shaken in her recollection that he had confessed to a killing. 'He said, 'We've killed somebody.' That's what I heard,' she asserted.

Both defendants had changed their story the day before the trial opened, now admitting that they had been involved in moving the car but maintaining that they knew nothing about the shooting until afterwards. It was, the prosecution claimed, an eleventh hour attempt to 'tailor' their defence to the evidence against them.

When his defence case opened, Jordan claimed that he had changed his statement because 'I was scared that I'd be getting other people involved, the people who was owed the money, that I'd be in danger from them as well as Gogo.' Jordan now claimed that following the phone call from Gogo, in which he made it clear that the 'nasty' would not be paid for, Brett was contacted by 'other people', namely, those who had supplied the drugs. Jordan claimed that he and his brother agreed to move this car about, believing it would be used to 'rough up' Manny. 'I thought that he was going to get a few punches and a few kicks,' he testified.

On the Friday before the murder, Jordan had texted his girlfriend, who wanted to know why he couldn't make a special meal they had planned. 'I'm telling you all because of them fucking pakis, that's why I'm skint, I hate them,' his text said.

His explanation for this text excluded the heroin double-cross. Jordan claimed that his cousin and uncle had agreed to build a car wash for Gogo after he had introduced them, but they hadn't been paid. 'Gogo and Chach started to say that me, my cousin Dean and my uncle were ripping them off on the price and they weren't going to pay them. I kept telling my uncle and Dean, "Don't worry, we'll get the money, I'll sort it out." All the time Gogo was telling me I wasn't getting anything. I didn't want it to look like I was getting bullied off them. I owed our Deano some money. I paid him £300 because I felt responsible for them not getting their money, because they had been introduced through me. This was two weeks before the messages. I was just annoyed that I had no money to go out and get something to eat because they ripped my cousin and my uncle off and I had to give my cousin some money.'

Jordan went on to admit telling the gunmen where Manny lived, but denied any conversation about heroin, hand grenades or guns. It had been, he insisted, Butterworth's idea to park the car on his drive because his mum was away, and the twins had simply gone along with it, knowing the car was

stolen and not wanting it on their driveway. He claimed that
he was in his mother's house at the time of the murder, with
Brett. The phone call from Gogo on the night of the murder
had left him 'beyond scared – I thought that someone was
going to come to my mum's house and shoot me, kill me.

'I went in my mum's room and told her we needed to get
out the house quick, we were being blamed for something. I
took her up to my grandma's up the road … Me and Brett
thought it would be best if we just got off. Anywhere, just
away from my mum's and my gran's.'

The bulk of the money they took with them had been saved
up by Brett, who had been planning to move to Australia.

Jordan would later say, 'If Gogo got his hands on us, he
would torture us. Suicide was the only way out.'

First of all, the twins got a lift to Manchester. Dropped off
somewhere near the Mancunian Way and disoriented by
panic, they then decided to head back towards Oldham,
Royton in particular, because 'we thought no-one would find
us there'. Then, after a couple of hours, 'we decided to get a
taxi and go home. Then we thought, nah, we can't go home, so
we headed towards Liverpool, to kill ourselves.' After checking
into the Campanile, they downed the cocktail of booze and
pills, smoked a few spliffs and 'just set off walking', before
jumping into the shipping canal.

During his defence, Jordan also identified the men seen on
his drive by John Butterworth but insisted they had nothing
to do with the heroin deal, or the guns. They were just
'Facebook' friends who they had previously partied with in
Ibiza.

Brett said he had been dragged into the dispute when the
Khans leaned on his brother. 'I thought it was because I didn't
know Manny and Gogo, so I wasn't scared of them, although
Jordan told me about them,' he said. 'I was sort of an outside
party. I tried to defuse the situation but Manny laid the law

down and told us what was going to happen, we had to get him some drugs and that's what happened.'

Brett said he spoke to 'a person, that person spoke to somebody else and passed on Manny's number. That's all I had to do with it. I didn't even mention quantity or a drug.' With the supplier breathing down their necks, Brett was, in his own words, 'prepared to go along with a situation' in which Manny was 'roughed up' because he felt he had no choice. He claimed John Butterworth was lying to 'help his case with the police' and denied making admissions to the paramedics. He did remember Paula Rimmer's eyes though.

The twins' claims of being falsely accused were not believed.

'You may think we shall never know the full history of the background of this case,' said defence counsel Richard Marks when guilty verdicts had been returned on both the twins and they stood in the dock, in their matching suits, waiting to hear how long the inevitable life sentence would be. 'You may feel', he added, 'that these two defendants, on any view, were well out of their league.'

He said there was no indication in Jordan Francis' past that he was violent or involved in gang activity or major league drug dealing. He felt his client had been duped.

'One can't ignore the part in all of these events played by Gulfan Khan, one can't ignore what is known about him,' he added. 'One can't ignore the fact that when one might expect him to be here supporting his family he has instead chosen to absent himself and go back to Pakistan. You may well feel that he has a good deal to answer for in relation to the events that led to the terrible killing of his brother that night. You may well also feel that there were others involved in these events, clearly others who were pulling the strings, others who were calling the shots and you may also feel that the events of which the jury heard in Runcorn are not the acts that one would ordinarily connect with ruthless killers, but were rather the acts of terrified young men caught up in events way beyond their control.'

Peter Birkett QC, defending Brett Francis, made a similar plea for leniency for his client.

'This is a case in which fundamentally decent young men were drawn into the sort of dispute between drug gangs which is characterising life in our cities,' he said. 'Jordan sought the help of his brother Brett, they are very close. Brett wanted to help and help he did. Initially they tried to negotiate their way out of their predicament, as we have heard they actually went in person to see Gulfan Khan in hospital to see if the matter could be solved. They were recruited, we suggest, to a plan to execute revenge and violence upon the Khans.'

A revelation from the QC followed – proof only of the twins' closeness.

Asked if there was anything he wanted to disclose following the jury's verdict the previous afternoon, Mr Birkett said, 'Brett confessed to being in the car, contrary to the evidence he gave in his defence – although he still maintained the plan had only been to "rough up" Manny – in the role of a spotter, to point the victim's house out. Brett was not the gunman. The next point I make, I make with some diffidence because I'm conscious that it can make no difference now, nor can it make any difference to your honour's sentence. He volunteered to me that Jordan was not in the car at the time of the shooting. Whether that is right or wrong, that can't now be resolved.'

Sentencing, Judge Michael Henshell said he found Brett's eleventh-hour assertion 'quite impossible to accept'. He went on, 'It has been suggested that you were both playing out of your league. The facts of this case indicate that you certainly had connections in the world of drugs and the violence that goes hand in hand with the trade. Whether or not you were what is described as the prime movers, it's perfectly obvious that you were fully involved in putting together some of the people together with Amran Khan for these drugs to be sold and, as the jury has found, you were fully involved in this dreadful murder.'

The twins had been party-loving ladies' men. They had been regular faces at boat parties on the Med and in Manchester's house music scene. From now on, their greatest pleasure would be the lifers' hobby of bird-keeping. They had been born together, had killed together and shared a cell together. Now, they would spend the next twenty-eight years behind bars together. As they were jailed, there were shouts of 'rot in hell' from the public gallery. The twins smirked back, bullishly jutting their chests towards the Glodwick contingent, their former friends, who had turned out in force to see them sent down.

Two other men, identified as the pair the twins had been seen talking to on the driveway, were subsequently charged with murder. Police believed that the men were the suppliers of the drugs that had been ripped off, and that one of them had supplied the murder weapon. However, while they admitted meeting the twins and discussing the drugs debt, the two men said they merely discussing a plan the twins had about 'jacking' Amran Khan's car as payback, not killing him. They were acquitted of murder.

IN MARCH 2011, Gulfan 'Gogo' Khan arrived back in the UK after eighteen months in Pakistan. The car hire boss, about whom much had been alleged in court, had put out the word that he intended to return, and all ports were put on alert that he was wanted. He returned only after a number of men, including his colleague in the car-hire firm, Mohammed Hafiz, had been found guilty of the murder of Nasir Hussain, meeting officers shortly after touching down at Leeds-Bradford Airport from Islamabad. He was promptly arrested and questioned on suspicion of Hussain's murder.

   In June 2011, Gulfan Khan answered bail and was released
without charge. Two other men were, at the time of writing,
still wanted by police in connection with Nasar Hussain's
murder.

Epilogue

JUNAID Khan was killed during the same spike in gun violence that claimed the lives of Amran Khan and Nasar Hussain. In 2011, about two years after Junaid was blasted to death with a machine gun in Chadderton, four men were cleared of his murder at Manchester Crown Court. Police in the town feared the verdict would stoke trouble in Oldham, and prepared for a new wave of gunplay.

Junaid Khan had spent much of his time working behind the counter in his dad's shop. He was more of a streetwise jack-the-lad than a gangster. He had grown up in the Werneth area of Oldham, a close-knit community rife with feuding Asian clans, hardmen and drug dealers, and he had been in a good few street fights. Whoever shot him, in July 2009, was absolutely determined to kill him. He was stalked to a quiet street in Chadderton where he was ambushed by a gunman, probably armed with a MAC-10. 'You motherfucker,' shrieked the assassin as he shot him in the back, then riddled his legs, buttocks and groin with bullets as he lay on the floor.

The police investigation found that Junaid Khan had been involved in a personal, 'respect' feud with a family linked to the drug trade in Werneth, and that tension between them had increased in the weeks before his death. The twenty-one-year-old was said to have been so frightened that he had taken to wearing a bulletproof vest behind the shop counter. He had also gone to Glodwick seeking help, a bold step since Glodwick lads and Werneth lads don't always see eye to eye. At the premises of Pennine Vehicle Hire, Junaid asked Amran Khan – later to be shot dead himself by the Francis twins – how much it would cost to get someone shot in the buttocks. Had the job ever gone ahead, it would undoubtedly have been contracted out to Simeon Henderson. As it turned out, word of Junaid's enquiry got back to the men he was feuding with, apparently increasing the animosity.

Police and prosecutors were convinced they had a damning case against four men they believed could be linked to the murder by witness testimony, circumstantial evidence and phone traffic. They were astonished when the jury returned not guilty verdicts against each of the accused. But another, more welcome surprise was on its way. A surge in gun crime in Oldham, expected in the aftermath of the acquittals, never happened.

Some ten miles south of Oldham, another community was also enjoying a respite from bloodshed. Inner-south Manchester, the area historically most troubled by gun crime, saw a prolonged and very welcome period of relative peace. This was largely attributable to the success of Operation Cougar, the initiative launched in 2008, and the work of anti-gun crime police from the Xcalibre Task Force in the Metropolitan division, which encompassed troublespots in Moss Side, Longsight and Fallowfield. These cops had responded to each surge in gun violence by evolving their techniques to the point where they smothered the scene, following gang members, stopping and searching suspects, meticulously recording the movements of likely characters and encouraging bad lads to leave the area. By their regular presence, and by supporting the families of victims of gang warfare through prosecutions, they built up an enviable intelligence network. At the first hint that certain premises might be being used to hide a gun, they would obtain a search warrant and turn the property over.

They also used devious means to take guns off the street. In one memorable sting, a fake shop was set up in the Moss Side area selling combat inspired clothing of the kind that would appeal to gang members. By January 2010, its customers included members of the Doddington-affiliated Moss Side Bloods and local youth who had grown up with them. The shop was staffed by undercover officers called 'Pablo', 'Richie', and 'Sue', who put it about that they were in the market for guns and found a supplier in Marc Billingham, who boasted that he had a well-connected pal who could help. Billingham presented himself as some kind of underworld armourer and said he could supply a MAC-10, Glock and Beretta handguns, and even an AK-47 assault rifle. In reality, Billingham was scrabbling around. He dug up a gun from its hiding place in a local park and convinced his mates to give up their weapons, because there were some idiots in town who would pay anything for a 't'ing', or gun. In an eight-week period, in exchange for £9,000, Billingham sold the officers a Reck Miami self-loading pistol and four bullets, a ME38 replica handgun which had been converted to fire real bullets, an ME38 revolver airgun and a blank-firing replica.

By cleverly using an unwitting insider to turn guns over to the hands of the police, the undercover operation undoubtedly prevented shootings. In April 2010, within weeks of Billingham's last transaction, the Moss Side Bloods and the Gooch clashed in broad daylight Moss Side when the Bloods tried to rescue a couple of their mates who had been barricaded in a house in Gooch territory by their rivals. Had this incident happened in 2007, it's a fair bet that shots would have been fired. As it was, the gang members went at it with bricks, bottles and sticks – raw street-fighting of a kind rarely seen in an area where, all too often, conflict had been settled with the gun.

A few weeks later, some visiting Birmingham hoods were showing off to the local girls in a £45,000 Audi TT in the car park of an Asda store in Hulme. This incensed the Bloods, who threw a shopping trolley at the car. The Birmingham posse returned to the city soon after seeking revenge and opened fire on a group of young people in Great Western Street, injuring an innocent teenage girl and an MSB associate. The activities of MSB clearly posed a danger to others in the neighbourhood, but it was a danger tempered by their own limited access to firearms: nobody from MSB fired back at the Birmingham drive-by team.

In October 2011, Marc Billingham was jailed for ten years. In an editorial on the same day, the *Manchester Evening News* revealed the extent to which gun crime had plummeted in Greater Manchester. In 2007–8, GMP dealt with 146 'firearms discharges', of which thirty-eight were confirmed as gang-related. In an equivalent period between 2010 and 2011, the number of firearms discharges had been slashed to forty-six, a seventy per cent drop. The number of gang-related shooting had fallen to just three, a ninety-two per cent drop.

In the summer of 2011, scenes of youths rioting and pillaging in English cities prompted a great deal of soul-searching about gang culture and the issues of class, race, inequality, aspiration and morality that lay behind it. It was ironic then that the Gooch and the Doddington, so often the focus of national media attention in the past, had so little part to play in the debate. The disorder had begun in Tottenham, north London, after police shot dead a young man, Mark Duggan, in mysterious circumstances. In London, where black people are five times more likely to be stopped and searched than white people, resentment boiled into protest in the aftermath of the killing. Fuelled by a combination of social grievance and material greed, rioting and looting broke out on high streets across the capital. In London, it was reported that rival gang members had put aside their beef and united to make war on the police and clean out the shops. But in Greater Manchester, where the chaos descended on August 9, gang members were conspicuous by their absence. Of the army of people dragged through the courts in the aftermath of the disorder, not one was identified as having any association with the Gooch, the Doddington, or any of their splinter groups. Contrary to the notion that most of the rabble rousers were young and black, the majority of those involved in the Manchester disturbances were white. And, outside of the city centre, it was the deprived, largely white areas of Salford and Wythenshawe that saw the most trouble. The Moss Side carnival, an event marred in previous years by gang tensions, passed off without incident the weekend after the rioting.

Back in 1981, young people, black and white, had rioted for two days in Moss Side against a backdrop of high unemployment and institutional racism. Social exclusion intensified in the aftermath, creating the perfect climate for gangsterism to flourish. The Britain of 2012 is undoubtedly a less racist, more sensitive place than the Britain of 1981. But, nationwide, those social problems that allowed a gang and gun culture to take hold among a subsection of young black males in inner-city areas remain. While black people make up less than three per cent of the British population, ten per cent of youngsters permanently excluded from school in England are black, and about fifteen per cent of the prison population in England and Wales is black. In a bold speech in November 2011, Liberal Democrat leader Nick Clegg spoke of how there were 400 more young black British men in jail than there were in top universities, how black football players had a one in 500 chance of getting into management, and described how African-owned businesses were four times more likely to be refused a bank loan than 'white firms'. Clearly British society, and the black community, has some way to go.

In Moss Side, the 'black' area historically most associated by gun and gang crime, there are plenty of reasons to be optimistic. Of the thirty-two council wards in the city, it ranks sixth for primary school attendance and tenth for secondary school attendance. The number of young people not in education or training is below the city average, some three times lower than in the Sharston area of Wythenshawe, for example. It is in the top ten wards for life expectancy, and people there have the lowest chance of dying from cancer in the city, with only affluent Didsbury West and city centre residents faring better. While rates of youth offending are relatively high, Moss Side has the lowest levels of 'serious acquisitive crime' in the city of Manchester, and eighty-seven per cent of people say they are happy.

The message from the statistics, culled from Manchester City Council's *State of the Wards* report, is clear. It is simply not accurate to say that Moss Side is the most deprived, socially excluded, bleak or neglected neighbourhood in the city. Even in 2007, as gun violence raged, the demand for homes on the Alexandra Park estate exceeded council stock, and house prices were healthy. Today, attractive housing developments on the east side of Moss Side retain families and young professionals in the area. If a gang culture were to persist among a section of the area's youth, it would be because the past casts a long shadow. Other inner-south Manchester areas affected by gang crime, such as Hulme, Fallowfield, Ardwick, Longsight and Old Trafford, also generally fare better, when it comes to statistics relating to deprivation, health, quality of life, and school attendance, than deprived corners of Wythenshawe and east and north Manchester with a limited history of gun crime.

As poverty cuts across racial lines – Manchester is the fourth most deprived local authority in the country – gang culture does too. But historically, of all the gangs in the region, inner-south Manchester's Gooch and the Dodding-ton and their offshoots have been the most troubling. Not because they committed the most crime, but because they were most willing to use firearms and would do so for rela-tively petty reasons, endangering the lives of anyone who happened to be around at the time. For that reason, the decline of gun culture and the improved prospects for young people in Moss Side is a victory for the whole city. Neverthe-less, there are still ghosts to be exorcised. There is still a subculture of young males who cling to the gang mythology, people who would make Moss Side and neighbouring areas of south Manchester their battleground. The challenge that community organisations face is to help youngsters in south Manchester move beyond the history of gang trouble by addressing the problem of low aspiration. The Reclaim men-toring and leadership project is one organisation which has been working hard at this across Greater Manchester. And for ten years, the community group Carisma sought to steer young people away from gun crime through activities in an annual Peace Week. In 2012, Peace Week's tenth year, the group said they did not think they could afford to do it another year because of funding cuts. It was a loss to the city, but at least the organisers could be satisfied that the years they had spent raising awareness of the problem had helped bring about the longest local lull in shootings in recent memory.

A potent sign of how the gangs no longer held the power they once enjoyed came when seventy-two-year-old Cecil Coley took on armed robbers who forced their way into his florist's shop. The gang of four included two notorious broth-ers, Gary Mullings, a veteran of the Young Gooch Crew who had been acquitted for the murder of a Longsight teenager, and Joseph 'JJ' Mullings, an Old Trafford Crip who had been questioned over the death of Jessie James. They attacked Mr Coley and a pal, robbing them of cash and valuables, but

Mr Coley fought back, stabbing and killing Gary Mullings. Mr Coley was eventually told he would not be facing any charges, while the surviving robbers pleaded guilty to robbery and firearms offences and were jailed.

There remains deprivation and disaffection in other areas of Greater Manchester, of the kind that fuels violent gang culture, and new frontiers periodically open up. In March 2012 the *Manchester Evening News* reported that at least six warring gangs were behind a spate of shootings in Salford. While the tough estates of Salford have spawned some of the region's most violent and organised criminals they have traditionally been selective in their use of the gun, which makes suggestions of a 'turf war' worrying. In 2011, two people were shot dead in Salford within months of each other: local hardman Lee Erdman, and Indian student Anuj Bidve.

However, the sheer number of tools available to the authorities these days is cause for hope that Greater Manchester will never see a return to the violent intensity of the Gunchester days, or of their post-millennial hangover, the period detailed in this book. Cell-site evidence, automatic number plate recognition and the extensive CCTV network make it hard to hide these days. DNA analysis has improved, and police have the National Ballistics Intelligence Service database at their fingertips. The last Labour government's law and order reforms, which included minimum tariffs for gun criminals, witness anonymity, and the allowance of bad character and hearsay evidence, have empowered the courts and the public. It might be a vain hope that gun crime will ever completely disappear from the streets of Greater Manchester, but it is harder than ever to get away with it.